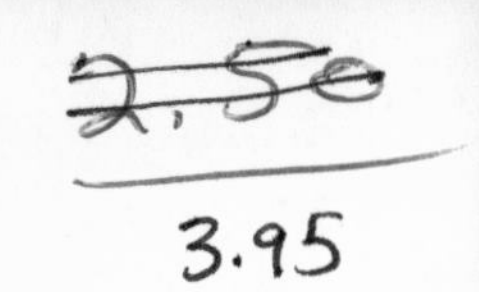
3.95

D1071267

Companion
of
Eternity

For what is the voice from heaven that resounds in the Scriptures but "Know thyself, O man, and know Me. Me the source of eternity, of wisdom and of grace; thyself, My creation, My likeness, My delight. For I have destined thee to be the companion of My eternity."

JOHN AMOS COMENIUS (1592-1671)

Companion of Eternity

W. GORDON ROSS

Abingdon Press
New York
Nashville

COMPANION OF ETERNITY

Library of Congress Catalog Card Number: 61-6394

SET UP, PRINTED, AND BOUND BY THE PARTHENON PRESS, AT NASHVILLE, TENNESSEE, UNITED STATES OF AMERICA

Dedication

From working with a host of
Berea students through the
years, it now seems clear
I have learned more from them
than they from me.

In dedicating this volume
to them, I do so without
holding them responsible
for its limitations.

Contents

Introduction

THIS IS AN ELEMENTARY WORK AND IN A SENSE IS A SET OF VARIATIONS on the theme: What is man? This is hardly a new or original question; yet it is one to which man himself needs desperately to give renewed and dedicated attention. The dominant problem of our world and time is the *human* problem. The dominant human problem is *religion,* the most multidimensional of all human concerns—from a conviction of the goodness of the natural universe, through a concern for the welfare of animals, to an interested attitude and action in behalf of human personality, and even on to a belief in eternal destiny. There are of course exceptions to or qualifications of the foregoing, even under the aegis of some kind of religion. Some religious points of view have affirmed the "evil" nature of the material world. "Reverence for life" has had to make adverse decisions against some particularly destructive forms of life. Religion has its own dark chapters of violating personality. Also, some forms of naturalistic or humanistic religion do not affirm any doctrine of eternal destiny.

The two aspects of the theme with which the present work is concerned are *potential* and *worth.* But the span of possibility for discussion is vast. There are those who say or imply that man is little more than a protoplasmic blob of dubious potential, appearing on the cosmic scene almost by accident. Alongside such a notion the idea of worth is, of course, entirely relative. Far removed from this outlook is the conviction that man is a special creation, deriving his worth from his inclusion in a divine plan. The present work conducts its operations between these alternatives, but sets its primary sights on the latter.

The key terms used in subsequent chapters to indicate the focus of human potential and worth are *personality* and *person.* They are not used herein as synonyms. For instance, if man has an eternal destiny in any real sense, usage calls for the term *person.* On the other hand, in so far as there is a developing interest on the part of science in peculiarly human data, one speaks of the scientific study of *personality*.

My outline is necessarily selective. In dealing with the theme of human potential I have limited discussion to three areas of conspicuous manifestation of potential: language, science, and religion. The theme of worth is considered in its relation to science, its affirmation in religion, and the validity of the principle itself.

The present task may be called an experiment in perspective and communication. Achievement of perspective is not an enterprise of the same order as either science or religion. It can never attain the kinds of precision realized by science. It is not marked by the depths of commitment and conviction one finds only in religion. Yet it is important for both science and religion—to avoid narrowness and intolerance, and to develop appreciation and co-operation.

Quite likely there is no such thing as an objectively assessed, freely chosen, and fully practiced perspective. Subtle and powerful determinants exert force upon us all. We are, in Tennyson's words, "part of all that [we] have met." Yet, we are repeatedly talked to and argued with as though we should be able to assess, to choose, and to practice this or that perspective. It is often implied that some self-determination is not only possible, but also incumbent upon us. Take the scientific point of view! Think, feel, and act religiously! Consider every subject philosophically! The exact nature and precise limits of our potentials are not determinable, but there are possibilities and responsibilities peculiarly relevant to man.

As far as it is possible, with hope of achievement, to experiment in perspective it is entirely appropriate to do so. Though we may not do so as specialists, we can at least do so with a fundamental appreciation of contributions of specialists. The difficulties and risks are great. How can the nonspecialist appraise the work of the specialist? This question is also applicable to the specialist in discipline *X* with regard to specialty *Y* in which he has no experience. No human being can ever be simply a specialist and nothing else. No one really says this is possible, but many arguments based on the supposed security of a particular specialization are in danger of making excessive claims as to the range of its applicability.

There are at least two grand divisions of any elaborated discussion of perspective: that of spectator and that of participant. The most relevant verb applied to the spectator is "to see." This is particularly the case in such a language as Greek, wherein there are various verbs for various kinds of "seeing" (with the physical eye, with the mind, and with comprehensive understanding—βλέπω, εἶδον, θεωρέω). The participant develops additional and improved understanding of something, like music, only after he participates. It is supposed, therefore, that participant-perspective relates "seeing" or "hearing" and "doing" so that perspective in general is improved.

If we think of perspective in sufficiently general terms, we could apply the term to any and all points of view, and in this sense everyone has some kind of perspective. It would be possible for a static perspective to impose upon all data a set of requirements ignoring all questioning and criticism. That such conditions obtain we well know, and they call to mind the Myth of Procrustes,[1] one of the most meaningful of all ancient myths.

I have sought in each chapter to be aware of existing perspectives and to explore possibilities and lines of communication with other interests and concerns. Where there is difference of opinion or conviction, I have tried to let the "opposition" speak fully, but without forgoing the right to affirm with confidence on certain issues, even though the eminence of the "opposition" be forbidding. It is hoped this is done with becoming diffidence.

There are certain things the present work is *not*. It is not a "contribution to knowledge," but rather a report of "discovery"—not the spectacular discovery of new knowledge, but of the richness to be found in communication among human beings especially if one is more willing to listen and respond than to tell and control.

It is not an "empirical verification" of challenging hypotheses. Empirical verification is usually thought of as objective procedure deliberately planned. An intimation that something in our general and unplanned "experience" commends itself is thought to smack of "subjectivity." While there is some truth to this, it seems a bit arbitrary to try to rule the latter out of court too summarily.

This work is not the product of specialization; neither is it a protest against specialization—but against the fractionalization that results from a misunderstood and misapplied specialization.

That it is not an adequate defense of my position is due as much to limitations on my part as to any other reason. The following chapters are exploratory rather than apologetic, conversational rather than polemic, experimental rather than doctrinal, reflective rather than dogmatic. And the question, What do you mean by "person,"

[1] Procrustes, in the Greek myth, was a brigand who stretched or "trimmed" captives so they would fit his bed, thus symbolizing the practice of forcing data or subjects to conform to a previously chosen and inflexible "norm."

"potential," and "worth"? is my own question as much as it is that of any critic.

It is inconceivable to me that these pages would be of any interest to the professional and the specialist. The one thought to be suggested at the moment, however, is that we are all of us *persons,* whatever else we may aspire to be.

Man in a cosmos without God is an utter orphan, but with God, he is an errant "child." In either case, he is a creature of potential—to become either fully human, if natural potential is realized, or to achieve stature as a religious person when performance is added to intrinsic status.

A special word of appreciation is due the Lilly Foundation for financial assistance in making available essential time for some basic study and inquiry. Mention should be made of Dr. J. Clayton Feaver of the University of Oklahoma to whose persistent urging this project owes much, both for initial impetus and continuance. A special palm goes to a tolerant and helpful family, particularly my wife Helen for her critical acumen.

CHAPTER I

What Is Man?

PHILOSOPHY HAS GRAPPLED WITH THIS QUESTION—MAN IS A RATIONAL creature, a political animal. Religion has considered it extensively—man is a child of God, a participant in meaningful creativity. Now science, or rather a congeries of specialized sciences, has approached this question from a variety of angles—man is an animal, a psychophysical organism, a product of an evolutionary process, a personality. Nonspecialized reflection speculates—man is the creature that laughs, the one that sheds tears, the being that talks.

The question seems to be a quotation from Ps. 8, but this psalm is not about man so much as it is about God. The writer implies that we already know something of what man is, therefore, it is hard to understand why he should engage the divine attention (vss. 3-4) and why such honors should be conferred upon him (vss. 5-8). It is as though the writer were implying, "We would not have thought to set this high a value on him." There is no clear-cut affirmation of inherent dignity and worth, but there is a strong suggestion of *imputed* status and privilege. A basic theme of the present work is that the affirmation of human worth, whether innate or imputed, is one of the most persistent and one of the most violated of doctrines. And, strange to relate, in no century has it been more persistently affirmed and more extensively violated than in the present century.

Throughout the centuries many insights and flashes of understanding have been concerned with our question. They have been the work of poets, seers, prophets, and spiritual geniuses, as well as of ordinary people. They make a better collection of wisdom than the notions people have had about any other theme. When human beings have been dependent entirely on their insights and capacities for reasoning and learning, they have gained a better understanding of man than of any other subject. Yet, definitive and conclusive answers have not been readily forthcoming. In recent times, a new and powerful instrument—science—seems to make it possible to approach more nearly to definitive answers. Thus, will there be a science of man? So far we have a whole family of near sciences dealing with various aspects of the complexity we call man. These social or behavioral sciences are practically unanimous in a profession of loyalty to the scientific approach. This new enterprise links man with nature more definitely than ever, and, correlatively, with animal. While this may seem correct procedure at the present level of scientific development, it does or will revive the question of whether nature provides the sufficient total context for man's existence and significance.

Man and Nature

It is a problem of tremendous proportions to try to fit these two concepts together. Modern science tends to see nothing but nature. When it began to investigate that which was not man, the problem did not seem so great. When it turned to the study of man, however, special questions developed. If the scientist as scientist had seen nothing but nature, not including man, what happened when man was included wholly within nature's scope?

If we put man into nature, what does that do for man? What does it do for nature? The simplest answer is, nothing particularly, but the whole question is more often avoided than faced. In the first place it is simpler to assume that there is nothing but nature; therefore, man is simply a special manifestation of natural forces. This can hardly be the entirely objective judgment essential to science, because man as scientist of man is both subject and object. This does not prove it to be a wrong judgment, however. One suggestion is that putting man into nature puts purpose into nature while taking it away from man. Yet if nature is a purposeless system of law, as is often said, and man, a creature capable of purposive action, as is also said, then we use purpose ambiguously. Purpose, in the sense of final cause, was "taken out" of nature a long while ago, at least as far back as the days of Bacon. The concept that Bacon criticizes is the personification of nature, or rather nature regarded as divine [1]—a typical Greek notion. According to Bacon, nature should be thought of and investigated in

[1] Cf. *Advancement of Learning,* III, iv.

terms of strict and universal causal sequences. Thus nature is now to be thought of as the area of efficient causes and not of conscious purpose. Therefore, if nature is the area of physical or efficient causes, and if man is entirely a part of nature or included within nature, then is man subject entirely to the same sorts of causal sequences that are characteristic of nature? Is so, man has no freedom, and any tendency to believe in freedom would be simply another type in the variety of causal sequences.

When the scientist today studies man, interesting developments transpire. If he gives attention to chemistry—which certainly is part of the context of human existence—the question of causal sequence is pretty much the same as in the study of chemistry elsewhere. It has become a commonplace to say that man is "worth" only so much at the chemist's counter, or that man's body contains only a few dollars' worth of chemicals. This has been a sensational piece of information, but it does not say very much at that. It is scandalous to think of how many questions concerning man it leaves unanswered—though it was never offered as a complete answer. The "worth" of two dollars worth of chemicals contrasts sharply with the worth implied in liability and insurance claims which often reach huge amounts. Moreover, chemistry could not forever ignore life (bios), thus biochemistry becomes a special study.

The science of psychology in the study of man encounters something not so accessible as the chemical composition of body. Behavior, memory, learning, emotion—these become objects of special studies. Most scientific psychologists, however, as scientists, may well agree there is no sharp line of demarcation between man and nature.

Has the idea of final cause threatened to creep back into thinking about nature? Notions at least vaguely similar to this have never been entirely absent from human thinking, and attempts have been made to revive a doctrine of purposeful direction in human evolution or social progress generally. We are told that we could make this world a veritable paradise "if only we would set our minds to the task." Presumably this means that by the employment of purposeful activity at the strictly human level we could build any kind of world we want. These are not full-fledged doctrines of final cause, however.

There is a sense in which religion is peculiarly relevant to man, whereas nature is the area of the investigations of science. To try to understand these two concepts in terms of their congruence we would need to say that both religion and science are natural developments. There is a tendency today, however, to make a sharp distinction between these two natural developments. Religion is interpreted as neurosis, science as our hope for the future; religion as a block on progress, science as our only avenue to truth, and so on. I see valuation in process here, but if value judgments are set aside in favor of strict description, it would be difficult to see any kind of distinction. From such a point of view there is no real distinction between, for example, a field mouse and a field marshal. We are still far from adequate description, however, and it is not possible to eliminate value distinctions entirely from our considerations—even of nature. Man needs value distinctions, even though it is true that the very process of valuing will, in its total scope, include devaluing *in extremis*.

Man and Animal

Man, as scientist, studies rats in a maze. Man built the maze and planned the obstacles, the rewards, and the hidden—until learned—pathways to the rewards. Presumably man is free to build a maze that has no pathway to the goal and no goal. Presumably he is free to make the obstacles unconquerably difficult or even lethal. By and large, however, man is not capricious in his controls. Whether the rat would agree might depend on his capacity to comprehend the "higher aims" to which his career is being dedicated.

Yet, the procedure of studying rats in mazes is based on the assumption that there are certain common denominators in rat behavior and human. The fact that man, as scientist, does not consciously experiment with human beings as he does with rats—there are exceptions to this [2]—is based on an assumption that there is also a difference between the rat and the human being. Thus we have two sets of assumptions, the first based on a comprehensive naturalism, the second based on norms not scientifically founded.

Is man also in a maze? Who built it? Does it have a sure pathway to a reward? Is the reward a "thing," such as food, or a condition, such as blessedness? Anyone could extend this list of questions, and it should be said immediately that there is no assumption here that they would in every case be "proper" questions. Also it is quite obvious that some of the questions might contain implications which would be challenged. Yet, all such questions could be matched with proposed answers. We need not for the moment consider the problem of how these proposed answers have been arrived at, or whether they

[2] See Norman Cousins, "Dialogue in Warsaw," *Saturday Review* (June 28, 1958), p. 9. The article contains reports on operations by Nazi authorities, using Polish women as medical "guinea pigs" without their knowledge or consent.

have any special validity. But it is entirely appropriate to raise some questions involving implications beyond the stated purpose of the experimenter who puts rats into mazes for the purpose of constructing a scientific model for intensive study. Only in imagination is it possible to detach ourselves completely from all contexts. Everything that is or that happens is inevitably in a whole series of contexts.

None of the occurrences that transpire in the laboratories are any worse for the rats—and some might even be better—than what would happen if all the rats were turned out into the "big world" to fend for themselves. Also, in the laboratories they are presumably fulfilling a lofty function. Whether the extra hazards in the outside world would result in their developing greater vigor, alertness, and additional talent it would be difficult to say. But what sort of function they would then be fulfilling is something of an open question. Koheleth's question is still a tantalizing one, "Who knows whether the spirit of man goes upward and the spirit of the beast goes down to the earth?" (Eccl. 3:21 R.S.V.) Yet there are people today—representatives of psychic research—who claim to have some experimental results that have a bearing on such questions as Koheleth's, but they are not yet fully accepted in the household of science.

Already we find ourselves confronted by at least three challenging assumptions. There is the operating assumption in the laboratory and the maze that there is sufficient similarity in biological and mental processes of man and rat for us to learn significantly about the former through deliberate experiments with the latter. A second assumption that hovers about—though not an operating assumption—is that man and rat are destined for the same end—complete oblivion. Though entertained by some people, it is vigorously challenged by others and is perhaps not likely to become a unanimously accepted operating assumption for society generally. A third assumption is that man has special functions and responsibilities. This is a more complex assumption than the former two and takes us into the realm of religion, whether humanistic or theistic, and into the loftiest and most daring assertions of faith. Also it renders entirely naïve and inadequate a too easy and simplified identification of man and nature if this assumes that the connotation of man is exhausted in impersonal and purposeless connotations of nature.

The problem of man's "maze" is a general and theoretical problem of the largest possible scope, perhaps even beyond solution—depending on how we interpret solution. It is also a specific and individual problem of peculiar importance to every person, as a person—more than as a body or mind or personality. The general and theoretical aspects will lead eventually to a consideration of the nature and significance of all of life and existence, a consideration not containable within the walls of the laboratory with its operating circumscriptions. The specific and individual aspects may even be concerned with the tiniest details of personal history and daily existence. Within any personality these two aspects inevitably merge. This is so much the case that when we consider what people say, we cannot always be sure whether we have a problem of theory or of diet, whether one's remarks are purely philosophical or are emotionally motivated, or whether some statements that have objective form are or are not subjectively determined. The objective validity of a person's statements may be unrelated to the psychological motivations prompting them, where there are such promptings.

Then there are certain questions which seem related to the whether and the what of man's maze. They are questions concerned with meaning, destiny, significance, evil, the sufferings of the innocent, and purpose—on all levels of context. Yet, such questions are not always at first glance what they seem to be. They may be straightforward questions calling for discussion if not answer. Even so, the first asking of some may have emotional and psychological associations which subtly affect the questions ever after. It is not always possible to dissociate oneself completely from emotional or psychological origins of certain types of questions. It is difficult, for example, to ask such a question as, Why should that tree fall just when *I* come along? without some emotional identification with notions that this was arranged with me "in mind." It is easy nowadays to call such a point of view primitive and immature. Such a question as, Could God call me as He did Amos? is not so easily disposed of however. A universe subject to capricious agencies that aim tree trunks at one for some reason, or none at all, is quite a different notion from the idea of a purposeful God who is Creator and who is meaningfully identified with humanity in moral and spiritual experience. However easily some people may feel they have disposed of this type of idea, it has not been with the same cogency of reasoning as with polytheistic, fatalistic, or mythological notions.

Questions about the nature and validity of the idea of God are legitimate questions for man—wherein he subtly transcends at least the more constricted interpretations of nature. And there are legitimate questions about man's maze—though I do not insist on the use of this word. I use the term for the time being only because the very idea and purpose of a maze for rats has anthropomorphic origins. As with so many scientific devices it is a model, considerably simplified, of a real maze which calls for a mode of behavior similar to human behavior as it tackles problems. In fact a recent author says, "A scientist is rather like a rat in a maze. Both proceed by observation, insight, hypothesis, and trial, and for both, the hypothesis may arise from mere hunch." [3] This might better have been put the other way, "A rat in a maze is rather like a scientist . . ." since man, whether as man or as scientist, was already working away in his maze long before anyone ever thought of setting up a model with the rat as performer.

If now we try to specify the different features of man's maze we soon discover its complexity, or perhaps even the inappropriateness of this figurative use of the term maze. Is there a goal, aim, or objective for human existence? Is there a divine dimension to be considered? Is there something we are meant to be? Any reader is well aware of the two main categories of answers: those that do and those that do not allow for any idea of God. Both might well claim a concern with and interest in human welfare, though reasoning to support this would vary. The goals of the rat in the maze are directly related to some obvious and definable goals growing out of biological needs primarily. They are therefore natural goals to meet natural needs. If it were to be said that a proper goal for man is to be a religious person, and that this goal has divine justification, this would also be natural, in so far as valid, but the two usages of natural would not be the same. The use of the term "natural" by the uncompromising naturalist disallows any notion of divine will or transcendent purpose. He excludes these by definition, which means at the level of basic assumption and presupposition—a truly philosophical level.

Let us indicate some goals for man which have been widely discussed. Happiness is often said to be man's chief goal. Salvation is often considered to be man's proper goal. In recent decades much attention has been given to emotional maturity. Its importance is affirmed in the following:

Emotional maturity is the most important thing in the world. In the words of my colleague, Leon Saul, it is truly, "The basis of mental health, of morality and ethics, of social cooperation." More than that, "It is the only healthy, long-range answer to mankind's central problem, namely, man's

[3] William S. Beck, *Modern Science and the Nature of Life* (New York: Harcourt, Brace and Company, 1957), pp. 55 ff.

inhumanity to man. What helps children develop normally toward emotional maturity helps mankind to make peace and brotherhood into realities."[4]

Of the three terms mentioned, "salvation" sounds like a religious term, "emotional maturity" like a psychological, and "happiness" could be either or both. The use of any and all of them calls for expansion of connotation of terms like nature and animal when we propose to link them with the term man, unless we choose to operate with restrictive connotations for nature and animal and let our connotation of man conform.

Science and Man

As implied above we have for some time now been rubbing away at the line of distinction between man and nature and man and animal. Who are the "we" attempting this erasure? How did the line of distinction get there in the first place? What is the justification for denying a distinction?

Who are the "we" attempting this erasure? This is comparatively easy to answer: moderns, naturalists, monists, positivists. These are labels rather than specific answers, however. The "we" would include anyone satisfied with nature as an all-inclusive term to designate our total context. It would include all who repudiate notions of the divine, of spiritual reality, and who disavow any claims that man is a special creation with a special mission and destiny. It would include those who believe that such statements as "every person is a child of God" are sheer poetry with no ontological reference. Of course they could still affirm that man has special responsibilities and that there are values requiring human acceptance and actualization. There would still be the question as to whether a ready recognition of such values and responsibilities was simply inherited or grounded in a strictly naturalistic or animalistic sanction.

How did this line of distinction get there in the first place? There are no records of the first glimmerings of this notion. But we do know a number of chapters in the history of thought devoted to themes of man's origins, nature, and destiny. We can always start with the Platonic theory of a body-soul dualism. For Plato, the soul was an immortal resident in a temporary and restricting abode. The idea did not originate on Greek soil but was an adapted importation from farther East. There was the earlier Egyptian Book of the Dead giving

[4] Edward A. Strecker, *Basic Psychiatry* (New York: Random House, 1952). p. 7.

detailed information concerning the journey of man into the beyond, with the weighing of his soul, his meeting with Osiris—if he was qualified—and even his taking examinations. Again, the book of Genesis notes that man became a "living soul" (2:7). This does not imply a strict dualism and is therefore quite different from the Platonic dualism. But the "living soul" of Genesis was made master over the animals, which is at least a jurisdictional distinction. But how ever the distinction may have been conceived of in early days, human beings have always tended to think of man as subject to special obligations incumbent on no other creature; as involved in possibilities and privileges unique to him; as the appropriate master of the things of this world. At least one net result has been that man is the one religious creature, or person, in the whole of creation. At the moment we simply recognize the complex fact that we are still trying to ascertain whether this is due to chance, deliberate purpose, strict causal sequence, or fortuitous mutations. Whatever we decide will affect our interpretation of man as religious person.

What is the justification for denying a distinction? There is no definitive and generally accepted answer to this, although it may seem that science comes nearest to doing so. But this is doubtful if we are to use the term "justification" strictly. It would be better to say that science is still working on the subject. We can discern at least three large scale hypotheses concerning man in modern times: man the machine, man the organism, man the personality. By referring to certain books we may ascribe these designations respectively to the eighteenth, nineteenth, and twentieth centuries: La Mettrie's *Man a Machine* (1742), Darwin's *Origin of the Species* (1859), and Allport's *Personality* (1937). Our immediate concern is with the third designation.

The present century has witnessed the development of scientific studies of personality, of efforts to identify, analyze, and define personality. Thus, science seems finally to have reached the citadel. To characterize man, the concept of machine seems less satisfactory than that of organism, as it seems less satisfactory than that of personality. This may seem to reverse the procedure urged in the principle of parsimony—the selection of the simpler of alternate hypotheses. Let us consider this in another way, however.

Science, as it approaches the citadel mentioned above, encounters special difficulties. These are intensified by the very fact that science is concerned with certain kinds of strictness: in use and definition of terms, in method, and identification of data. Man is a peculiarly complex area of data for scientific inquiry and a serious challenge to attempts—so essential to science—to measure, check, and experiment on or with. It is by no means certain that the data can be completely "quantified." Is the whole man simply the sum of discrete parts? Will the assembled reports of various specializations give us the answer? Can the data be eventually "reduced to a science"? As man reads accounts of himself, whether as machine, organism, or personality, he may well ask, Is *that* what I am? or Is that *all* I am? There is one peculiarly stubborn question which science may never completely answer: Is there any fundamental difference between what nature does and what "I" do? Nature arranged the chemical processes that take place in the body long before "I" came to know there was any such thing as chemistry. Nature arranged for the heart to work in a certain autonomic manner. Nature built an incredibly complex and concentrated computer which is the brain.

There are, however, some remarkable things that nature will not—perhaps even cannot—do, things that are left to man. Some seem obvious enough to us: administer justice, practice mercy, relieve the oppressed, love neighbor as self, love God, teach kindness, meditate, save lives, distinguish between good and bad—anyone could extend the list. It also seems possible that man could do the opposites of any of these: oppress, kill, exploit, et cetera. Also it seems that sometimes man is not capable of doing any of these if his reason is "dethroned," his emotional conflicts beyond his control, or his freedom impaired.

If anyone wants to make a case for nature it could be said that it is merely a manner of speaking to say that man does these things, or that nature does all this through him; that all of it is simply a matter of modes of functioning, all of which are "natural."

The question still remains, but two reminders are in order: it is no basis for belittling science, and human experience discloses an inveterate tendency to start with a closed case.

Many people do belittle science in one way or another. They rejoice to call attention to what they say science cannot do—"Science will never explain the miracle of life!" "Science would destroy poetry if it had its way." It is less than mature to rejoice in the limitations, alleged or real, of science. It is more like a confession of some deep uncertainty than it is a victory song—and even victory songs are not noted for the numbers of beatitudes they contain.

A classic example of starting with a closed case is provided by the book of Job, wherein the three friends who approach Job to "console" him hold to the inflexible premise that only the guilty suffer. To them it is not open to question or debate. The scientist, as man, is not entirely free from this tendency, and in the history of religion there are alarming instances of the practice. Yet, though it is to be found *in* religion and *in* science, it is not *of* either religion or science. Yet the errant sons of man can bring disgrace on the family, whether in religion, science, or whatever.

Is Man What He Does?

The attack on the idea of substance as held in ancient and medieval times has been widespread and pronounced. This has resulted in a widespread shift of emphasis from essence to function, from being to doing, from entity to performance. The contributions of John Dewey have been vastly influential in this regard, and, to many who have been influenced, the supporting arguments seem to have the force of self-evidence. Concerning man, the argument would say that we do not need to try to find out what he is so much as what he does, how he operates. We could state the nub of the argument informally as follows: man is not a distinct entity, separated from all his equipment such as body, emotions, and the like. He is not a lever-operating engineer sitting in the background, unobservable and inaccessible—even if he were such, we could get at him only through his various manifestations, actions, performances. Thus we do not need to try to find out what he is for we are being constantly confronted by what he does. Therefore, there is no need to try to locate *him*. Man the entity is dismissed in favor of man the set of functions.

Thus the next few paragraphs are devoted to some provisional answers to the question, What is man? They will be partial, but contributory. Most of them will be in terms of what man does, but not all of them. The present argument raises the question of whether there is a strict dichotomy between "is" and "does," and whether these two types of answers are mutually exclusive and irreconcilable.

Man is the only name-giving creature. This is a form of uniqueness, but of what kind is not perfectly clear. If language were said to be a divine gift, this would affirm a special kind of uniqueness. If, however, we said that man is simply that area or context where language shows up as a mode of functioning, and that, given ample evolutionary time and process, any creature could learn to talk, we would imply only a relative sort of uniqueness. Gerald Heard's short story "Lost Cavern" tells about talking bats. While this story is science fiction—without descending to the lower levels of science fiction—yet it could not have been written without a profound comprehension of many of the features of language.

Man is creator and builder. For unnumbered centuries ants have built the same kinds of colonies. There is no Dior among peacocks to introduce new styles. The beaver is satisfied with the same type of dam-building "machinery" used by remote ancestors. The bloodhound can track down one who has fled, but he seems not to have thought of adding a microscope to his equipment. A dog bays at the moon, but can never predict an eclipse. Man, however, can exercise creativity in all of these areas, and occasionally some creative genius among human beings will do something that even others of his fellows cannot do, and that he himself does not understand. I suggest at this juncture that man's creativity has nowhere been more evident than in science and religion.

Man is nature's self-conscious artist. We are often told that the greatest painter could not reproduce nature's artistry. But it is not the mode and manner of man's artistry simply to reproduce. His artistry, self-conscious as it is—nature's is not—gives form and articulation to his imagination. Moreover, man's art is not limited to rare geniuses, but, as art teachers are affirming today, human nature generally has artistic capabilities. The heyday of children's art is certainly upon us. It is not completely clear whether we should say man *is* artist or that he *does* art.

Man is the focus and agent of religious achievement. He is a religious person. He becomes a religious personality. In the total scheme of things he essentially is something that calls for the use of the adjective "religious." Also, what he does during his existence here may reveal his status as a religious person. In other words, "is" and "does" are both relevant at this point. I am also saying that the term "religious" can apply in some sense to persons even if what they do is classifiable as irreligious. This work will make a distinction between "religious person" and "religious personality." The word "person" will designate something peculiarly appropriate to religion, and "personality" something appropriate to science. The first will be used to mean only that which is intended by such a phrase as "inherent worth of persons," and the second will refer only to what is indicated by such a phrase as "the psychology or psychological study of personality." This does not mean that person will be used as the equivalent of soul, or that personality will be precisely synonymous with functioning organism. Personality has a distinctly human dimension that functioning organism does not, and its use here does not close the door on the question of a possible distinction between man and nature, however unorthodox this might seem to naturalism. Person is used here so as not arbitrarily to exclude the concept of man as a child of God.

We could continue: Is man the creature that laughs? Or must he share honors with the hyena? Is he closest to the angels? Is he on occasion lower than the beasts? Is he the only creature capable of feeling sorry for people he never saw and of hating people who never did him a wrong? Is he the only creature that consciously reasons? There are many people quite willing to drop all or at least some of the question marks and convert the foregoing into declarative sentences. Other statements drawn from the literatures of the world could be put along with these. Let us include one such from a significant poet. It seems to say that man is two things, not the time-honored dual distinction of body-soul, but rather something like saint-sinner. The poet says it this way:

> In me, past, present, future meet
> To hold long chiding conference.
> My lusts usurp the present tense
> And strangle Reason in his seat.
> My loves leap through the future's fence
> To dance with dream-enfranchised feet.
>
> In me the cave-man clasps the seer
> And garlanded Apollo goes
> Chanting to Abraham's deaf ear.
> In me the tiger sniffs the rose.
> Look in my heart, kind friends, and tremble,
> Since there your elements assemble.[5]

"Damaged Goods"

When we work with human beings we work with "damaged goods." The human creature does not show up in the context of social existence as an unblemished product. He is not labeled "Passed by Inspector X" or "Guaranteed to be in perfect working condition." And if, once in a great while, he does not show up in the context of human existence, but in a feral context, he will be even more "damaged," generally speaking. What are the possibilities, potential and inevitable?

Hereditary equipment seems to be a compound of debits and credits.

[5] From *The Heart's Journey* by Siegfried Sassoon. Used by permission of Harper & Brothers.

Discoveries and developments in the field of biology since 1920 tend to validate the dictum that truth is stranger than fiction. The opening of doors to the amazing worlds of the gene and the virus, to mention no others, reveals incredible performances. There are other doors yet to be opened, if indeed they can be. It now is revealed that we are often at the "mercy" of the hidden "codes" or "programs" in the genes. Moreover, the genes themselves are potentially subject to the influences of background radiation, a newly discovered feature of our dynamic universe. Thus it looks as though some Mr. *A* was predestined or fated to have some affliction, for example, cancer, because he was in that line of descent wherein an individual gene, influenced by radiation, experienced a mutation that set the hereditary stage for his case of cancer. This is only one spectacular and dramatic possibility in the whole concourse of biological and hereditary patterns. If, in the language of mythology, Fortune smiles, or does not, in the language of the modern information theory, genes are coded with the "language" that "says" whether it shall be debit or credit for the inheritor.

If Otto Rank is correct, one's very entrance into this world is hazardous. According to his "birth-trauma" theory one can never be sure of completely recovering from the psychic shock of the radical transition from a "world" of blissful security to the troublous journey toward self-dependence. While this particular theory has been challenged—by Freud and Ferenczi, for example—the general subject of psychic shocks and wounds has become one of the most challenging and disturbing catalogues of possibilities to confront man since the days of demons. At the same time there are few topics showing a greater compound of fact and fancy.

A modern psychiatric dictionary lists a greater number of actual afflictions than the horrendous fancies which fill the mythologies of the world. One startling statistic will serve as an example. The *Psychiatric Dictionary* compiled by Leland E. Hinsie and Jacob Shatzky [6] lists nearly 250 examples of terms ending with the combining form "-phobia," from achluophobia to zoophobia. These are acquired fears. One may well wonder at the creative genius that was able to say, before the days of dictionaries,

> and by a sleep to say we end
> The heart-ache and the thousand natural shocks

[6] New York: Oxford University Press, 1940.

> That flesh is heir to, 'tis a consummation
> Devoutly to be wish'd. To die, to sleep;
> To sleep: perchance to dream: ay, there's the rub:
> For in that sleep of death what dreams may come,
> When we have shuffled off this mortal coil,
> Must give us pause: there's the respect
> That makes calamity of so long life.[7]

How ever much competence and wisdom we may have potentially or may subsequently develop, yet we are all subject to threats from within. And for the moment we do not need to have recourse to doctrines of original sin and total depravity, or to theories of a clamorous Id, or of a superego that "does make cowards of us all." We need only a modicum of reasonable imagination to raise the question of whether future generations may deplore our ignorance in some areas, even as we deplore the ignorance of bygone generations. For example, consider the extent to which people of early centuries spread germs and infection in utter ignorance of either germs or infection.

Perhaps the miracle is that in the midst of so much damage and threat of damage, man can spiritually transcend it even before he learns how or develops the desire to eliminate it. He can and often does die triumphantly in the midst of trouble, threat, and damage that lay violent hands on his normal securities. So that well might we continue to grapple with the question, What is man?

[7] William Shakespeare, *Hamlet,* Act III, scene 1.

CHAPTER II

Questions and Questioning

Man Asks Questions

THIS CHAPTER WILL INTRODUCE AND PAY RESPECTS TO THE HUMAN capacity for articulating questions, and will introduce some significant questions and question situations vitally related to the theme of the entire book.

The ability to think up and articulate questions is a remarkable combination of curiosity and speech. The cat has acquired a reputation for curiosity, but until it acquires the additional capacity for speech, we still have *some* basis for a distinction. According to folklore, curiosity tends to be lethal for the cat. If we interpret folklore as symbolism, man's curiosity may turn out to be lethal for him.

The term curiosity is notoriously ambiguous. We often think of curiosity as a noble impulse and basic to the enterprise of science. On the other hand, Emerson speaks of the "low curiosity" that would like to "pick the lock of the future." [1] Many adjectives are attached to the word, referring to the motivation or aim: idle, prurient, intemperate, gossipy, intelligent, and the like. A classic judgment directed against one type of curiosity is found in John Calvin's *The Institutes of the Christian Religion:* "Great shrewdness was discovered by a certain pious old man, who, when some scoffer ludicrously inquired what God had been doing before the creation of the world, replied that he had been making hell for over curious men." [2] Calvin directs varied judgments against questioner and answerer and implies thereby that the very nature of the question of the "scoffer" reveals the motivation.

[1] Cf. "The Over-Soul."
[2] Book I, Ch. xiv, sec. 1.

An idealistic consideration of the place that curiosity may have had in human history is manifest in the following:

> While it is generally admitted that the capstone of the edifice of science is its modifications of the conditions of human life, so as to add to the enrichment of human civilization . . . nevertheless the real motive which spurs on the true-hearted scientist is not practical but a burning curiosity to find out the truth.[3]

Here too are judgments, both comparing and contrasting with those of Calvin. Sometimes people will use a quotation like this, contrast it with one like Calvin's in order to "prove" that religion discourages curiosity, whereas science is a magnificent product of the inquisitive spirit of man.

The importance of questions for the study of nature has been stressed. Francis Bacon speaks of "putting nature to the question."

> The scientist asks definite questions of nature and according to the sort of question he asks he will get a different sort of answer, and therefore a different sort of science. . . . This method of question and answer was described by Francis Bacon as "putting nature to the question." [4]

This poses the problems of what sorts of questions to put to nature and of how to go about getting answers. There are also problems relating to the questioner, What motivations prompt the questions? and To what uses will the answers be put? As to the first, there are "right" and "wrong" questions to put to nature, as well as right and wrong ways of obtaining answers. If we say there are "right" and "wrong" motives for the asking of questions, however, new connotations creep into our use of these adjectives.

Thus, we should speak of "good" and "poor" questions to put to nature. In the past there have been innumerable questions concerning nature, and innumerable answer attempts, both good *and* poor. Consider such a normal question as, What are the stars? Before he finally obtained a good answer, man asked and answered many other questions about the stars. Which stars control my destiny? Do they revolve in a purer context than ours? and many others. Some were futile and poor. Gradually man learned not to ask them, though he still asks poor questions in many areas.

[3] Daniel S. Robinson, *The Principles of Reasoning* (3rd ed.; New York: Appleton-Century-Crofts, Inc., 1957), p. 220.

[4] Mary B. Hesse, *Science and the Human Imagination* (London: Student Christian Movement Press, 1954), p. 36.

Methods of obtaining answers make a lively topic. Perhaps the most famous method is the "scientific method." Uncounted texts in the sciences will give attention to it in early pages. The discussions are usually simplified, but strictly speaking the whole subject is far from simple and clear. A great many people who study the sciences come out as technologists rather than scientists. A scientist never ceases to raise further questions.

The problem of motivations prompting questions can become perplexing and obscure. Questions can be the results of impulsions ranging all the way from simple requests for information—How far to the next town?—to subtle and complex questions that grow out of motivations too deep in the inner life for either questioner or hearer to understand, or perhaps even know about. Questions thus can be related to emotional health.

In his *People in Quandaries*[5] Wendell Johnson says that a "scientist" abandons a question when he realizes it is unanswerable. This implies that the scientist is one who is able to abandon a question that is unanswerable, and who is able to recognize questions that *are* unanswerable. This may be overly idealistic. The people who are most persistent in articulating such questions are usually not able to cease questioning by merely deciding to do so. It would be the counsel of perfection to ask them to quit. They are in the grip of compulsive motivations.

In our day the problem of uses to which answers are to be put has become poignantly significant, beyond anything we had ever dreamed. The outstanding phrase in this connection is "peaceful uses of atomic power." In the past "pure science" felt no compunction about asking questions and obtaining answers, since it was able *not* to give attention to the *uses* of the knowledge acquired. This is not so easy now. It is far less easy than ever before to ignore "applied science" or the applying that can be done by nonscientists.

We turn now to a brief outline of the "question situation," something existing only in a human context.

The questioner. He of course is always a human being. The extent to which animals are questioners may be of significance, but need not concern us here. The questioner is now an object of study, an object of scientific questioning, and we might add, at last. This service has been performed by the psychological sciences.

The subject matter of questions. Questions can be asked about any-

[5] New York: Harper & Brothers, 1946, especially Ch. III.

thing, and as such would frustrate neat classification. Fortunetellers still have much business because enough people are willing to pay for answers to "lock-picking" questions about the future. Opinions vary as to what is considered allowable subject matter for serious questioning. Some scientists will not agree that extrasensory preception is proper subject matter for scientific questioning. Others will say that psychologists of personality are asking futile questions about "depths" or "personal wholeness." Representatives of religion often suggest that questions of the laboratory type are inadequate for study of religious experience.

Modes of answering. The history of answering questions would be funny if so much of it were not pathetic. Consider the blundering and consequent suffering in the story of "answers" to such questions as to how to cure illness, how children should be dealt with, how to detect crime, how to test credibility of witnesses, and so on. This history includes such devices as oracles, magicians, chicken entrails, signs in the heavens, among others. Humanity has not to this day reached an exactly enviable stage of maturity in the modes of answering they are willing to employ.

Answers. Many times in human history good and valid answers to questions were not recognized as such at the time. People have always tended to judge answers with self-confident recklessness, committing countless errors in the process—often because of inertia, prejudice, or fear of the new. But judge they will. And *all* answers will be used.

The linguistic formulation. With the instrumentality of language questions can be "detached" from questioners and converted into objects of study themselves. Or they may be used as pedagogical devices. They can be discussed. They can be considered in terms of their presuppositions and implications. They can be put back into hypothetical situations and studied as to psychological significance, and this would involve study of questioners. Man would never have become so conscious of his curiosity or his questions had he not acquired or been endowed with language. He needed language so that his curiosity could become fruitful, so that any natural tendency to curiosity could be brought into consciousness—that is, so he could *ask* questions. In other words, since the asking of questions develops into such a tremendous enterprise, language may be entitled to the major credit for this. Language is essential in a number of ways.

In the first place the articulation of questions helps to keep an inquiry alive. Whether animals ever have questions "in mind" we need not say, but it takes language to *keep* questions in mind.

Again, language makes the communicating of questions possible. With language you may learn what my questions are, and vice versa. The subject matter may not be present or even existent, but your questions can, through language, become my questions. A hunting dog may seem "inquisitive" about the possibility of birds in a field if he encounters another dog already starting the search. But this is not communication in the strict language sense.

When language is committed to writing, questions can become permanent. They can be communicated not only to contemporaries but to succeeding generations. Even stupid and senseless questions can be recorded for permanence. We may fail to detect the senseless quality of some questions for centuries!

Finally, language enormously facilitates thinking about questions, making possible questions about questions. True, we do not often demonstrate virtuosity in thinking about questions, and too often we are uncritical in our acceptance of proposed answers. Language makes it possible to make even greater mistakes and commit more and more fallacies, as well as to ask more questions of the improper and unanswerable variety.

Man Is Questioned

In preceding pages we had occasion to introduce certain aspects and implications of the human enterprise of asking questions. We come now to the selection of certain special questions for the present work. They are not questions that we can consider in terms of adequate answers, but rather that they are universally relevant questions. The most we can expect will be a kind of "educational acquaintance" with them. Readers may recognize the source of this phrase:

> Every systematic science . . . seems to admit of two kinds of proficiency; one of which may be properly called scientific knowledge of the subject, while the other is a kind of educational acquaintance with it. For an educated man should be able to form a fair off-hand judgment as to the goodness or badness of the method used by a professor in his exposition. To be educated is in fact to be able to do this.[6]

This involves obligation rather than privilege. From the work of experts and professionals come reports of profound and far-reaching inquiries into the "heart of things." The most that we can do, usually,

[6] Aristotle, *De Partibus Animalium,* 639 a 1 ff.

is to endeavor to acquire at least an "educational acquaintance." This has been one of the assumptions of such "general education" as generations on the wane have endeavored to commit to generations on the rise.

Two of the special questions referred to above are: What is my psychological condition? and, What is my religion? They are universally relevant to human beings; they are difficult to answer; and, if faced up to squarely, they *could* be very embarrassing. It is tempting to add the seductive word "really" to each question. But psychology is a very young science, and we are repeatedly told that "religion" cannot be defined.

Vast resources are being drawn upon today to underwrite efforts to find ways of answering the first of our two questions. The mighty instrument of science is at work on this task with its techniques of measurement, analysis, controlled experiment, and kindred procedures. Shall it concentrate on the organism and thereby stay close to the more established science of biology? Or shall it concentrate on the subtler "personality"? A booklet called *Measure Religion* is indicative of the trend.[7] It was Thorndike who suggested that "if it exists it can be measured."

Resistance will be offered to measurement and analysis, especially if it means people should abandon valuing in favor of description. When our very selves are being subjected to measurement and analysis, "frail human nature" can hardly stand dispassionately to one side and await the objective verdict. Two solemn fears would often haunt: that we might be shown to be inadequate or defective, or that what we held to be important might be "explained away." Many deplore what they call the "paralysis of analysis."

The universality of the first question is utterly obvious, even if we were not to use the adjective "psychological." And science is entering this area as investigator. The article of faith back of this has nowhere been stated more tersely than by David Hume in the eighteenth century: "There is a general course of nature in human actions, as well as in the operations of the sun and climate" [8] On the basis of this he dreamed of introducing "the experimental Method of Reasoning into MORAL SUBJECTS" (title page), of laying the foundations for a science of man, and of doing a "naturalistic" history of religion. The dream is more vivid than ever today.

[7] Ernest J. Chave (Chicago: University of Chicago Press, 1939).
[8] *Treatise of Human Nature,* Book II, Part III, sec. i.

The relevance of the second question may not seem so obvious or universal. This would imply (as I intend) that everyone has some kind of "religion." Not everyone will agree. It will be argued in subsequent chapters.

It was said that our questions could be embarrassing. Why? It is not too embarrassing usually to be told that one's blood count is low, or that he has a vitamin deficiency, or that he needs a tonic. Of course it would be a shock to be told one has cancer. All this is not embarrassing in the sense that some psychological reports would be, however. To be told that one is emotionally immature, full of irrational hostilities, subnormal in this particular, abnormal in that—such reports could cause special embarrassment. Many people still avoid consulting "psychological" doctors. Families are often more embarrassed to have it intimated that "mental" trouble afflicts a member of the family than if the difficulty were injury from irresponsible car-driving, hang-overs, or general physical disrepair.

If qualified persons were to prepare reports on our religion, we might discover that it is different from what we say it is; or that the religion we practice is one we hardly know we have; or that our rejections of religion are really religious battles; or that the tenets of the religion we socially profess are skillfully modified by another religion more congenial to our private striving for advantage and power; or that our "real" religion is naïve and misguided devotion to "false gods." The total history of religion betrays much emotional immaturity. It would be difficult to conduct a controversy on any intellectual level if our emotional development is still done up with safety pins.

While complete answers to our questions are hardly to be expected, there are better opportunities today for getting certain kinds of light on both questions than ever before. Ancient man tended to believe that the "heart" was an impenetrable area:

> The heart of man is more dangerous than mountains and rivers,
> more difficult to understand than Heaven itself.
> Heaven has its periods of spring, summer,
> autumn, winter, day-time and night.
> Man has an impenetrable exterior;
> and his motives are inscrutable.[9]

[9] Taoism. Quoted in Robert E. Hume, *Treasure-House of the Living Religions* (New York: Charles Scribner's Sons, 1932), p. 81. Used by permission of Bernard Quaritch Ltd.

"The heart is deceitful above all things, and desperately wicked: who can know it?" (Jer. 17:9.) One can imagine psychology saying that this question, formerly thought insoluble, is now on the way to solution with the rapid development of personality studies. Would that mean progress toward finding out what religion is?

True, the claim to offer a psychological explanation of religion—or some aspects of it—has more point than the same type of question using the name of any other science. Psychological explanations have "pepped up" daily conversation with a whole new collection of seemingly technical terms: neurotic, phobia, rationalization, and others. Psychological contributions are still in a somewhat ambiguous state, however. On the one hand are the "floating dogmas," often uncritically accepted as "new truth": Religion is authoritative and dogmatic; religion is a form of illness; religions are all the same. On the other it is sometimes said that modern psychological studies of fear show the wisdom of an ancient affirmation, "True love casts out fear." [10]

If . . .

A complex of questioning gathers about the uses of the word "if." We introduced this section with a fragment of conversation:

"What do you think of me?"
"Is that a serious question?"
"Yes."
"Then I'll attempt an answer because I do have one."
"What is it?"
"I believe you are a religious person."
"I have never been so insulted!"
"Sometimes you must explain what it means to be insulted. I've often wondered. Are you insulted if you don't admit you are? Are you insulted if there is no intention to insult? I had no notion I was insulting you. I thought I was being descriptive."
"Why did you call me a religious person?"
"That would involve definition, and I was consciously using a partial definition—one it seems to me should be part of the definition."
"What is it and how does it relate to me?"
"I said 'religious person' because I believe that you really care about people."
"I hate people!"
"Here we go again."

[10] Cf. Oskar Pfister, *Christianity and Fear,* tr. W. H. Johnston (New York: The Macmillan Company, 1949).

This fragment, plus some additional bits not recorded here, transpired almost accidentally. Yet it would be difficult to find a casual bit of conversation with more opening gambits for a consideration of the themes of this work. It is tempting to say that *if* we understood this little episode completely ("all in all"), then we would know what *religion* and *person* are ("what God and man is"), or that *if* there is a divine mind, then it understands how these speakers "got that way" and what they were to become—that is, *if* the Whole is represented in the particular, or *if* the totality of events is caught up in a universal and unvarying series of casual sequences. These are sizable "if's." In this paragraph we have deliberately made oblique references to Tennyson and Laplace, to the former for his use of "if" in his poem "The Flower in the Crannied Wall," to the latter for his references to how the past and future could be read "if" an infinite intelligence surveyed any particular event in its totality. Both references testify to the currency of notions among the general public which were inspired by scientific developments of the eighteenth century and by presuppositions current at the time as to how this universe operated. That they evinced a certain naïveté we may assume, but the importance and the currency of the hypothetical connecting of concepts and events continue. We give attention to the importance in science and to the currency in certain speculations concerning human welfare.

If x, then y. The simple term "if" is an index to a now demonstrated human capacity—the ability to connect concepts whereby contributions to the advancement of knowledge become possible and to understand many kinds of causal operations. This has been put graphically:

> A question of the form: If I do this, what will happen? is strictly scientific. As a matter of fact, science can be defined as a method for, and a body of information obtained by, trying to answer only questions which can be put into the form: If I do this, what will happen? The technique of it, fundamentally, is: Try it and see. Then you put together a large amount of information from such experiences. All scientists will agree that a question —any question, philosophical or other—which cannot be put into the form that can be tested by experiment (or, in simple terms, that cannot be put into the form: If I do this, what will happen?) is not a scientific question: it is outside the realm of science.[11]

The popular style of this paragraph may engender the notion that the author is operating with a strict dichotomy, that there is a sharp

[11] Richard P. Feynman in *Frontiers in Science*, ed. Edward Hutchings, Jr. (New York: Basic Books, Inc., 1958), p. 315. Used by permission.

line between the realm of science and "others," and that procedures for the former are clear cut and unequivocal. True, there is an uncommon strictness in scientific procedure with its goal of precision. We, therefore, may well imagine the scientist shying away from such a formulation as "If there was a just God, he wouldn't let all those injustices prevail."

A second comment is found in Norman Campbell's *What Is Science?*:

> If we could imagine ourselves without any experience of the external world derived from our senses, we might doubt whether there actually are such relations concerning which universal agreement can be obtained. . . . But we all know from our experience that there are such relations and we know of what kind these relations are. They are of the kind that have just been indicated; the universal relations that we can state are between events which are such that, *if* one event happens, *then* another event happens.[12]

There are, that is, relations between events whereby we can depend on recurring sequences, and even do some predicting. David Hume's critical analysis of the causal relation was not so much an analysis of the relation *between events* as it was of what we call *knowledge of* this relation, an analysis of the mental habits that enable the mind to make a "jump" from the experience of *constant conjunction* to the assumption of our knowledge of *necessary connexion.* And yet the same Hume also said, "Effects always correspond to causes."

Thus, in relation to themes in the present work, we have only a proximate understanding as to how the hypothetical formulation, so important in science, can indicate fruitful inquiry. Consider the following formulations: If we are to understand religion then we need to understand man; if we would understand man then we need to know biology; if we are to understand anything, we need the scientific approach; if we are to be free, then we must know (the) truth. It may be a bit early to know with precision which of the foregoing are more valid, more fruitful. The requirements for inquiry after the mode and manner of if *x,* then *y* are severe. And the maximum possible observation and experimenting are requisite. The primitive may have said, "If we beat the tom-toms when the sun goes into eclipse, it will soon pass away—it always has." With hindsight we can say confidently that he certainly fell short in observing and experimenting. Or if people have said—and they have—that "if you beat a child enough

[12] New York: Dover Publications, 1952, p. 38. Italics in the text.

you will tame him," perhaps they felt secure in their reasoning, but science would immediately remind us that the relationship of the x and the y in this case was woefully misunderstood.

If only. . . . There is a note of pathos in some of the "if" uses of this type, whether intended by writers or not. The first one comes from Herman J. Muller's "Will Science Continue?" It appeared in the *Bulletin of Atomic Research Scientists,* December, 1952, and was reproduced in *Readings in Philosophy of Science:*

Man is a minute mote in the vastness of nature. He has only just begun, through science, to see the world for what it is, and to find large-scale ways of controlling it in his long-term interests. *If only* he will settle the sorry, shameful conflicts between groups of his own kind, he may then proceed to contests with nature which are really worthy of him.[13]

It is not clear whether it is implied that the scientist should proceed forthwith "to contests with [human] nature which are really worthy of him." Should *human* nature be studied and treated the way nature is, in "long-term interests"? The so-called stricter scientists are often captious in their criticisms of the very scientists who are approaching this most difficult of areas of data—personality and personality depths. Is the settling of the "sorry, shameful conflicts between groups of his own kind" a scientific problem, to be approached by the scientific method? Whatever the case, it is obvious that norms and imperatives are involved. Muller is aware of this. He says, later on in the same article,

Finally, we must face the problems of human nature itself, for these present us with the greatest tasks of all. We shall then find that the transfiguration of man, by man himself, into a being ever nobler not merely in body, but, more important in spirit, is a direction of progress which will require our utmost resourcefulness and wisdom, and which is never-ending in its possibilities.[14]

The next reference is from an address presented by retiring president George W. Beadle at a meeting of the American Association for the Advancement of Science, December, 1956.

Man's evolutionary future, biologically and culturally, is unlimited. But far more important, it lies within his power to determine its direction. . . .

[13] Philip P. Wiener (ed.) (New York: Charles Scribner's Sons, 1953), p. 424. Used by permission. Italics supplied.

[14] *Ibid.,* p. 425.

But knowledge alone is not sufficient. To carry the human species on to a future of biological and cultural freedom, knowledge must be accompanied by collective wisdom and courage of an order not yet demonstrated by any society of men. And beyond knowledge, wisdom, and courage, faith, too, will be essential. Man must have faith in himself. He must have faith in the rightness and goodness of his goals. And many would add that he must continue to have spiritual faith.[15]

The cynic stands hard by, ready with the question, Why don't you just give up if you realize that it takes all that, and that man has never demonstrated such collective wisdom and courage as would be required? The cynic's question is precisely the same kind of reaction—rather than response—that stimulates the spiritless conviction that everything that has been tried has failed—education, politics, religion, civilization itself. And the cynic, we may note, is often a tiring idealist.

Of course presidential addresses and articles for public consumption often have something of the promotional quality in them. One finds an occasional deferential use of honorific terms like "spirit," "spiritual," and "faith" looming up, though many individual scientists reject them out of hand, but not all of them. In either case, however, such terms are not characteristically scientific.

The "if" is introduced in the following quotation almost as an afterthought. It evidences an awareness of problems at least hinted at in the preceding paragraph: "Science and mankind, and religion, too, for that matter, would profit *if* all men would live closer to the ideals expressed and practiced by the more devoted men of religion and science." [16] While the "and religion, too, for that matter" may sound a bit like a public relations gesture, yet the whole statement is a good example, for all its brevity and apparently incidental quality, of the realization that there is a problem that is not exactly in the laboratory, but certainly is in the larger context in which the laboratory finds itself.

A more subdued example of our linguistic formulation is the following, but which at the same time directly calls attention to the pathos of vastly extensive human plight: "We have the tools and the technology to feed everyone in the world with our present resources. And yet it has been estimated that 80 percent of the world population

[15] Reprinted from *Science* by permission from the American Association for the Advancement of Science.

[16] James R. Newman (ed.), *What Is Science?* Ward Clyde Allee, "Biology" (New York: Simon and Schuster, 1955), p. 250. Italics supplied.

normally suffers from undernutrition or malnutrition." [17] The chapter is not primarily concerned with either the ways to arouse the will and interest of people, or the political and social organization essential for getting the food to the 80 per cent. Rather it is concerned with the interpretation as to what food is. The author's interest is in the "nutritional aspect of processing foods." Thus, when his biological and technological competence is coupled with a *modus operandi* for arousing interest in people, and the formation of political and social techniques of distribution, vast problems will be solved.

Muller said that it is "first necessary to know," but other than that, all the foregoing statements refer to something that man must do, or be, or want to do or be—that is, all except the one from Borsook, and it does so by implication. Knowledge we have, also technological competence, material resources, tools, equipment, machinery. What is lacking? It is not primarily a scientific problem—unless the interpretation of the scientific enterprise be broadened to include an active concern with values and human welfare as well as with a scientific approach to the human datum. One may suspect that the ridicule directed at the more human sciences—by scientists in the name of scientific "strictness"—conceals a subtle fear of the very magnitude of the problem. On the other hand, scientists, as scientists, do have a point in their criticisms and interpretations as to what can be called a "science," but this, by implication, disallows the presumption of the omnicompetence of "science," which presumption has been toyed with in modern times, what we might call the "Tower of Babel complex."

Our final *if* is a spirited affirmation of what will "save" our world, if it is to be saved. Perhaps the author, A. H. Maslow, offers this as an answer to the question of the preceding paragraph (What is lacking?):

> I believe that the world will either be saved by the psychologists or it won't be saved at all. I think psychologists are the most important people living today. I think the fate of the human species and the future of the human species rest more upon their shoulders than upon any group of people now living. I believe that all the important problems of war and peace, exploitation and brotherhood, hatred and love, sickness and health, misunderstanding and understanding, the happiness and unhappiness of mankind will yield only to a better understanding of human nature.[18]

[17] Hutchings, *op. cit.*, Henry Borsook, "We Could Feed the World," p. 80.

[18] "Toward a Humanistic Psychology," in the symposium *Our Language and Our World*, ed. S. I. Hayakawa (New York: Harper & Brothers, 1959), p. 186.

Many psychologists and friends of psychology have *thought* this without being willing to say it quite so categorically. As a statement, however, it represents an answer, or what the speaker believes to be an answer to the problem of the alleviation of the pathos referred to above.

Yet, there is a dark cloud on the horizon. It has been psychological knowledge and psychological techniques, put to certain lamentable uses, that have given us one of the ugliest of modern terms: brain-washing, with its unholy disregard of the principle of worth of persons.

CHAPTER III

Language

PERHAPS EVERYONE HAS HEARD MARK TWAIN'S TONGUE-IN-CHEEK compliment to the French children—that in France even the little children speak French. It is far easier to be amused by this observation than to be amazed by the fact that any children anywhere can and do learn language. Familiarity with the fact lulls us into the supposition that it is "obviously natural." There is nothing obvious about it, beyond the bare fact that it is. Most of the questions that are easy to ask about language are either very difficult to answer or are unanswerable. Beyond the generalized notion that it followed a process of natural development along with the increase of mankind's cranial furnishings, little or nothing is known for sure. Was there ever a time when mankind had a vocabulary of only a dozen words or so, with no recognizable syntax? There is no answer. Yet we may feel like saying that there must have been. What was the first real word ever uttered? We cannot be sure whether this is an improper question. On the other hand, was such a first word something like "swish," or some other onomatopoeic term? Let us take a look at some of the natural questions concerning this "natural" accomplishment.

Do we know how language began? Is there in human nature a language-making instinct? Are there any known primitive languages—primitive in the sense of having few words, no sentence structure, and limited syntax or none? If a newborn child were separated at birth from all human associations, but put in an environment permitting it to stay alive, would it develop a language of its own? Or if some human infants were subjected to such an experiment but associated with each other, would they as a group develop a language as they grew up? Could a human child learn a language the way the hero of Tarzan fiction did? If the answer to all these questions is no, as is probably the case, ours is perhaps the first century to realize this with regard to all such questions. The remarkable instrument of language has never been so thoroughly and professionally studied as in the past few generations. The names of Jespersen, Sapir, Usener,

Cassirer, Whitehead, Urban, and others constitute the bright galaxy of students of this as yet mysterious accomplishment of *homo loquens*.[1]

There are other questions perhaps not quite so unanswerable as the foregoing, though that may be debatable. Why are there so many languages? How did the notion of magic words ever arise? Why can't animals learn to talk? What is the language spoken in heaven? After a child learns to talk, is it conceivable that he might be able to speak words and sentences in a language he was exposed to during the first twelve months of his life but not later? Why is it easy for a child to learn three languages at the same time, whereas many adults have difficulty learning one new language? Is communication the sole purpose and function of language? Do people learn to talk because they need to? Were the voices that spoke to Joan of Arc—or anyone like her for that matter—nonhuman? Is language essential to thinking? Are there "thoughts that lie too deep for tears"? Is it possible to know something and not be able to explain it? Is music a language? Some of these questions have been answered for centuries, but today the answers are being reconsidered and in some instances rejected. Some of the proposed answers of the past are being replaced by new ones. In some cases the questions themselves are being rejected, or at least revised.

Man is a name-giving creature, the only one. This is a basic feature of the language process. It would be hard to find a more realistic statement in ancient literature concerning language than Gen. 2:19. This passage says that Adam (man) gave names to the creatures. Even so, fallacies still persist. As long ago as Plato's *Cratylus,* the Fallacy of Natural Names was discussed and rejected. It persists, however, although it may be no more than a speech habit handed down from generation to generation. A man, reporting his first experience with an opossum commented on its peculiar behavior. Then, as though coming into an important realization, he said, "All of a sudden I realized why they are called 'possums."

Perhaps a tentative summary of reminders would be in order at this point. Some of these reminders have impressed us as discoveries, once we consider them critically. It would be a case of something which might seem natural to uncritical observation. For example, to

[1] Cf. the significant discussion of this term in W. F. Zuurdeeg, *An Analytical Philosophy of Religion* (Nashville: Abingdon Press, 1958), p. 59 ff., *et passim.* Zuurdeeg acknowledges the influence of Georges Gusdorf's *La Parole* (Paris: Presses universitaires de France, 1953).

some people it seems natural to conclude that it would take a pendulum "twice as long" to swing through a two-foot arc as through a one-foot arc. It may seem natural to suppose that primitive people speak primitive languages, or that mankind has a language-making instinct. Our selected list of reminders, based on some modern study of language, would include: 1. There are no known primitive languages; 2. There are no known simple languages; 3. There is no known human culture without language; 4. There is probably no language-making instinct; 5. Language makes reasoning possible more than its being a result of thinking and reasoning; 6. Language is a fallible instrument; 7. Learning to talk depends in part on a "babbling instinct" that human children have, and which animals seem not to have. On this last point Susanne K. Langer calls attention to the significance of this babbling proclivity in her *Philosophy in a New Key*.[2] In a more recent work, Roger Brown, commenting on this reference in Langer's work, reminds his readers that "the aesthetic pleasure or sound-play assumptions do not explain the most important thing about babbling, the fact that it drifts in the direction of the speech the infant hears." [3]

Each individual person is not so much a name giver as he is a name user. It is not now necessary for each person to name very many things. As he enters into human society, most things have already been named. It is necessary only to learn the names already given. Yet, name giving continues in another way. Anyone can "name" something to suit himself in a way that passes far beyond the relatively simple process of labeling, cataloguing, or classifying. We pass into the jungle land of human emotions when we find people giving names that are not names in the strict sense, but indexes of how the speaker feels. Description and labeling pass over into judgment. "Mr. X spoke for an hour on the subject of proposed legislation to equalize franchise privileges of citizens." "Mr. X gave a long-winded and radical harangue on some starry-eyed notions about voting." These two hypothetical quotations could refer to the same speech. The first one is presumably a description. The latter is a severe judgment. The former could be emotionally neutral. The latter is anything but neutral. The first is reportorial. The latter is condemnatory.

Two things are suggested by the preceding paragraph, and together they present the uniquely human problem in a special way. In the

[2] Cambridge: Harvard University Press, 1942, pp. 116 *et passim.*

[3] *Words and Things* (Chicago: The Free Press of Glencoe, 1958), p. 199.

first place, the individual human being probably has the capacity and potential to reproduce the whole human achievement as far as language is concerned, yet he could never do this alone. The development of name giving, of language, has been a group achievement. But the capacity and potential require a focal point for realization—the individual human unit, the person. We know, or seem to know, that an individual child detached at birth from all human associations would not learn language. But if all newborn infants at a given time were detached from all other human associations than themselves, by some drastic, cosmic experiment, presumably, in time, they would develop language, or rather their remote decendants would. Presumably, this is what did happen, in some sense. That is to say, if man has had non-language-using ancestors, somewhere along the line language developed or was invented. In the process there developed in the individual human unit something as physical as vocal cords suited to speech and something as subtle as the capacity for symbolic representation. In the second place, this magnificant accomplishment is remarkably corruptible in a variety of ways. This takes us far beyond problems of mere error.

The corruptibility is partly due to the fact that though these activities have emerged into consciousness, troubles can still develop in the depths below the conscious level, can have baneful effects, can produce perversions and distortions. The constructive operations of language use will function best when personality growth and development are characterized by health, wholeness, and intelligence. When personality is subjected to those stresses and strains that affect its health and hinder its progress toward wholeness, language use is correspondingly affected. There are so many ways for this to happen that it would take much space simply to list the names of language fallacies and perversions. One recent author has said:

> There is a language of personality maladjustment. You have to use a certain kind of language—or you have to use language in a certain way—if you are going to worry, or to regret, or to hate, or to develop and maintain an inferiority complex. Leaving any consideration of language behavior out of a discussion of personality would be somewhat like leaving the cheese out of a cheese souffle.[4]

We may consider the corruption of language from a different perspective. Instead of looking at maladjustments of language and of

[4] Wendell Johnson, *op. cit.*, p. 243.

personality in terms of the personalities and speech of individual people, let us take note of social and political dimensions:

The most effective way of making people accept the validity of the values they are to serve is to persuade them that they are really the same as those which they, or at least the best among them, have always held, but which were not properly understood or recognized before. . . . And the most efficient technique to this end is to use the old words but change their meaning. Few traits of totalitarian regimes are at the same time so confusing to the superficial observer and yet so characteristic of the whole intellectual climate as the complete perversion of language, and change of meaning of the words by which the ideals of the new regimes are expressed. If one has not one's self experienced this process, it is difficult to appreciate the magnitude of this change of the meaning of words, the confusion which it causes, and the barriers to any rational discussion which it creates. . . . The whole language becomes despoiled.[5]

It is not clear from the foregoing quotation whether the author had Thucydides in mind, but certainly a report from that gifted Greek historian presents a situation that has some startling resemblances:

Revolution thus ran its course from city to city, and the places which it arrived at last, from having heard what had been done before, carried to a still greater excess the refinement of their inventions, as manifested in the cunning of their enterprises and the atrocity of their reprisals. Words had to change their ordinary meaning and to take that which was now given them. Reckless audacity came to be considered the courage of a loyal ally; prudent hesitation, specious cowardice; moderation was held to be a cloak for unmanliness; ability to see all sides of a question inaptness to act on any. Frantic violence became the attribute of manliness; cautious plotting, a justifiable means of self-defence. The advocate of extreme measures was always trustworthy; his opponent a man to be suspected.[6]

The following quotation from George Bernard Shaw shows a reversal of this kind of procedure. Here we find in a speech by Don Juan in the play *Man and Superman* something that offers itself as a correction of a prior corruption in name giving, or as suggested earlier in this chapter, name using:

In this Palace of Lies a truth or two will not hurt you. Your friends are all the dullest dogs I know. They are not beautiful: they are only decorated.

[5] Friedrich A. Hayek, *The Road to Serfdom.* Copyright 1944 by the University of Chicago, pp. 157, 159. Used by permission.

[6] *The Peloponnesian War*, tr., Richard Crawley (New York: The Modern Library Inc., 1934), III, ix, 82, 189.

They are not clean: they are only shaved and starched. They are not dignified: they are only fashionably dressed. They are not educated: they are only college passmen. They are not religious: they are only pewrenters. They are not moral: they are only conventional. They are not virtuous: they are only cowardly. They are not even vicious: they are only "frail." They are not artistic: they are only lascivious. They are not prosperous: they are only rich. They are not loyal, they are only servile; not dutiful, only sheepish; . . . not masterful, only domineering; . . . not disciplined, only cowed; and not truthful at all.[7]

While man is the name giver, it is no doubt obvious that names already assigned present numerous questions of great variety and difficulty. To begin with we state a question that seems simple and obvious. Since there are many names, is there an object for each name, a referend to which it refers? If we say no—as might seem to be the obvious answer—we could ask how it is possible to use such names or terms in discourse. If there are names for things that do not exist, we obviously can carry on conversation as though they did. A common explanation is to distinguish at least two orders of existence, such as spatial, existing in space, and conceptual, existing only in the mind. But the problem of name object or name referend, seen in the form of the persistence of the tendency to hunt around for an object or referend for each name, as "parts" that can be separarated. For instance, consider the subject "ghost." It is possible to get into a controversy as to whether ghosts exist. In the process it is easy to ignore completely the problem of how this name ever got into the human catalogue of names. Man is a persistent name giver, for this he is entitled to credit, and thus even to give a name like "ghost" to "something" is an example of this laudable tendency at work. It is also an indication of capacity for error, however—granting for the moment that ghosts are not real. This is not so laudable perhaps. What is the cause of this type of error? In other words, we have the outlines of a universal type of problem. What does man do when he names "something"? How can the important process of name giving be continued, while all seek ways to eliminate or at least play down error? Is the making of errors always of the same type? Most readers will probably detect the possibility of getting into controversy at this point concerning a word like "sin," a term allegedly congenial to religion but uncongenial to science.

[7] Act III. Used by permission of the Public Trustee and The Society of Authors.

There continues to float around through human mental experience the notion that for every name there is an object to which it refers. This is taken account of in the following: "The mind tends to believe that there is a real object for every thought it entertains. This tendency to objectify is so deeply rooted in man that he comes only gradually and reluctantly to the recognition that there may be objectless thoughts." [8] This quotation need not be taken as a definitive and clarifying psychological analysis, but it does at least denote the locale of a persistent problem. Moreover man sometimes tries tricks with this general problem, such as:

"Nothing" is a noun, isn't it?
Yes.
And a noun is the name of a person, place, or thing, isn't it?
Yes.
Then if "nothing" is a noun, and if a noun is the name of something, "nothing" is therefore something.

A parallel notion equally persistent is that "everything has a name." This takes more than one form. There is the form, already referred to, that we may call the fallacy of natural names. It shows up in the story of the person who praised the astronomers for their ability to "find out" the names of the heavenly bodies. Another form is the belief that if anything "doesn't have a name" there is something mysterious about it. A young man reported that in his home community there was talk about a mysterious animal that roamed the woods, but had not yet been seen clearly by anyone. When he asked a man for the name of the animal, the man replied, "It doesn't have a name!" Under the circumstances this was not the same as saying that mankind "had not got around to naming it yet." This is only a step away from the persistent notion, widely held through many centuries, that a name is much more than a mere label or identification tag; a name is a thing in itself. This notion persists—not without some reinterpretation—in such concepts as "good name" and "bad name." If you destroy a man's name, you have harmed an important possession or attribute.

We now consider some of the aspects of the problem of names in its relation to religion, as compared and contrasted with the same problem in science. No enterprise has ever given such strict and ex-

[8] Ledger Wood, *The Analysis of Knowledge* (Princeton, N.J.: Princeton University Press, 1941), p. 130.

tensive attention to the task of naming as has science. In a sense, science is almost regarded as an ideal fulfillment of man's name-giving propensities. Science adds a very strict set of stipulations: name the things that are; define the names; check your observations so as to know whether there is something "there" to be named; be especially critical of hearsay; be chary of giving names to the supposed furnishings of mysterious, unseen, and invisible "worlds"; specify in cases of uncertainy and doubt, or if possible, investigate; avoid intemperate guessing; eliminate ambiguity from terms used; study the mental processes that lead or lure into fallacies of and with language—such as hypostatization, reification, fallacy of the absolute dictionary, and a host of others. None of this means that a scientist cannot enjoy stories about Sherlock Holmes, since the doughty sleuth was only a "fiction." Yet Darwin records that he lost his taste for poetry, Shakespeare, and kindred interests; and in a way it is easy to ask, Why not? There is a type of plausibility in the scientific prospect of a purification of language in the direction of precision in usage, and in pruning away all vague, nebulous, and undefinable terms. Yet it would require, for full development, much more knowledge than we may ever have. It would also require some radical adjustments in human nature to eliminate, or attenuate those imaginative, aesthetic, and intuitive capacities that add color, richness, and warmth to language possibilities. It is again conceivable that this will evoke the query, Why not?

The extent to which one is swayed by the considerations in the preceding paragraph may determine the degree of disfavor into which religion may fall. For if we make exclusive use of the strict stipulations that are congenial to science, many of the names and much of the terminology customarily associated with religion come under suspicion. A number of questions arise. For instance, each item in the set of stipulations listed above may seem an adequate basis for a sharp question to be directed against many religious terms, or what are nominally regarded as religious terms: spirit, soul, divine will, supernal realm, God, providence, eternal plan, destiny in eternity, and may others. If we try to settle such problems quickly, crisply, and conclusively, then it may seem we do so by simply asking questions, How can you know that there are such things? Why suppose these are real existents? Are these susceptible of any kind of verification? These questions have only a limited relevance, how ever forceful they may be up to a point. In the first place, the problem of naming is by no means limited to the problem of locating clearly identifiable things to which names may be given.

To say the least, this limits the function of language unduly. In the second place, it is often quite important to try to ascertain what human beings are trying to do or say when they apply names. That errors may arise we readily grant. It is a much more important task, however, to ascertain what people are trying to do in the use of language—in its various uses, not in just trying to give names to things as they find them. This is a field of inquiry scarcely opened yet. Even in the use of such an admittedly ambiguous term as "spirit," it is not enough simply to decide there are no spirits, that we may therefore drop the term. What have people thought they were doing; what did they intend to do; and what have we found out since the word became established in usage that will throw light on their stumbling efforts? It is too easy to write off the errors of the past and repose confidence in supposed "new truth without error" of the future. We forget that profound wisdom can be tucked away in the efforts of the past, and that our present and future work will traffic in errors whose magnitude would alarm us if we knew what future critics would say about them.

How great is the contrast between religion and science with regard to the problem of name giving and name using? That is one question, and it is by no means solved yet. This is partly due to limited understanding, but more than that, we too easily apply the same types of norms to both areas. That is, we do if we say that since science verifies the existence or nonexistence of an object in *X* manner, therefore religion should do the same. This is right in certain limited ways. But if science uses a method to ascertain the suspected existence and location of, for example, Neptune, shall religion be told to use the same method to ascertain the existence and location of divine love?

A second question concerns some supposed origins of some examples of name giving. This makes it possible to ignore any problem of whether these terms denote reality of any kind. Thus our second question may take the form of inquiring whether the genetic fallacy is being committed. Attempts have been made to ascertain the psychological origins of such concepts as the divine, immortality, God, and others. For many people these psychological explanations may have the feel of proof, yet they hardly have any firmer status thus far than attractive —or sensational—plausibilities. A question such as, What is the scientific proof of the existence of God? is frequently not a bona fide question, especially if it hides the prior assumption that there certainly isn't any God. This decides the question ahead of time, guaranteeing that it is a futile question. Translated out of such a context it would be

What is the scientific proof of something that doesn't exist? There is nothing open about this question. In another sense, what allowance is made for the question of whether scientific proof is a proper and relevant approach to such a problem? In so far as there is a problem here, the question might become, What is the scientific proof of something that is not amenable or accessible to scientific proof? Neither is this an open question. Thus we may ask: Wherever there is a name, is there a single mode for ascertaining whether there is a referend to fit? It is difficult to see any adequate basis for saying there is. The attractiveness of the promise of single explanations is as much due to a feeling of gaining control of data as it is to a clear-eyed perception of a mode for acquiring knowledge.

What has been said is in no sense a derogation of the enterprise of science. It does nothing more than raise a question about some interpretations of science and of its applications. The same general type of question applies to the "other side." This is thought to be such an old and established conclusion that it might seem unnecessary to mention it—namely, that religion has been accused of dictating to science, and prescribing norms for its use. Certainly things have happened that had this appearance, depending how we are using the term "religion." Was it religion that told a developing medical science that demons caused certain kinds of illness, or religion that told this or that astronomer what he could or could not find in the celestial regions? It is much easier to say that religion did all this than to say that human interpreters did it. The latter would require a more complex explanation, more critical appraisal, and a certain amount of suspension of judgment. It has been popular to say that "the world is a stage." Oftentimes it is more like an unruly courtroom, with the people all too ready to volunteer assistance to the prosecutor, too willing to bypass the jury, too ready to rush to a verdict, too emotionally involved to examine anything so pedestrian as details of evidence. I will illustrate with the report of a conversation which will serve as an elemental, and probably over-simplified, example:

"What is the scientific proof of immortality?"

"You are not asking for arguments for?"

"No, just scientific proof."

"Perhaps the only thing that actually calls itself scientific proof would be some of the reports from psychic research."

"Bunk!"

"You asked for scientific proof. It seems you might at least respond with scientific criticism."

"What do you mean?"

"'Bunk' is not scientific criticism."

"I never thought of that."

For present purposes we concentrate on one special example of name giving and name using. A famous term that has sometimes been a legal term, sometimes dramatic, sometimes psychological, but never sensational, is "person." There is a verbal form—personify. There are adjectival forms—personal, personable. What is the meaning of person? Or, what is *a* person? How was the term used originally? It is easy enough to assume that early definitions were based on inadequate knowledge. Recent definitions may be based on more knowledge, but hardly adequate. Yet it would be naïve to expect man to await adequate knowledge before using terms, names, and words. Aside from knowledge, there have been and are intimations, intuitions, guesses, suppositions. Many turn out to be erroneous, but not all.

The argument—rather suggestion—of the present volume tries to make a working distinction between "person" and "personality." The former term is, as far as this book is concerned, more closely related to religion, and the latter to science. The numerous books of the past twenty years representing scientific efforts—particularly in this country—to study man in some sort of presumed "wholeness" tend to use the term "personality." We are more likely to find scientific studies of personality than of person. Yet at the same time the phrase "sacredness of personality" often appears. But it does not sound like a strictly scientific concept, how ever much individual scientists may subscribe to it. In so far as sacredness of personality suggests a tie that an individual scientist may feel with religion or ethics, yet there is no unanimity of opinion that sacredness of personality is a strictly religious notion. Thus, in my discussion, I use the phrase "worth of persons" the more nearly to harmonize with the attempt to make a distinction between person and personality.

This introduces a crucial question—a more crucial one we could hardly imagine. Are we suggesting that person is meant to refer here to something that may not be included in the usual connotations of personality—particularly those set forth in psychological treatises? Are we referring to something "over and above"? Yes. Such an answer may evoke vigorous protest. It will seem I am here trying to smuggle in that which, for so many, is an abandoned notion—soul. It will be argued that I have no empirical evidence for such a referend. It may be said I am merely articulating an article of faith. Or it may be pointed out that I am reluctant to release hold on a notion handed down from the past and that I am simply using another term—person—to preserve what I can of such widely discarded notions as "soul" or "spirit." There is some plausibility of an apparent sort in each objection, though none of them can be called conclusive and definitive. They represent articles of faith also, in different ways. If they seem, in some cases, to rely more on demonstrable evidence, this is because there has been a prior preference for traffic in demonstrables, and it tends to close the case prematurely against that which is nondemonstrable.

The point is that we see no way of doing full justice to certain persistent religious claims by trying to stay within the limits of a strictly scientific study of personality, at least as it is understood and practiced today. Those who flatly reject the religious claims may feel a certain security in an assumption that nothing is beyond the purview of the scientific approach and that questions implied in religious claims are conclusively and negatively closed. Those who do not consider the questions so absolutely closed cannot be so sure. What religious claims? For one type of answer we may offer the title of a recent symposium, *Man's Destiny in Eternity*.[9] Surely no one would suppose that the participants in the symposium are in unanimous agreement on all points. Then there are other claims indicated by such terms as purposes of God, spiritual life, idea of God, and others. No one would claim that these are univocal terms, but neither is personality nor nature.

Thus, in reference to our opening question, What is man? I offer as an answer—or as one type of answer, or as one of many attempts at answering—*person*. But this is two answers: (1) the answer of science's attempt to study personality, and (2) the subtler answer of religion—which we are trying to indicate by the word "person." One reason for this is that people are forever trying to fit these terms into a "spectrum" that issues from our opening question and that spreads all the way from the barest of physical answers—"man is two dollars worth of chemicals"—to a baffling, yet appealing answer—"man is a child of God." Certainly the scientific study of personality endeavors to take full account of the physical, physiological, and biological bands

[9] Garvin Lectures (Boston: Beacon Press, 1949).

in our spectrum. It does not—because it cannot do so in the same manner—study the worth of persons, especially in its relation to such elusive and controversial themes as "God's will and purposes," "the spiritual life," "eternity," and others.

There is a severe limitation in the use of the figure of the spectrum. The spectrum in the analysis of a light source is a more or less perfect analysis of what "really is" in the source. Moreover, there is no preferential status of one band over another and no conflict between them. The use of this figure indicates all sorts of questions. What does our spectrum show to be the real nature of the subject under analysis—man? Our spectrum is a whole series of different, and even conflicting bands, yet all profess to indicate something real and even in some instances claim to be inclusive. Moreover, the various bands in our spectrum may represent different modes and methods of analysis or study. These modes and methods will inevitably affect the language with which results and conclusions are announced. The method that at present enjoys preferred status as one that is self-conscious and presumably describable is the scientific method. The apparent sharpness of its results, however, is dependent on a very strict set of conditions. Thus it is quite limited—so far—in dealing with two matters related to this chapter: The precise origins of language, and the meaning of person toward the upper end of the spectrum alluded to above.

There are numerous other names, terms, or phrases that invite attention. Most of them are subsidiary to *person,* for example, vocation, call, dedication, divine mission. Limitations of space preclude our giving attention to these.

The first few paragraphs of this chapter introduce some questions concerning language, most of which seem natural enough, but some of which prove to be surprisingly unanswerable. Suppose we condense all these partial questions, dealing with certain aspects of language, into one omnibus question: What is language? Today as never before it is possible to begin to comprehend the size and difficulty of this question. As we become better and better acquainted with its size, with its implications, and with its many subordinate questions, the whole subject begins to be forbidding, even alarming to some, and too big to tackle or "too hot to handle." Blank walls show up on some proposed roads of investigation.

Neat and tidy notions and beliefs about language abound, most of them inadequate or wide of the mark. Fallacies in both the interpretation and use of language show up in such profusion that in a weak moment we might ask how intelligible communication is ever possible.

Voltaire, usually good for a satirical observation on human matters, said, in this regard, "Men use thought only as authority for their injustice, and employ speech only to conceal their thoughts" [10] This may differ from maxim 1073 of Publilius Syrus, yet Voltaire might say he could approve the last part of this maxim: "Speech is the mirror of the soul: as a man speaks, so is he."

We have some notions as to what an ideal language situation could be, but corruptibility and corruptions of language experience and language use are notoriously present even in this enlightened age. It is between the ideal and the wholly corrupt that most human beings live. Here they employ language in all its remarkable variety and in unnumbered examples of partially successful, partially unsuccessful efforts at expression and communication. "Let's talk it over" has become an ideal to many. It depends, of course, on at least a minimal degree of desire for mutual understanding. Without this desire "Let's talk it over" can become a series of devious maneuverings for advantage, of using language to conceal ulterior purposes, and of the deliberate employment of clever fallacies decked out in the habiliments of plausibility. The normal, nominal, and probably naïve definition of language as a means of communication overlooks the fact that it can become a great perverter of communication and, strange to relate, without seeming to be so.

One of the seemingly natural questions arising in any attempt to take another look at language is being abandoned because of the extreme difficulty, not so much of obtaining an answer as of knowing where to turn to tackle the problem. The question is: What was the origin of language? Of course there have been speculative attempts to answer. These are listed in almost any encyclopedia article on language. Perhaps the two favorites among these are the theory of divine origin—language a divine gift, and the generalized notion that it has followed some evolutionary principle. On the latter point, Susanne Langer said, very graphically: "Between the clearest animal call of love or warning or anger, and a man's least, trivial *word,* there lies a whole day of Creation—or in modern phrase, a whole chapter of evolution." [11]

What language is, basically and fundamentally, becomes difficult to state in at least two ways. In the first place it is necessary to set aside the customary notions and definitions, because most of these are simply

[10] Dialogue 14, Le Chapon et la Poularde, 1763.
[11] *Philosophy in a New Key,* p. 103.

afterthoughts. And in the second place it is not easy to formulate a statement that is simple and clear. Attempts in this direction need to be explained—the definition needs to be defined! We may, however, turn to Sapir for an excellent effort:

It is probable that the origin of language is not a problem that can be solved out of the resources of linguistics alone but that it is essentially a particular case of a much wider problem of the genesis of symbolic behavior and of the specialization of such behavior in the laryngeal region, which may be presumed to have had only an expressive function to begin with. . . . The primary function of language is generally said to be communication. . . . The autistic speech of children seems to show that the purely communicative aspect of language has been exaggerated. It is best to admit that language is primarily a vocal actualization of the tendency to see reality symbolically, that it is precisely this quality which renders it a fit instrument for communication and that it is in the actual give and take of social intercourse that it has been complicated and refined into the form in which it is known today.[12]

Language is so taken for granted that we forget we hardly know what it is or realize the hazards and risks besetting those who would presume to make use of it. Did it start in a word, and if so what was the first word? Another student of the subject said:

Everyone thinks he knows what language is: a meaningful sound, a sociable noise, a passing to and fro of signs, which men make chiefly with the mouth and take in through the ears and by means of which they communicate with each other—though gestures, hands, eyes, etc., also help. No one denies that behind this shifting pattern something is at work that may be called Force, or Meaning, or Will, or Mind, or Body and Soul of Man, or anything else. But as soon as we inquire what this "something" is, opinions begin to diverge widely. . . . Origin of language is attributed by psychologists to the psychic part of this disposition, by phoneticians to the bodily part, by sociologists to the communal life of man. The clash of opinions becomes most violent when it comes to the problem of the *value* of language. Overestimation stands against underestimation. On the one hand language is thought to be error and illusion, a veil hiding truth, self-deception; on the other it is looked upon as the first and most important educator of our thought, even as itself thought.[13]

[12] "Language," *Encyclopaedia of the Social Sciences*, pp. 158-59. Copyright 1948 by The Macmillan Company and used by their permission.

[13] Karl Vossler, *The Spirit of Language in Civilization*, tr. Oscar Oeser (Harcourt, Brace & Company, 1932), pp. 1-2. Used by permission.

In addition to the complex problem of the relation of language to personality and personal relationships we need to recognize, as we can, how such large scale enterprises as science and religion understand and use language. The statement, sentence, or proposition is centrally illustrative of the wonder of language. We turn therefore to statements—religious and scientific.

CHAPTER IV

Statements

PEOPLE HAVE LONG BEEN AT LEAST DIMLY AWARE OF MANIFOLD POSSIbilities of language usage, both favorable and unfavorable, both enlightening and misleading. Socrates was accused of manipulating language so that *X* could be speciously proved to be non-*X*. No one can say for sure how old the phrase "oily tongue" is. On the other hand, the words of the sage were long ago considered to be "life unto those that find them." (Prov. 4:22.)

One of the profound puzzles is how man became able to manage the transition from word to statement or sentence. Someone has said that if one wants to acquire a "feel" for the mystery of language he should observe a child as the young one manages the transition from nouns to pronouns. An even subtler wonder is the transition from words to sentences. Benjamin Lee Whorf suggested:

> Because of the systematic, configurative nature of higher mind, the "patternment" aspect of language always overrides and controls. . . the name-giving aspect. Hence the meanings of specific words are less important than we fondly fancy. Sentences, not words, are the essence of speech.[1]

Religious Statements

There is no precise and clear-cut method or standard always enabling us to distinguish clearly between statements that are religious or scientific and those that are nonreligious or nonscientific. Yet some general distinctions can be made by almost anyone. Such is the flexible usability of language and the variety among psychological modes and moods, however, that statements, apparently religious or scientific, can be emptied of meaning or made use of for purposes other than religious or scientific. "Oh, I believe the Old Book from kivver to kivver" may not be fundamentally and primarily a religious statement if the speaker is simply inviting an exercise of the franchise in his favor. Yet we

[1] Whorf and J. B. Carroll, *Language, Thought, and Reality* (New York: John Wiley & Sons, Inc., 1956), p. 258.

have no authority for conclusively classifying it as a nonreligious use of a religious form until we understand the particular situation with its motives. "Science proves that this product destroys more germs than any other similar product now being made" may have had something happen to it after it left the laboratory, if in fact the primary aim in the laboratory was to do what the statement intimates. Yet again, it is as easy in this instance as in the former to leap to a conclusion not solidly grounded, no matter how much suspicion there may be. But let us consider religious statements and scientific in this order.

By way of introduction we may say that religious statements are primarily those found in the sacred scriptures of the world. But many of the statements within these scriptures would be ruled out by any strict classification. To say that some king died when he was forty years of age is not necessarily to make a religious statement. At this point we indicate a collection of statements drawn from the world's sacred scriptures which represents something of an attempt to distinguish the more definitely religious affirmations and imperatives in them; although this is not precisely the way the editor of this collection has stated his purpose.

Robert E. Hume, compiler and editor of *Treasure-House of the Living Religions,* states his purpose as follows:

> This book aims to present the quintessence of the religious wisdom of the world since the tenth century before Christ. . . . It is intended that these pages shall contribute to an increase of positive knowledge and also to a general increase of faith, hope and love for all mankind. . . . The fullest fruit of the religious life comes, partly in attaining the proper relation of man with the Supreme, and partly also in proper sympathy between man and man. . . . This book is designed also to serve as a scientific source-book for a comparative study in the fields of active religions.[2]

Thus, the first point is that *if* there are such things as religious statements, there is no problem in locating some of them quickly. When people start reading them, however, anything can happen! Some will not understand many of them. Some will find something that inspires them mightily and induces in them a new life. Some will raise philosophical questions. Some will offer scientific criticisms. Some will find and use statements which they will want to turn into inflexible dogmas and will try to bind other people to them. Some will be fascinated.

[2] *Op. cit.,* p. vii.

Some will be amused. Some will respond to literary artistry. Some will deplore the perpetuation of what they consider primitive modes of thought. Some will find what they believe to be the "quintessence of the religious wisdom of the world," as the above quotation has it. Some will be untouched and unmoved. It would take a supernally wise court to adjudicate all the claims made or implied in these attitudes.

Thus, a religious statement is not a fixed entity with an inevitable functioning, not an existing causal agent whose effect can be predicted precisely, not an existent whose "essence and attributes" can be studied as the geologist studies rocks or as the chemist studies molecular structures. What does the scientist do with them or about them? In a sense some religious statements seem to have no significance whatever for science or the scientist. Scientists have rejected many of them as meaningless, invalid, improper, unverifiable, and the like. It is easy to list some of the critical judgments leveled against many supposed religious statements—if not against religion in general—by science. They, or certain ones of them, are said to be nonempirical, a priori, inadequately formulated, question-begging, unsupported, not the result of any definable methodology, and dependent on undefinable terms.

Such criticisms and judgments are directed against what the statements claim to say. Wherein such statements are affirmations about something presumed to obtain or exist, but which science believes does not exist, the argument would be that the statement is simply wrong. This kind of objection says that such statements do not denote or connote what the speakers or writers claim they do. The objections might then be amplified by insisting that if those who composed the statements originally had used a better method for finding out what ought to be affirmed about existence or existents, they would have made more nearly valid statements. Their "labels" would have been nearer to the facts.

Leuba has endeavored to argue that the more eminent a person is as a scientist the less likely he is to subscribe to certain types of religious statements.[3] There is a problem as to whether the questions in Leuba's questionnaire may have had some influence on results by the way they were phrased. His question concerning belief in God was put to a group of students with the following results: when they were confined to Leuba's definition the group voted 21 per cent yes, 38 per cent, doubtful, and 41 per cent, no. When they were allowed some lati-

[3] J. H. Leuba, "Religious Beliefs of American Scientists," *Harper's Magazine* (August, 1934), pp. 291-300.

tude in contributing to the definitions themselves they voted 84 per cent, yes, 11 per cent, doubtful, and 5 per cent, no.[4]

All this is not to imply that science *always* objects to religious statements. Many scientists are deeply religious men, thoroughly committed to affirmations and imperatives of religion as expressed in religious statements.

However, the point here is to indicate something that has happened which puts the whole problem of statements—of whatever kind—into a new light. Statements are part of the subject matter of a whole new area of data to which science is giving attention. The concerns and criticisms indicated above have not been abandoned, but new methods, new ways of looking at the data, and new approaches have yielded results not heretofore anticipated. Some of the procedure is to give attention to and to seek answers for new kinds of questions. Some of them are as follows: What is the psychological condition out of which specific statements develop? What was the original impetus or impulse for a given statement, or type of statement? Are these the same for all subsequent uses of the same statement? What are the psychological effects of the statements? Why would anyone ever make a statement about demons? What sorts of laws operate in that area of activity which includes the making of statements? Thus the whole problem of meanings of statements suddenly becomes much more complex than the simple consideration of the dictionary meanings of words in statements, and hence of the statements. Why would anyone ever make such an affirmation as "God is holy"? Why should anyone ever have proposed the imperative, "Love thy neighbor as thyself"? Let us observe that the "why" can be considered in more ways than one. We may try to answer in terms of attempting to verify the existence or nature of God by empirical methods. We may try to give a psychological explanation for the origin of statements. This may or may not involve the question of existence of what the statement refers to. Two sorts of meanings are thus implied, the normally linguistic, and the psychological.

Much of the controversy concerning religion has been due to a confusion of meanings of religious statements. Much of this has involved the unconscious. This compounds the confusion, partly because it is not always recognized as such. For example, a man might say, with great fervor, "My heart bleeds for all the lost of the world." If this is

[4] Cf. Report in *The Journal of the National Association of Biblical Instructors*, 3, part 1 (1935), 13.

true, there is perhaps some nobleness in the man. If it is not true, we have a complex problem in the making, and it is relevant at this point to go into the details of the possibilities. If the man makes the remark and believes it to be true when it isn't, we have a case of self-deception. The new science of human personality has thrown a great deal of light on the universal problem of self-deception—both varieties, the conscious and the unconscious. If the statement is not true and the man himself knows it isn't, he is consciously using the statement as a technique to deceive.

Again, if the statement is true, it may have some good effects. But if it isn't true, whether the man himself knows it or not, many people may be perceptive enough to be suspicious. Some will feel—perhaps partly unconsciously—that there is something wrong, without quite knowing what. They will miss that essential "ring" in the statement —the ring of confidence or certainty. To some he will be a "cracked bell." One thinks at the moment of Lincoln's famous remark about fooling people, but Lincoln did not offer explanations as to why it is that some people are more easily fooled than others. So it is that some people, because they are often perceptive in an intuitive sort of way, would "know" or "feel" that the statement did not ring true. Some students of personality would venture the generalization that *any* use of the statement quoted above is almost automatically under suspicion, that it is too likely to be an index of sentimentalism, self-adulation, romanticism, and kindred conditions. Thus, the possibilities of variety in meanings are complex. But this does not mean we cannot learn to understand these complexities. Let us summarize a pattern for at least elementary consideration of them.

First let us note that much controversy has not been about the literal meanings of statements. Many times people have thought certain controversies were about definitions of terms or meanings of statements when as a matter of fact the controversy was due to the people's feelings about the terms or statements. These feelings were, in many instances, due to other things—not always obviously relevant. This whole subject is so complex and involves so many ramifications that analysis is very difficult—there are so many components to classify. A controversy—or agreement for that matter—between any two people, whether on religion or not, can be quite different from that of any other two people. It might therefore seem impossible to find any common denominator.

Modern climate of opinion, influenced as it is by science, encourages the assumption that each case would exhibit a discernible rationale—

had we the opportunity and preparation to investigate adequately. It is further believed that all the elements of each controversial situation could be subsumed under some comprehensive science, such as psychology. It would be left to other sciences to investigate other aspects of the statements especially as they claim to say something about the external world. For example, if "God created the world six thousand years ago" were to be considered a religious statement, a geologist might want to say something about it in terms of geology, whereas a scientist working with the material of human psychology might want to look into the psychological factors of all statements about God.

Let us now look at an elementary pattern for the consideration of religious statements. First we might raise the question of validity. Validity is a broader and more flexible term than truth. Thus the poet might say of his beloved, "Her eyes are limpid pools." The literalist might object that if her eyes *were* limpid pools she would have a very hard time seeing, and moreover she would have to be always holding her head back except when there was a freeze. This illustration may be guilty of levity, but the general problem is as real as hunger. Thus, the statement is not literally true, but could still be valid as a meaningful form of language use. Literal meaning and objective verification are fundamental and important in certain contexts—scientific, for example. If we are to restrict the use of language to literal meanings and objective verification, however, then language becomes a very limited vehicle. Of course responsibility goes both ways. If the poet desires the freedom of poetic license, he must not demand that people accept poetic statements as dogmas. This may seem never to happen, but it does in subtle ways, particularly in relation to religious statements.

The second element in the pattern concerns the use of religious statements. Standard procedure in religious circles has included their use as doctrine and as teaching, and as such they are taught to oncoming generations. Immediately this raises the whole question of methods and content of teachings. Nowadays, if we take account of what some educational psychologists are saying, we would be better occupied if we gave more attention to learning than to teaching, with its transmissive implications. Religious statements are also used in worship, both public and private and there have been other uses. A question which is very easy to ask today is, What are the effects on people of language in general? More specifically, What are the effects of the more distinctly religious statements? For a long while to come there will not be adequate research in this area—partly because of the complexity of the material, and partly because of the not always discernible presence of variables. There are numerous assumptions, often rather vaguely formulated. It is assumed for instance that it is good to hear good things, but bad to hear bad things—leaving aside for the moment any discussion of meanings of good and bad. A girl reports that her mother admonished her when she went away to college, "Now don't you come back here with any ideas." A father objected to a son's reading Plato because "Plato's ideas weren't so hot." A friend of a certain school liked the school but warned against "presenting stuff to young people too idealistically." Some people will urge others to "read religious classics because they give comfort, inspiration, and guidance." There is *some* truth—in varying degrees—in all these and the thousands of similar suggestions one hears. Quite possibly the modicum of truth in some instances is different from that which the speaker suspects. Also, people are not always clear as to just how they are using some of the key terms quoted, for example "ideas," and "idealistic." It would be quite interesting to know precisely what effects are likely or inevitable if people read and reread selected material over a long enough period of time for the results to "take." It would be very difficult to conduct such an experiment because of the large number of other forces operating to produce similar, or other, effects at the same time. Submission to the possible influence of "good" statements, however, can hardly fail to yield constructive results. Personal witness does not have the same status, considered scientifically, of a verified hypothesis, but it may be nonetheless valid, effective, and influential. Someone paid tribute to the influence derived from a persistent reading of Dante's *Divine Comedy,* even when as a young reader, he frequently did not know what it meant. Someone else commenting on it said, "I hardly see how 'The Inferno' could ever be beneficial, though I can well believe it would tend to perpetuate some thoroughly irreligious ideas." Two such opposing comments are at one in assuming some influence of the poem.

The third element in the pattern is the misuse of statements. This theme may be introduced with a reference to the misuse of a nonlinguistic symbol. Some of the stories coming down to us from the Crusades report the allegation that the great two-edged swords of Crusaders which were of the general shape of a cross were at times of sufficient potency that when held up before the onrushing Turks they struck the enemy down instantly. The most elementary logical inquiry could ask devastating questions of such a report. If the symbol were so potent, why was it that the Turks were not drastically and conclusively defeated? Why won't that happen today when we use this symbol? What is the relationship between such usage and the original message of the Cross? The ascription of such lethal power to something of whatever shape is a magical notion. Even if such a notion is believed and therefore has psychological power, it would never stand up under any kind of critical scrutiny.

The misuse of religious statements is a far more extensive and complex story than the misuse of physical symbols. Details of the former will almost never be as clearly distinguishable as details of the latter, however. All sorts of motivations operate to impel misuse of religious statements. They include ignorance, prejudice, emotional involvement, frustrations, misunderstanding, maladjustment, and maybe even sin. Were Negroes enslaved because of the story of Ham in the Old Testament? (Gen. 9:22-27.) Or did this story provide a rationalization *after* they were actually enslaved? In either case a story in a scriptural record is misused, whether it be called a religious statement or not. Those who burned witches for the sake of Jesus had a severely distorted notion as to what "sake of Jesus" ought to mean. Much cursing is a dubious trafficking in religious terminology. One who entreats the Deity to consign someone's soul to hell, should at least allow the question to remain open as to whether such drastic judgment is objectively merited. How often do we hear a person, under stress of damning someone's soul, taking the trouble to append a codicil, "unless it should transpire that I have erred in my judgment in the present instance, in which event, dear Lord, please forget my request and forgive my intemperate impetuosity." It is of course true that sometimes such modification and repentance follow after some lapse of time, and upon active reconsideration. In such a case "true" religion is belatedly exemplified after "false" religion had its say.

The fourth element in the pattern may be called the psychological situation. Two very famous ancient documents are directly related to this question. Plato's *Republic* has much to say about submitting children to the stories about the gods. All this is too well-known for repeating here. Suffice it to say that just as Plato believed in the psychological effects of good religious statements, so was he convinced of the psychological effects of bad statements. There was a problem of validity—God must not be spoken of in a misrepresenting way—and also a problem of psychology—wicked stories of gods will have an unfavorable effect, especially on tender minds. The other document says, "And these words, which I command thee this day, shall be in thine heart; and thou shalt teach them diligently unto thy children, and shalt talk of them when thou sittest in thy house, and when thou walkest by the way, and when thou liest down, and when thou risest up." (Deut. 6:6-7.) Some years ago at a conference on religious education in Cincinnati, Ohio, a rabbi made the point in open discussion that religious education was not new, and he adverted to the Deuteronomic instructions for integrating the great religious statements of their tradition into the very fiber of daily life. All these instances have implications concerning the psychological situation. There is the assumption that causal relations are in operation. Not until modern times was there ever any systematic and searching attempt to discern and formulate these principles. To be sure there is the "rational psychology" of the Aristotelian-Thomistic tradition, and it may claim the status of science—or at least philosophy—but it is not welcomed unanimously into the modern household of scientific psychology. Also there is the stout claim that the ancient Hindus were psychologists in ways and to a degree that modern science has been slow to appreciate. Ardent students of Shakespeare, Homer, and other greats in the field of creative literature are very quick to tell us how great these men were as psychologists. But none of these psychologists denies the power and influence of religious statements, as well as other types of statements.

The first and fourth elements in the above mentioned pattern are the main ones. Let us consider them from a somewhat different angle. Since it is frequently urged that psychology is not yet sufficiently established as a science, it might be the counsel of caution not to assume yet that it is. Since within the wide house of psychology itself there are serious controversies as to whether the studies of the depths of personality can claim scientific status, it might be even more the counsel of caution to hold off for a while. However, it is being assumed here that we may venture—if we are careful—to speak of the psychological sciences. The main point of the present discussion does not need to await decisions regarding these controversies. Furthermore the present discussion is presented with diffidence. If the direction is reasonably valid, this is as much as could be hoped for under the circumstances.

Concerning religious statements, it may well be that psychology as a science would prefer that statements—statements generally, not only those classifiable as religious—increasingly conform to scientific criteria of validity:

1. The use of precisely definable terms;
2. Renunciation of claims to having access to such modes of justification of statements as may be said to come through dreams, special visions, revelatory experiences, and the like;
3. Experimental verification.

The primary concern is with validity or truth of statements. Is the sun a god? Are there many gods? Is there any God at all? Is there only one? Has man an eternal destiny? Do gruesome stories harm children? In other words, what statements are valid answers to such questions? Moreover, what statements would be valid comments on these questions?

If the criterion of verification in the manner of science as at present understood be limited to empirical verification, we are faced with the question of what to do with statements that are nonverifiable in this manner. It has become so customary to differentiate between statements of fact and statements of value that it is easy to fall into the notion that this dual classification is exhaustive. Also, it has become easy to extol the one and discredit the other. Further, it has been easy to assume the former are verifiable, hence more meaningful, and the latter expressive, hence less meaningful. These are neat distinctions, partly because they are primarily surface distinctions. Putting all value statements into one class on the basis of surface appearance is the height of over-simplification. This would be the case even if there were no known method for clearly distinguishing between the two kinds of statements. Yet some people have distinguished between value statements, for example, between such statements—direct or implied—as "Moloch likes the smell of the burning flesh of children" and "You ought to love your neighbor as yourself."

Such a statement as "God is holy" is difficult to test by means of scientific verification. Some people today simply call such a statement meaningless, or nonsense—implying that it does not admit of verification in sense experience. If this is the proper and only way to appraise such statements, then we could confidently assume that as soon as enlightment spreads sufficiently, all such statements would die a more or less natural death. In fact it has already been affirmed—and in the name of science—that religion itself is due for eventual demise. A great many individual statements from the days of the race's infancy have "died." Some have been retained, however, and both those that have died and those that have survived could, in one sense, have been loosely classified as "religious statements." We have never clearly defined the precise criterion whereby religious statement can be separated from religious statement, or whereby we can distinguish in every case which ones are sailing under false colors and which contain imperishable wisdom. Distinctions have been made, however, and before those making the distinctions knew how to validate them. We have to give the human species—*man*, whom we cannot precisely define—some credit for the exercise on occasion of a wisdom he does not understand and which he does not always know he has. To be sure, all the while other kinds of distinctions are being made which will prove not to have been wise.

The astonishing thing is that it was in this "twilight era" that such wisdom—if that is the name for it—was acquired and exercised—along with the errors, some tragic. It was this era when most of the famous religious statements were formulated, and often lived out in faithful practice. But references to and assertions of "fundamental human wisdom" must sound a discordant note to ears attuned to the less poetic music of empirical verification, objectivity, facticity, laboratory technique, quantification, and similar terms.

We spoke above of psychology as a science and how it might deal severely with religious statements. We may also think of science as psychology and detect a new kind of modern approach to the problems posed by religious statements. When psychology gets into the picture, the attitude that science can take toward religious statements is something new. It reveals a new, possible dimension of science heretofore unrealized and unanticipated. It reveals areas of inquiry not heretofore known. Eventually it may be that new interpretations of scientific method will be revealed. Of course we need to remind ourselves immediately that all this cannot be said without challenge. Unanimous agreement is not possible yet, even among those classifiable as psychologists. We are dealing with direction of effort, possible perspective, and not with uniform conclusions. One key word related to all this is personality. Science as psychology has a contribution to make to work with our opening question, What is man? This contribution says, in effect, man is a creature of "depths." And out of these depths proceed some of the achievements as well as some of the distortions of language.

We confine ourselves here to one type of contribution that science as psychology makes to the understanding and exposition of religious statements. This enterprise will help to provide some new criteria for distinguishing between religious statements that have validity—in some cases, unsuspected validity—and those that do not. It will do better at this task than at the task of trying to determine which religious statements—if any—are revelatory in the more strictly religious sense.

Scientific Statements

The use of language for scientific purposes is our next consideration. If we are to use such a phrase as "scientific statements," it would refer to statements empirically verifiable; descriptive of natural processes, formulations of natural laws, descriptive of scientific procedures and aims, and objectively definable. Such statements would not include characteristics of other types of statements and other uses of language, such as poetry, myth, figures of speech, certain kinds of speculative formulations, value claims, or language of worship.

This does not, however, represent a hard and fast distinction. It is quite possible to borrow terms, although there might be some change of connotation in the process. It is possible to write poetry about scientific achievements, as it is possible for science to salute the "wisdom" in speculative and literary compositions. And there are other possibilities that anyone can indicate.

When the linguistic formulations of one type of language use are judged by the standards appropriate to some other type, difficulties of which disputants are not fully aware can develop. Poetic use of language is not appropriately and fairly judged if the strict methods of the laboratory are imposed. Poetry complains, it may be, of the cold, unfeeling quality of scientific language. Some have feared that the continuing advance of science would destroy aesthetic values and the linguistic formulations of these values.

Clear and definitive standards do not exist for each and every mode of language usage, although there are many examples of rules and standards for language. The oldest and one of the most famous is grammar. This does not refer to a particular usage of language, but in some sense to certain rules for most usages. That certain exceptions have been recognized is illustrated by the famous phrase "poetic license." A less tolerated type of exception is illustrated by the reproach implied by such terms as "colloquial" and "provincial."

Even the general requirement that any particular example of language usage must "make sense" is not universal. The phrase "make sense" becomes highly ambiguous if we lay it down as a presupposition—inspired by science—that all language usage makes sense, in that, along with the movements of stars, the growth of cells, and the motions of wind and weather, language use makes sense because it is part and parcel of some kind of universal causal sequence. This stretches the meaning of "make sense" beyond its uses in reference to language with emphases on denotation, connotation, and the like. To most people "tongue-speaking" does not make sense as language, although a psychologist might say it makes sense as a manifestation of psychological conditions. It would be uncharitable not to listen to the tongue-speaker's own explanation as to the sense of his utterances, no matter what we might think of it.

In a sense it can be said that science has directed and concentrated an enormous amount of attention on certain features of language use to the exclusion of some other features. Among these emphasized features are precision and verifiability. If this sometimes seems to result in unintelligibility, it is rather the other way around. For instance, "there is a roughening above the greater trochanter, and a forward displacement of the clavicle at the acromic, clavicular joint" is *not* less intelligible than "he's got a busted shoulder," although it may seem so to some people at certain times. Of course, this provides opportunity for occasional fun at the expense of the "technical people."

Scientific statements, in so far as they exemplify precision and verifiability, are therefore representative of a spectacular chapter in human accomplishment. In the process numerous general and vaguely valid statements—"He is sick"—have given way to a host of specific statements as to what, precisely, the sickness is, with a separate statement for each example. Thus, "He is sick" can become separated into a thousand "technicalized" statements requiring special training to understand.

There are special difficulties that stand in the way of "reducing" religious statements to statements of scientific type. In the first place, many religious statements are in the imperative mood, or if they are in the indicative mood they make liberal use of the notion of "ought." Love your neighbor as yourself; you ought not to worship false gods; human sacrifice is wrong. None of these statements—if we classify them as religious—can be verified in the same way as simple categorical statements such as "He has a ruptured appendix."

It is possible in some sense to translate some religious statements into scientific. Instead of saying "Love your enemies," we might translate and say, "If you love your enemy, you will tend to produce such and such a result; whereas if you hate, other results ensue." But something is lost in the translation. "If you want . . ." and "If you do not want . . ." are, by implication, not differentiated. In the original we are admonished. We are confronted with an imperative, with an "ought."

Another type of difficulty is that religious statements often deal with inaccessibles. A datum that is inaccessible is of no use to science as science is now understood and practiced, not that all scientific data are directly accessible. If science seems reluctant to concede the possible reality of inaccessibles and the possible validity of statements relating to these, there is good reason—up to a point. There have been so many statements in human history concerning inaccessibles that it is not difficult to entertain the suspicion that they are all alike. Also, the development of understanding of how human beings generate notions concerning inaccessibles has thrown light on the mysteries of demonogony and the like. This reluctance can be a matter of temperament or of climate of opinion. As such it does not prove anything. We are still left with the problem of distinguishing between, for example, YHWH and Moloch, God and Thor, "God is love" and "Whirl is king," eternal destiny and complete oblivion—that is, of distinguishing between them in terms of plausibility, if not verifiability in the restricted scientific sense. If a scientist believes in God, what has that to do with his science? What *should* it have to do with it? There is no unanimous agreement on how to answer such questions, though many suggestions have been made, some even dogmatically. On the other hand, if we argue for the plausibility of statements concerning inaccessibles, we imply a measure or degree of accessibility, which introduces a kind of qualification of the term "inaccessible." God is inaccessible for the laboratory, but accessible to faith and commitment. If, in the name of the laboratory, with its management and measurement of much of the data it works with, we impose the requirement of accessibility on the datum God, we may question his reality if he does not respond. If, on the other hand, we doubt his reality to begin with, we are limited to speaking of faith and commitment as merely psychological conditions.

It may be that in the long run religion must affirm the ultimate remoteness but relative approachability of certain inaccessibles, whereas science must continue to traffic only in accessibles. That this involves risks goes without saying; that it does not close the door to co-operation may be less obvious. With regard to certain kinds of problems religion and science are a constant embarrassment to each other. Nowhere is this more evident and conspicuous than when they settle down to their various uses of language, both in terms of their own characteristic affirmations, and in the criticisms and questions they direct toward each other. Philip Wheelwright presents a relevant reminder: "To declare a religious statement true is at once to declare something about the ultimate character of the universe, to declare that certain ways of responding to such a universe are more appropriate than other ways."[5] These same words could be used concerning science, but the meanings of the two sets of statements would not be the same.

If it eventually should develop that their most characteristic statements are mutually exclusive, then we might say science and religion are basically incompatible. But such a turn of events is not yet conclusively indicated, though everyone will not agree with this.

[5] *The Burning Fountain* (Bloomington, Ind.: Indiana University Press, 1954), p. 296.

CHAPTER V

Definition and Meaning

ARISTOTLE CREDITED SOCRATES WITH HAVING "FIXED THOUGHT FOR the first time on definition." [1] Some modern Aristotle could credit science with having fixed thought on new ways of achieving precision in definition, except that this achievement is already being trumpeted up and down the land by scientists and friends of science.

The following pages give some attention to the process of defining and consider its peculiar problems in relation to person and religion. We find the subject of meaning arising not only in relation to definitions of terms, but also in situations having nothing to do with definitions of any terms that may be used.

If not the first step, at least an early one in the process of defining is to give a name to something. The choice of the particular name will be the first indication of what the definition is to be. Two matters are involved here: the choice of the particular name decided upon, and the preliminary notions as to what the thing is that is being named. Somehow and somewhere in the mists of antiquity and in the depths of human nature, there developed the strong conviction that everything must have a name—everything that existed or could be thought to exist. The names of many things erroneously suspected of existing make a long list of terms designating fancies—goblin, elf, troll, gnome, Elysium. An exception of a sort may exist in minds that believe there are things without names. But a universal question is the one Moses attributes to his friends, "and they shall say unto me, What is his name?" (Exod. 3:13.) Of course there is a special feature of this report. It seems to assume that the name asked for already existed.

[1] *Metaphysics,* 987b3.

What type of awareness or acquaintance brought the various types of named "somethings" to man's attention? There is much variety in the answers and attempts to answer this question—sense experience, mystic experience, imagination, fancy, hearsay, insight, invention, and others. The vagaries of human experience are such that one may stubbornly vouch for the existence of something unseen—"There's a law that causes parents to give names to their children that they are supposed to have"—and another just as stubbornly disavow the existence of something seen—"There ain't no such animal"—the comment of a doubter on seeing his first giraffe.

There may be differences as to the part of the "something" that is comprehended in the naming—external appearance, inner essence, functioning, or some special aspect. It has often transpired that names thus given are understood in different ways. "Illness" might be given as a name to an observed something, but interpreted to be a "judgment." Or the name "demon-possession" might be used on seeing some overt demonstration, but given to the supposed cause of the demonstration.

Thus, how man, the name giver, understood the something to which he was giving a name was from the start a matter of greater complexity and importance than he could ever have comprehended, at least in the earlier chapters of his history. Thunder interpreted as a "voice," dreaming of a departed one interpreted as an actual return visit, a storm on one's birthday regarded as a judgment, blue eyes interpreted as evidence of an evil spirit, prognostications "read" in peculiar arrangements in fowl physiology—all these and thousands of other examples give evidence of fallibilities in man's interpretation of those somethings to which he has given names. These examples of error should be balanced against examples of accuracy and validity. Ideally, man progressively eliminates or grows out of error and progressively accumulates valid knowledge. Such ideal accomplishment advances and refines definition. That we fall short of the ideal should be fairly obvious.

Very few people ever participate in the basic process of conferring names on things and of deciding on preliminary definitions. By the time anyone comes into the world, there is already an extensive deposit of words and definitions in wide use, thoroughly standardized and continually being subjected to transmission through formal education or informal "social osmosis." Thus the process of learning or absorbing definitions is not even a fully conscious process.

To be sure there is some variation in terminology in every age.

New words are added, some old ones dropped, and continuing words often encounter changes of definition. In any age, questions may arise concerning definitions; criticisms will be made of some long-established terms and their meanings; new suggestions will be offered for new definitions—but most of this will be in the context of already-learned, taken-for-granted, and habitually used language. The critical and questioning efforts will be the work of a minority, and they will not always be appreciated.

Eventually the problem of definition brings three important considerations into focus:

1. Basically, the definitions of terms are what people, language users, name givers, say they are.

2. The accuracy, validity, and appropriateness of definitions ultimately will depend upon the degree and accuracy of man's understanding of the world in which he lives, with its uncounted hosts of things to which he gives names.

3. For a thorough understanding of language usage, it is essential to understand what human nature is, and how its nature and conditions relate to the use and effectiveness of language.

To these three items we give some additional attention.

Words mean what people say they mean, but what people say can exhibit fantastic variety. We can speak in idealistic terms of definitions and meanings that words and sentences ought to have. Less idealistically, we may speak simply of the right of stipulation. That is, if the hearer is to understand the speaker, the speaker must employ common usage, or if he employs words in any unusual manner, he must stipulate. The speaker does have a right to use words to suit himself. A particular form of this has been more or less immortalized in Humpty Dumpty's remark to Alice in *Through the Looking-Glass,* though his statement was no doubt intended to illustrate some motivation of perversity: "When I use the word, it means just what I choose it to mean." Words do get their meanings and definitions from people, and if there is any choosing, man does it. But communication between people, to be communication, must involve some common denominators, some definitions generally known and accepted. If Mr. *A* wants to use "cat" where other people use "dog," there rests on him the obligation—at least for the sake of intelligibility—to obey some elementary principle of stipulation; that is, he should let his hearers know about his perversity. That this would complicate communication is obvious. Yet, in daily life worse complications transpire repeatedly, and are undetected. Mr. *A* and Mr. *B* can carry on a discussion using the same word, but with two distinctly different connotations, and without realizing it. Then they might wonder why they have so much trouble. Or, what is perhaps more likely, they may accuse each other of stupidity, perversity, or something else as bad or worse.

Thus, although people are notoriously creatures of habit, and especially linguistic habits, they make their own choices as to the meanings and definitions of the words. These choices are not necessarily free choices. They are only as free as one's understanding, intentions, and motivations. If we were to say, therefore, that there is a solemn responsibility on the part of people in their use of language, man's unique gift, the statement might be laughed off or taken seriously, depending on the degree of understanding and the sense of responsibility of hearers. Definitions are what people say they are. Words mean what people intend them to mean. In a poet's words, "The choice is always ours," [2] but the freedom of our choices is in proportion to our capacity for choice, and our capacity for intelligent choice is a measure of our humanness and our maturity.

In the second place, it was suggested that the accuracy, validity, and appropriateness of definitions ultimately will depend upon the degree and accuracy of man's understanding. This involves a number of things. In the first place, words that are the names of things should have definitions true to the actual structure and nature of the referends. To say that the sun is a divinity is less accurate than the suggestion of Anaxagoras that it is really a molten stone. This would be more easy to verify than terms and statements concerning imperatives claiming to be guides to human conduct or terms referring to the divine nature. Science's accomplishments in definition have made it impatient of terms characteristic of poets, prophets, and artists. The achievements of the sciences can be either the bane or inspiration of the nonscientist in his use of language.

In the third place, the most difficult of all tasks to master is language users understanding language user. This may often seem to present no problem at all—up to a point—but trouble may develop with unfamiliar terms, or unfamiliar connotations for supposedly ordinary words, or with sentences. A woman went with her husband to a conference and later reported, "I understood most of the words, but none of the sentences." Thus, there are times and occasions when people know they understand and when they know they do not under-

[2] Aldous Huxley, "Orion."

stand. But the most serious difficulties develop when language user fails to understand language user without realizing there is any failure of understanding. *A* may suppose he understands *B*, and *B* suppose he is understood. This means that failure to understand is not recognized as such, and if some awareness of trouble develops, it is more often than not "mis-located" by those concerned.

Moreover, the relation of language use to mental health and maturity is beginning to be studied on a heretofore unanticipated scale. Definitions of a disturbing sort can have emotional effects if users and believers are sufficiently committed to them.

We give some attention in following paragraphs to a peculiarly acute problem of definition. Religion is widely and variously used and defined. The subject will be dealt with more fully and positively in Chapter XI.

Defining Religion

The problem of defining the word "religion" is at least fourfold: (1) "something" to which the word was originally applied was already in process for many ages before the Latin-derived "religion" was even thought of. (2) There is some question as to what the original word meant, and as to its precise etymology. (3) Before the Latin word was employed, there were accents, dimensions, and manifestations in the complex enterprise which we would now call religion which were not comprehended in the original connotations of the Latin term. Thus, any use of the term today should allow for these ingredients. (4) If there has been any further enlightenment or extension of knowledge since the original use of "religion," these should be incorporated into modern definition.

On the other hand, there is a simpler aspect of the problem. It can be stated as a question: What do people have in mind when they use the word "religion"? It is possible to put the question to people individually, but people generally have many different things in mind—and in feelings—when they use the word. Thus, it might be a hopelessly difficult problem to assemble, classify, and detect common denominators in all the varied usages. It is most likely that people use this word with some general notion of whether it refers to something "good" or "bad." Moreover, the adjective "religious" can be applied to a bewildering variety of nouns. This would imply that the noun "religion" has an amplitude of definition possibilities, making its use in communication somewhat hazardous or adventurous. The use of the word often —if not always—involves both definition and judgment. Rarely do people begin a discussion of religion with the question, Are we in agreement as to the definition we are using? Even more rarely do they begin such a discussion with the question, What sorts of feeling do we have—often unavoidably—in the use of this and related words?

In this discussion I shall follow a simplified outline of the major aspects of the problem of defining religion. It is much less a dictionary problem than would be the case with many terms, perhaps most of them. In some instances, science has taught us how to suspend judgment on definitions of terms until we can more clearly identify the "somethings" to which the terms refer. This has a mature and ideal sound about it. But science has not yet taught us how to suspend judgment in all cases involving definition. Even scientists are capable of some degree of emotion with regard to certain terms—perhaps a modern example would be the term "extrasensory perception."

Histories of definitions of religion often begin, in the Western world, with a recognition of the comments of three writers. Cicero says that "religio" is derived from "relegere," to treat carefully.[3] Lactantius finds the derivation to be from "religare," to be tied to, to bind. "We are bound and tied to God by this chain of piety; from which religion itself received its name, not, as Cicero explained it, from carefully gathering." [4] Augustine suggests a derivation from "religere," to recover, though he does not hold to this idea consistently.

That it is not necessary to choose between these is illustrated by Thomas Aquinas, who quotes all three and discusses the complexity of the "something" which the word "religion" denotes.[5] This suggests that it may be a long time before there is a universally agreed upon definition. It may seem the linguistic ideal to divide up the connotations so that more precision would be possible—as science suggests. This would mean the eventual substitution of a collection of words for the one word "religion." This would be a loss if there is some "wholeness" that the word now refers to, how ever vaguely.

Since the name had already been applied before Cicero discussed its etymology, the main problem is the identification of the "something" to which it applies. This is the universal question. Speaking denotatively, what is it that people are "pointing at" in human experience when they use the word "religion" or its equivalent—if there is an equivalent? Is there some universal constant? Is there some inevitable manifestation classifiable as "religion," how ever varied the

[3] *De Natura Deorum*, II, xxviii.
[4] *The Divine Institutes*, IV, xxviii.
[5] *Summa Theologica*, II-II, Q, lxxxi, a, 1.

individual examples might be? Is it some transcendent norm to which human beings should be related and of which they are somehow aware?

Let us suggest some things to which observers and participants might have been pointing when speaking of religion. We may mention, without discussion, some aspects of human thought, action, feeling, and practice that have been denoted; some special kind of person; that subjective experience that is usually called mystical; certain kinds of ceremonial, ritual, or symbolic behavior; organizations of special types that we may call ecclesiastical; certain codes of behavior; creedal statements; recognition of and service to superior powers; special modes of dedication; and perhaps some others.

Are these the things that are referred to by historians? Histories of religion and introductions to religion have been far more numerous and ample than histories of definitions. This is inevitable because the extent and variety of the observable manifestations of the "something" are much more accessible to comment and discussion than the intricacies of etymology, definition, and connotation. All the histories and introductions record, make use of, or imply definitions of religion. Two examples, arbitrarily chosen, may not be out of order: "Religion is man's attitude toward the universe regarded as a social and ethical force; it is the sense of social solidarity with objects regarded as Powers, and the institution of social relations with them." [6] "As there are a great many religions, so there are a great many limitations, and I propose to define religion as: *A sum of scruples which impede the free exercise of our faculties.*" [7] Both quotations come from discussions of the problem of definition. They represent attempts to single out "essential features" of religion. That they differ strikingly is less to be wondered at than that, with such difference of definition, both can be classed as able works.

What happens if we turn to other languages? This can be an enormous and highly technical problem. Yet it also has its simpler features. We shall be content with referring to and indicating a few directions and possibilities.

Sometimes people with a yen for the sensational will ask, Did you know that the word "religion" does not appear in the Old Testament at all, and only three times in the New? I was once asked, on a uni-

[6] C. H. Toy, *Introduction to the History of Religions* (Cambridge: Harvard University Press, 1913), p. 1.

[7] Salomon Reinach, *Orpheus: A History of Religions*, tr. Florence Simmonds (rev. ed.; New York: Liveright Publishing Corporation, 1929), p. 3. Italics in the text.

versity campus, "Did Jesus have any religion? He never used the word." These questions perhaps were not intended to intimate that "if there isn't a word for it, it either doesn't exist or is unknown," but they do suggest these questions: What words were used? What did the words mean?

The standard equivalent for religion in the Hebrew Scriptures is the phrase usually translated "fear the Lord" or "fear of God." (See Prov. 1:7, 2:5; Isa. 8:13, 33:6; Neh. 5:9; Ps. 36:1; Deut. 12:3; Job 15:4.) In the *Apocrypha* and in the *Talmud* the same usage is found. There are those who see in this a proof that religion either grows out of fear or teaches fear—or both. But they are using a definition for fear which does not capture the connotation of the Hebrew term. This connotation includes such meanings as "reverence," "standing in awe of," and "service to." That it is possible to appeal to or make use of craven fear in the name of religion is of course obvious—just as possible as it is to practice injustice in the name of justice. It is even possible to set up a religion based on fear, depending on how broadly we want to use the term and apply special definitions to it. These things are possible in the complexity and variety of human experience.

The word translated "religion" three times in the New Testament in the King James Version of the Bible is *threskeia.* (Acts 26:5; Jas. 1:26, 27.) A fourth occurrence (Col. 2:18) is translated "worshipping." Its usual Greek meaning suggests ceremonies or visible forms. The references in James clearly suggest some distinctions between various professions of religion. The writer proclaims a distinction, as for example, between the vain and the pure. The object of his judgment is the type of religious observance. It is as though he were saying that a ceremony of worship before an idol is vain, but that social service in behalf of real need is really religion. That he does not bring up the subject of motives and motivations does not necessarily mean he was unaware of their possible significance. Moreover, he probably leaves it to the reader to discover the ultimate sanctions for the distinction between genuflection before an idol and ministration to human need.

What is the equivalent in the New Testament for the word "religion" if *threskeia* seems inadequate? Would it be some phrase in the Sermon on the Mount? Could it be *threskeia* redefined as seems to be done in James? Is it necessary that we find a specific word or phrase? The one word that comes as near as any is a verb, *agapao*. It occurs, in some form, in the Sermon on the Mount (Matt. 5:43, 44, 46; 6:24), although the noun *agape* does not. By the time of Pauline and Johannine authorship, however, the noun has become quite prominent. Whether anything can be made of this is an open question. A tentative suggestion is offered here, but with much diffidence.

Defining religion is not simply a matter of ascertaining what to put into a dictionary after the word. No word so deeply involves the actualization of the definition and its meaning in the lives of people as does the word "religion." If one says that people are religious, he presumably tells something profound and important about the people. If people profess religion or a religion, it is an empty pastime unless the profession indicates and declares something important about their dispositions and activities. To profess verbally some acquaintance with a dictionary definition of religion and yet deny the religion in thought, feeling, and action is a travesty, whether intentional or unintentional, conscious or unconscious. Religion at its best requires the highest kind of loyalty, honesty, and maturity—so much so that "at its best" it may seem unrealizable. The phrase "at its best" suggests direction. On the other hand, representatives of religion have long taken account of an incongruity between profession and practice. Whatever we call it—deception, hypocrisy, frailty, incompatibility—it is a perennial drag on the achievement of mature religion.

The transition from verb to noun can be something of an index of the temptations and hazards involved in the problem stated in the previous paragraph. Whether the New Testament usages of *agapao* and *agape* are evidence of or illustrate this is at the moment beside the point, but it is true that Christianity has suffered immeasurably from those professing it—perhaps more than from its enemies. One way to indicate this linguistically is to speak of it in terms of the transition from verb to noun. To this we now turn.

It appeals to what may be called the "pragmatic temper" of America to stress the verb rather than the noun. A preponderant concern with nouns is often said to be manifestation of a search for "substances" and "essences" which are thought to be "behind" the appearances. It is further suggested that a concern with verbs tends to keep us closer to behavior, action, conduct, and to the questions: What is the behavior like? What are the results? Would a different type of action accomplish better results?

Correlatively it could be argued that an overemphasis on the noun makes it subtly possible to "detach" it from behavior, action, and conduct and safely impound it in a creed, formula, dictionary, or encyclopedia, where we may profess it without really practicing it.

We might even make the profession obligatory on those over whom we can exercise some kind of control. It is a remarkable thing that the first of the great Creeds—The Apostles' Creed—almost completely bypasses the Sermon on the Mount. If we place the two documents side by side, we may well wonder just where the Sermon exerted any impact on the Creed. Should it have exerted influence? We may imply that it should have, but for the present we should like to regard this as an open question.

We may also, for the time being, leave as an open question whether this would apply to all religions that have ever had any extensive following. Limitations of acquaintance preclude a direct reply. It does, however, seem that human beings have a remarkable facility for such incongruities as combining a verbal profession of, for example, love, with a practice of hostility. Such incongruity is compounded by the addition of "rationalization," excuse, or by that champion of fallacies—giving a "good" name to a "bad" thing. The incongruity has nowhere been stated more graphically within the compass of a single sentence than by Strindberg in his play "The Father." In Act I the Captain comments on what he believes are the intemperate efforts of the nurse, Margaret, to evangelize him: "It's a strange thing that you no sooner speak of God and love than your voice becomes hard and your eyes fill with hate."

By now we realize that whatever the dictionaries or other formal documents may say about definition, whatever scientific and other professional treatises may say about the nature of things to which descriptive definitions should be faithful, whatever the formal definitions of moral or religious imperatives, human beings *do* participate in the formulation of definitions. If we do not do so by intellectual processes, we do so by the implications inhering in our practice. We can revise standard definitions by verbal manipulation or by borderline practice. We can appeal from the universal and theoretical—no matter how admittedly valid—to the practicalities of specific cases. Everything becomes relevant—from the dynamics of single acts, to philosophies of life and theories of the largest possible scope—whether overtly professed or unconsciously implied. One of the pioneers of American pragmatism, William James, touches on this theme in an interesting way.

In the preface to that admirable collection of essays of his called "Heretics," Mr. Chesterton writes these words: "There are some people—and I am one of them—who think that the most practical and important thing about a man is still his view of the universe. . . . We think the question is not whether the theory of the cosmos affects matters, but whether in the long run anything else affects them."

I think with Mr. Chesterton in this matter.[8]

Meaning

Definition and meaning may differ. In other words, there may be other meanings of a statement than the meaning derived from checking the words and phrases with the definitions found in dictionary and encyclopedia. What is the definition? is in a sense a very simple question, but, What is the meaning? can be far more complicated. The focal point and the area of concern for both definition and meaning are the human personality and the person. Also, religion is peculiarly susceptible to the problems and complications resulting from the variety and complexity of meaning. Moreover, the religious person is a unique center of meaning and is intimately related to whatever meanings of purpose and significance there may be in the total context.

We may speak of the meaning of a statement, of a poem, of a symbol, of a motion or action, of the particular articulation of a given statement at some specific time, of the meaning of life and existence. We may speak of wrong meanings, consciously and intentionally wrong, or unconsciously so. We may speak of absence of meaning and of meaninglessness. We may speak of a sense of meaning and of a capacity for apprehending meanings. Our "literal Lymans" and our poets have varying experiences with meanings. We may even speak of the meaning of a loss of meaning. Most types of meaning, however, are uniquely related to language.

When Mark Antony said that Brutus was an honorable man he meant that Brutus was dishonorable. In other words the intended meaning was the opposite of the apparently literal meaning. It is more or less customary to say that there were at least three possible levels or varities of awareness in this dramatic situation and therefore three possible meanings: that of Mark Antony, who knew very well what he was doing and what results he planned to achieve; that of the crowd, who did not vividly realize thy were being subtly nudged into the point of view of the speaker; and that of Brutus, who, had he heard the speech, would perhaps have been attracted at first by the literal meaning because it may have been what he wanted to hear. This hints at the generalization that there are risks in wanting to hear something because there is a possibility that you will hear what you

[8] *Pragmatism* (New York: Longmans, Green and Company, 1907, 1940), p. 3.

want to hear when, as a matter of fact, the real meaning may be something else.

The point, at this stage in our discussion, is that this incident in the famous drama illustrates difference in types of meaning. Shakespeare was primarily concerned to portray human nature in action. Here is an excellent example of what is called "literary psychology" —the acute and perceptive insights of a keen observer of mankind. This drama is not an academic, scientific, abstract analysis of meaning and meaning situations. It is not a step in a process of ascertaining the dynamics of meaning modes with the idea of formulating the "laws" of these operations, nor is it part of a linguistic analysis of varied modes of communication.

Today the subject of meaning has received academic, professional, scientific, analytical, and linguistic attention. Attempts have been made to investigate, analyze, and understand the dynamics of the various meaning situations in human experience. Language itself has been studied directly and there is now an impressive array of recent works on philosophy of language, semantics, and meaning. Account has been taken and classifications made of the various uses and functions of language, of the "diseases" to which language is subject —or to which human beings are subject in such a way that the diseases show up in the use of language. A variety of technical and semitechnical terms will meet even the casual reader—pragmatics, syntactics, and others such as the expressive, the poetic, the pragmatic, and truth functions of language.

To give "depth" to the problem, the psychological sciences are opening up the subject of the relationship of language and language use to the inner and deeper areas of personality. A simple, yet potentially horrendous example is the statement "I am afraid." A normal response to such an affirmation might be, "Of what?" If the answer to this question is, "I don't know," communication usually begins to falter. We now realize that a statement such as "I am afraid, but don't know what I am afraid of" may be and often is meaningful. Yet how many people, in unrecorded events through uncounted centuries, have declared such a statement to be "meaningless" or "silly" or "perverse." The works of Sigmund Freud, Oskar Pfister, and Rollo May, to name only three, are beginning to reveal the meanings in such experiences.[9]

[9] See: Freud, *Works;* Pfister, *Christianity and Fear,* tr. W. H. Johnston (New York: The Macmillan Company, 1949); May, *The Meaning of Anxiety* (New York: Ronald Press, 1950).

Perhaps it would not be out of place to call attention to an ancient narrative that illustrates very vividly the drastic and dramatic disparity between different responses of a person to the same words used by different people. Very few reports from ancient times so vividly illustrate the fact that there are depths to meaning situations which differ greatly from the literal. Moreover, the story is tantalizing in that it gives no hint of the degree of understanding, of the principal actors, of what was taking place. It is the story of Micaiah in I Kings 22. Ahab, the king, at the urging of Jehoshaphat, his ally, consulted the prophets as to the advisability of a campaign in Ramoth-gilead. Exactly what Jehoshaphat had in mind is not clear, unless he was questioning the validity of the project. Ahab, however, was prepared to meet the request because he had four hundred available prophets. With one voice they echoed the desire of Ahab. Any critical acumen he might have had was lulled into inaction by the dulcet tones of the "language" that reinforced his desires. Again Jehoshaphat demurred, asking for a "prophet of the Lord." This introduces the first harsh note in the proceedings. Ahab did know such a person but hated him. The reason he gave is one of the most vivid examples of a psychological "letting the cat out of the bag" in ancient literature: Micaiah did not "prophesy good" concerning the king. But he agreed to call Micaiah. A messenger instructed Micaiah on how to "vote." Micaiah's reply to this seems to be the usual, courageous, and independent declaration of the "true prophet." When he came before Ahab, however, and was asked the same question put to the four hundred, he dramatically surprised the king—and the reader—by giving the same answer as given by the four hundred. Why? He explained later, but with an explanation that would not be accepted by the modern mind, which would want a more naturalistic and psychological answer. In the same vein it might be asked whether he was being deliberately psychological in his contest with the king.

The climax came when the king responded to this same reply he had already heard, from a different source. In effect he called Micaiah a liar. But if Micaiah was a liar, why were not the four hundred liars? Were the meanings of the statements different, and was the difference subtly perceptible to Ahab? Even an elementary acquaintance with modern psychology of personality depths could suggest some tentative explanations of Ahab's motivations, both conscious and unconscious —much more so than of Micaiah's.

For spectacular virtuosity in the achievement of precision in the definition of terms and in the employment of language with clear and unequivocal meanings, the palm goes to science. The secret seems to reside in the development of procedures for the acquiring and the accumulation of precise knowledge. When we come to know precisely what air is, then we can formulate definitions that leave nothing to speculation or guess. When we learn the structure and constitution of stellar objects and formulate the laws of their operations, then we expose the naïveté and the fancy of definitions imputed to such terms as sublunary, supralunary, celestial, terrestrial, and empyrean. Even the great Kepler retained misguidedly precise notions concerning the "music of the spheres" and the musical parts "sung" by various planets. Multitudes of terms, such as genius, muse, enthusiasm, demonic, inspire, sortilege, diabolical, augury, and divination, shed some or all of their ancient meanings as knowledge about what they supposedly referred to is increasingly made clear.

This has had dramatic and even drastic effects on meanings of phrases and statements. Language, long since divested of its supposed magical qualities and potencies, shows up as a versatile but natural instrument for use in the bewildering traffic of meanings. This may be illustrated simply and briefly as follows: What is the meaning of the statement, "Milk is good"? The question can be answered in a number of ways because potentially there are many more meanings than one. If the statement is an example of the use of language to give expression to one's feelings and preferences, the statement could mean "I like milk." Or if a mother is trying to induce a refractory offspring to adopt some sensible eating habits, her use of the statement could mean "You ought to drink it." Some bit of additional meaning might be noted in the tone of voice and the inflection with which she says it. In the third place, a scientist representing the accumulation of knowledge referred to above could have a complex but precise meaning we could call a truth meaning or a logical meaning: "Milk is a protective food, rich in vitamins and minerals and proteins of high biological value, specifically caseinogen, lactalbumin, and lactoglobulin, and liberal amounts of the so-called indispensable amino acids—in the caseinogen—which cannot be synthesized by the organism out of materials ordinarily available at a speed commensurate with the demands for normal growth." This may seem too extensive to be called the logical meaning of the brief statement first quoted. Yet it is certainly an illustration of the detail and precision that go into the scientific enterprises of developing meanings through the extension of knowledge. A fourth potential meaning can result from the poetic use of language. Conceivably the statement could be used as a poetic tribute to motherhood. A fifth possible meaning comes from psychoanalysis which speaks of milk as "an unconscious symbol of mother-dependence, gastrointestinal fixations, and Oedipus ramifications."

While science has made such an extensive contribution to precision in definition and meaning, and partly as a result of this type of influence, religion has suffered some loss of prestige because of the variety and nebulous quality of the meanings supposed to obtain in terms and statements used in religion. Although an enormous amount of energy has been expended in attempts to formulate definitions and explications of meaning under the aegis of theology, there are those who satirize the whole enterprise of theology by calling it a "dead language." It is accused of trying to define terms that cannot be defined—providence, God, congregation of the blessed, the Fall, original sin, and the like. It is contended they cannot be defined in the manner the sciences employ in formulating their definitions.

Science's use of language is limited, how ever spectacular its achievements in the accumulation of knowledge, its precision in definition, and its verifiability of meaning. Science does not compose poetry; does not scientifically validate terms and statements dealing with values, norms, and worth—execept in limited ways; and does not conclusively justify imperatives and obligations—not primarily or extensively.

On the other hand, religion specializes in poetic language and in statements concerning values, norms, and worth and unblushingly proclaims imperatives and obligations. That this would put an intolerable strain on attempts to hew to the line of strict scientific procedure is obvious enough. That it would involve hazards and risks is also obvious. That it allows for speculation, faith, affirmation in absence of any evidence that science would accept is not only obvious, it is essential. It is relevant at this juncture to recall the words of William E. Hocking:

> Taking religious ideas literally and fixedly is, in fact, a modern and Western peculiarity. The Oriental mind realizes that the spiritual atmosphere in which either men or gods may breathe, must be *created;* it knows nothing of empirical truth in matters of religion, truth passively taken; and postulate joins hands with poetry in constituting the medium in which all spirituality may live. . . . We approach, in religious matters, the poetry of the Orient often with a literal-minded savagery, which must accuse us of some deeper defect than simple lack of humor—a lack, namely, of spirituality itself, which knows that the language of the spirit must be read by the

spirit also, and is not to be rudely transferred into empirical text-books of physics and of medicine.[10]

Lest it be thought that our author is in danger of presenting a dubious dichotomy or a one-sided picture, we need to observe that he also says: "Nevertheless, I must believe that the great heave of the West to get a literal and objective grip upon its major religious objects is an advance, and not a retrogression. We only drive men to make their religion all prose, when we threaten to make it all poetry and postulate." [11]

Thus we may raise a question as to how appropriate it is for science to analyze and judge religion solely by the standards by which it usually analyzes and judges. Individual scientists differ widely on how they understand and assess such a question as this. One may condemn religion out of hand for its unscientific methods and its vague definitions and meanings. Another may withhold judgment on religious claims. Another may be a deeply religious person. Another may say the universe has no meaning. Still another may aver we are all a part of the divine plan. It is a certainty, however, that no single "basket" will carry such an extensive burden of "eggs." Moreover, it is a bit early in the history of human experience to develop an unequivocal and universally acceptable method of "candling" to assess the acceptability of all the "eggs."

Finally, for present purposes, we may observe that in all the foregoing, the human person is present in some way. Furthermore, we may well ask, Is the human person a unique center and focus of meaning? If so, is this by convention? Or is there some eternal dimension? If these questions have been definitively closed, then we are ready, presumably, to formulate final definitions and statements of meanings. If they are not closed, we still walk by whatever faith we are able to develop or receive as a gift.

[10] *The Meaning of God in Human Experience* (New Haven: Yale University Press, 1912), pp. 149-50. Italics in the text. Used by permission.
[11] *Ibid.*, p. 150.

CHAPTER VI

Science

GIVING SUCH A TITLE TO A CHAPTER MAY BE AN ACT OF ARRANT presumption. On the other hand, to ignore science until we are thoroughly competent is a pretentious bit of "voluntary paralysis." It is not possible to ignore science. If we pretend to do so—when it would be thought we should not—we invite suspicions as to our motives. To tamper with the subject at all throws open the door to all sorts of possible charges—that we distort science, romanticize it, oversimplify it, underestimate it, misconstrue it, lack experience with it, resist it, use it to prove too much or to prove the "wrong" things, ignore its valid proofs, and no doubt many others. Even people officially classified as scientists may do some of these things. Thus the only recourse for the nonexpert is to try to see as clearly as possible under limiting circumstances, to make some effort to become acquainted and to try to understand.

There are some large scale concepts associated with the term "science." They include pure science; applied science; scientific method; the special sciences; the science of biology, chemistry, et cetera; the scientific study of personality, politics, religion, et cetera; the scientific attitude of mind; the spirit of science; the scientific spirit; and others. In this work we are concerned primarily with two matters: some understanding of the scientific enterprise and of its relations to personality and religion. The specific phrase "science of religion" has not caught on yet, at least in the way that "science of biology" has. Whether the reasons are obvious may be an open question. The phrase "science of personality" seems to be in the process of becoming established just in the present century. Though it would be admitted that the "science of" something or other has not yet become established, there are innumerable people who have no doubts about the appropriateness of and the possibilities in the scientific approach to anything whatever.

The world today believes in science. The prestige it has acquired is almost beyond estimation. We can assume, however, that there may be exceptions to such generalizations. Perhaps science is acclaimed more for what it has produced than for its emphasis on objective search for truth. Man is not famous for welcoming "new truth," especially if it replaces some "old truth." This is also true for many scientists who, as human beings, are not altogether immune to fixations in certain orthodoxies. It is not brilliantly characteristic of man to welcome the risks of progressive change in preference to feeling secure in old stabilities. To be sure, some people who rhapsodize about change may sometimes forget that not all change is progressive. Thus, anyone with the temerity to try to say, even on an elementary level, what science "is" takes his life in his hands so to speak. But it is impossible to avoid taking some account of this remarkable enterprise.

It may be well to begin with some general estimates that touch on the spirit and accomplishments of science.

> We have seen how science, henceforth the imperious master of human destiny, is forcing mankind to give up war by making it an all-pervading instrument of destruction so vast and complicated as to escape control. On the other hand. . . . We have never let ourselves be blinded to the fact that the forces of science are so new that the full extent of the revolution caused by them in human affairs is only beginning to be apprehended even by thoughtful people. The policies of nations do not quickly respond to the dictates of reason. . . . With the advent of science, other and still finer visions of justice and strange, new creations of art beckon at the door of the future. For science, by making industries interdependent, challenges old taboos and outward customs with new demands for social justice.[1]

The same author wrote, thirty-one years earlier, "It was a religion, not a science, which presided over the fall of Rome. Had it been a science, Rome might not have fallen when it did." [2]

These quotations are presented as examples of the general acclaim accorded science, rather than as any strict description of what science is. We need not assume, however, that all representatives of science would agree with these examples of acclaim—or any others.

My aim will be to give attention to some of the principal features of science in its impact on modern thought and feeling; to consider a particular area of scientific thought and activity—the psychological sciences; and to take up once again the question, always a live one,

[1] James T. Shotwell: *The Great Decision* (New York: The Macmillan Company, 1945), pp. 218 ff. Used by permission.

[2] *The Religious Revolution of Today* (New York: Charles Scribner's Sons, 1913), p. 36.

of relationships between science and religion. What the scientist himself says will be of value to others if they make some effort to understand. Subsequent paragraphs therefore are simply an attempt to achieve some perspective and some understanding of science in its relation to other subjects. If there is no communication, no mutual understanding, no co-operative effort, life will be chopped up into warring, mutually suspicious precincts. I shall occasionally quote the scientist, but not as an oracle or unquestioned authority on all matters.

For the present I shall try to single out certain features of the scientific enterprise and its relationships, presenting the items and discussion in arbitrary order. The first is the general connotation for the word "science" as understood and used herein. It refers, in the first place, to modern science. This distinguishes today's usage not only from that of the Greeks, or from reference to certain efforts of primitive man that are called elemental science, but also from medieval science. This is not to say there are not common denominators in all three. The features of modern science as distinguished, for example, from the Greek, include a revised definition and understanding of nature, the abandonment of the concept of "final cause," a revolt against supernaturalism, and extended use and revised understanding of the technique of experiment. It is possible, however, to be betrayed by seductive influences of the term "modern," influences which might induce a "we have arrived" attitude. Belief, formerly entertained, that the Greeks had achieved adequate and competent knowledge now seems naïve. This belief was epitomized by Dante's characterization of Aristotle as the "master of those that know."[3] Aristotle's "mastery" was indeed spectacular and varied, but it was not the achievement of knowledge whose finality could be taken for granted—and certainly not as dogma.

Modern science, or any other kind, remains an abstraction until it becomes actualized in some kind of performance—in attitude, approach, or methodological operations. Who will be able to, and who will practice modern science with its stringent requirements become major questions. Even more, to what ends will it be practiced? This is crucial. The "if" of H. J. Muller becomes acutely relevant.[4] If this quotation is taken seriously, it raises questions as to what sorts of aids science will require, and what types of impetus will nourish and direct this aid. Will it mean the enlightenment of people generally?

[3] *The Divine Comedy,* Canto IV of "The Inferno," line 131.
[4] See p. 38.

Or will it mean the assumption of power and control by some enlightened "board of directors"? The former is democracy, the latter, benevolent despotism.

In the second place, I mean science in its most advanced forms. That is to say, science is not thought of here primarily in terms of its origins nor explained in terms of an original impulse. The ultimate source of this vast enterprise would no doubt be a subject of great interest. Did man begin to be a scientist because he wanted to, or because he needed to? Is there something that could be called a scientific impulse or instinct? Need science ever be embarrassed by humble beginnings? Is magic with its emphases on prediction and control—of bizarre types usually—the ancestor of science? These are interesting questions, but they are hardly the way science is coming to be understood, defined, and used. More advanced science is coming to require more preparation, more interests, and more serious attention to the purposes of science and its relationships with other enterprises than we have anticipated. As the powers of science increase, the problems of direction and control of power become more urgent. From now on it will be hopelessly naïve to think of the fruits of science as automatically and exclusively beneficent.

In the third place, I mean grown-up and self-conscious science. Today science is a work for intelligent and mature people. It is not an enterprise solely for occasional geniuses who never fully understand what they are doing, who wait for "lightning to strike," whose laboratories are their crania. There is no intention here to belittle these procedures. In so far as any of them yield fruit, they have made their peculiar and significant contributions. Some of them may operate today. The very word "genius," though still used, does not now have the original connotations. Any dictionary that deals in etymology will make this clear. This is not to say that everyone has abandoned beliefs in and notions of psychic influences, directing forces—geneii or stars, demons, and the like. What we mean is that there is more general maturity and self-consciousness in the scientific enterprise than ever before, and consequently an enlarged understanding of what there is to be done and why.

There have been notable developments of awareness among scientists in this century—an awareness that is taking increasing account of the various contexts within which any enterprise must operate. The concept of context becomes of special significance. There is always some kind of context, for science, as well as for any activity or enterprise—social, political, cultural. Now we know as never before that results and influences can work outward from scientific thought and achievement. Powers, desirers, and users look on the work of science, sometimes with an ominous variety of notions about making use of the scientific community, asking for new accomplishments, wishing to make special use of what has already been accomplished.

Further, I mean to include in my usage some reference to science which has achieved so much and which, by common consent, is thought to be capable of further and further achievement. This can assume the proportions of utopianism, which I expressly hope to avoid. In fact this is exactly what has happened in those popular articles which give romantic and glorified pictures of what the utterly capable and carefree days of the distant future will be when science "really gets going." Everyone will have equipment—gadgets, necessities, and luxuries—not yet on present drafting boards. Judging by the pictures drawn to accompany some of these articles, everyone will be well-fed, well-dressed, and well-behaved. However, there is still a modicum of truth in the general picture. If we look back for something similar to this in older literature, we think naturally of Francis Bacon's *New Atlantis*. He anticipates a number of things which have actually come to pass. Thus the characteristic phrase "know-how" signalizes innumerable scientific achievements in modern times.

In the next place we need at least to take note of the fact that science—whether we speak of the word or of the enterprise—has been subjected to redefinition and reinterpretation. Reference has already been made to the distinction between Greek science and modern. There has been much redefining and reinterpretation during the past hundred years. True, one occasionally hears a captious criticism to the effect that all this change of definition or shift of point of view shows that science "doesn't really know what it is doing" and that it all illustrates how science "doesn't have any real respect for the eternal verities." Someone will say, "These doctors don't really know as much as they think they do. They're always changing their minds. If you have good common sense and practice it, the doctors would starve to death." These points of view may not need to be taken seriously, as arguments, but they do need to be taken seriously as human conditions. A mother of five children said to an unmarried nurse who objected to the mother's feeding her tiny infant black coffee, "How many children have you got? None! Well I've raised *five* and I *always* give them black coffee." It is not entirely unnatural that human beings seek some consolation in their limitations—especially when they are not understood to be limitations, and when the individuals are threatened by something new. The new will often involve some reinterpretation, some redefining—things that science supposedly takes a pride in doing. Yet scientists themselves are subject to resistance to change—but as human beings rather than as scientists.

A few recent titles on this general theme are A. N. Whitehead's *Science and the Modern World,* Herbert Dingle's *A Century of Science,* Werner Heisenberg's *Philosophical Problems of Nuclear Science,* and the popular though somewhat romantic *The Common Sense of Science* by J. Bronowski.

In the sixth place we may call attention to the fact that science intends to be a benefactor. This is a manner of speaking and is not intended to be a personification of science. It is possible, theoretically, for a scientist, or scientists generally, not to have beneficent intentions. We venture the question of whether it could be argued that science as an outlook and mode of procedure tends to encourage the benefactor idea. Or is it possible for fallible human nature—whatever this means precisely—to think of science as a mighty instrument of power, quite apart from any notions of benefits? About the only people who seem to develop this theme at the present time are science fiction writers—particularly the more sensational ones—and the noncomical comic strip authors who deal in interplanetary problems of control in which a few "scientists" are engaged in fantastic battles for cosmic supremacy. Presumably they are scientists in the sense of ability to achieve mastery over natural forces. The history of science presents some exceedingly interesting examples of wrestling with aspects of this problem and raises the question of the importance of moral and spiritual qualities necessary for the management of the powerful instruments that are science's achievements. The main point here is that, as of the present, benevolence is considered to be an aim of science. Yet, benevolence is not strictly science, as science is usually described or defined, but it is urged as an essential characteristic for the scientist.

What stands in the way of a predominantly or exclusively beneficent use of the achievements of science? What dangers are there that we shall always be threatened by destructive use of the achievements? What possibilities are there that science itself will deliberately set about to construct something that is intentionally and entirely destructive? It may seem obvious what the answers to these questions are. Yet, it is not certain what sorts of questions they are in the first place. Are they spectators' questions? Are they questions of participants? What sorts of implications do they involve? Are they subtle hints to the scientific community to sharpen their own and our sense of ethical and spiritual responsibilities as we become the beneficiaries of the knowledge that confers power?

We may call attention, in the next place, to some distinctions within the field of science itself. We speak of pure science and applied science; of intrinsic value of acquiring knowledge, but also of its instrumental value; of science as an ideal considered abstractly; and science as it may need to conduct itself in this world. This raises the question of the responsibilities of science and the scientist. It used to be urged in some circles that pure science had no ethical responsibilities, and that values generally were not properly a concern of science, as science. Within the past few decades, however, problems of ethics, values, and even politics have received increasing attention from scientists—if not from science. This does not represent so much a revision of the definition of pure science, as it does an extension of the understanding of science to include science in this world. It represents an increased perception on the part of scientists of their responsibilities in this world. It may be fair to say that the scientists now see more clearly their two-fold responsibilities: in the laboratory and outside the laboratory. There is, after all, something of a dreamlike quality in the concept of pure science if it is too completely detached from the problems of human relationships, civic responsibilities, and life in society in general. If the concept is too utterly idealistic, it gets away from the scientist as human being.

Does this seem to be forcing some nonscientific concerns upon the strict province of science? Whether the future will see the scientific enterprise giving attention to the training of the scientist not just as scientist, but also as responsible agent, as civic-minded manager of science's gigantic achievements, as moral and spiritual being remains to be seen. But it will have to be done somehow, even if it seems to be "coercing" science into a relationship with some things that are not exactly science, for example, morality, politics, religion, and the like. It is already happening that science in some places is being coerced into alliances and relationships that are not generally beneficent.

Thus, three developments obtain simultaneously: (1) science is inevitable and here to stay, (2) it is replete with actual and potential aids for human welfare, and (3) it is risky and dangerous in the hands of man. But what is new is that the same person can be making all three statements himself, and with something approximating equal force. In a more naïve time it may have seemed possible to discuss the benefits brought by science and forget the rest. Now, even a scientist must dwell on all three considerations. Two questions to which answers of various types and adequacy will be given—even within the same mind over a period of time—are: (1) What are the nature and extent of our dangers and risks? and, (2) What are the most appropriate of any possible solutions? In the next few paragraphs we see some people wrestling with certain aspects of these questions.

We need now to take note of some misgivings. We shall present only three examples. They have been articulated by men classifiable as scientists. The first comes from an Italian ballistics expert of the sixteenth century, Tartaglia. He was asked by a master of ordnance in Verona for some advice concerning the aiming of artillery:

> [After voicing preliminary plans, he suddenly reconsiders and goes on to say] But, since then, one day meditating to myself, it had seemed to me that it was a thing blameworthy, shameful and barbarous, worthy of severe punishment before God and man, to wish to bring to perfection an art damageable to one's neighbour and destructive to the human race, and especially to Christian men in the continual wars that they wage on one another. Consequently, not only did I altogether neglect the study of this matter and turned to others, but I even tore up and burnt everything which I had calculated and written on the subject, ashamed and full of remorse for the time I had spent on it, and well decided never to communicate in writing that which against my will had remained in my memory, either to please a friend or in teaching of these matters which are a grave sin and shipwreck of the soul.[5]

If the foregoing quotation evinces some misgiving about science, or at least the uses to which science is put, the next question from the same author may provide some basis for misgivings about man himself. The King of France, at least a nominal Christian, instigated an invasion of Italy by the Turks, to which threat Tartaglia responded as follows:

> Today, however, in sight of the ferocious wolf preparing to set on our flock, and of our pastors united for the common defense, it does not seem to me any longer proper to hold these things hid, and I have resolved to publish them partly in writing, partly by word of mouth, for the benefit of Christians so that all should be in better state either to attack the common enemy or to defend themselves against him. I regret very much at

[5] Quoted in J. D. Bernal, *The Social Function of Science* (London: George Routledge & Sons, 1942), p. 169. Used by permission of Routledge & Kegan Paul Ltd.

the moment having given up this work, for I am certain that had I persevered I would have found things of the greatest value, as I hope yet to find.[6]

The second example comes from Bronislaw Malinowski in his contribution to a symposium, *Science and Religion:*

> Is science responsible for my agnosticism and for that of others who think like me? I believe it is, and therefore I do not love science, though I have to remain its loyal servant. Science deals with truth and with evidence, and it develops a critical sense and a passion for full experience which spread beyond its own limited domain.[7]

This may stimulate us to recall Darwin's lamenting the fact that scientific researches had destroyed his appreciation of poetry.

In our third example, something approximating an alarmist note is sounded in the address delivered in November, 1945, by J. Robert Oppenheimer:

> What has come upon us, that the insight, the knowledge, the power of physical science, to the cultivation of which, to the learning and teaching of which we are dedicated, has become too dangerous to be talked of even in these halls? It is the question that faces us now, that goes to the root of what science is and what its value is. . . . We have made a thing that by all the standards of the world we grew up in is an evil thing. . . . We have raised again the question of whether science is good for man, of whether it is good to learn about the world. . . . Because we are scientists, we must say an unalterable yes to these questions; it is our faith and our commitment, seldom made explicit, even more seldom challenged, that knowledge is a good in itself, knowledge and such powers as come with it.[8]

These misgivings do not clearly identify the problem to which they refer, nor do they specify causes or remedies. They tend to concur in at least a general recognition of science as either good in itself or as a source or instrument of benefit, in spite of the risks involved. It is hardly credible that science would be discredited by scientists in any really damaging sense. It is true that warning or questioning voices have been raised ever since the seventeenth-century turning point in the rise of modern science. This does not refer to the "warfare" between science and theology as reported in such a work as A. D.

[6] *Ibid.*

[7] London: Gerald Howe, Ltd., 1931, p. 78.

[8] "Atomic Weapons," *A Treasury of Science*, ed. Harlow Shapley, *et al.* (2nd ed., New York: Harper & Brothers, 1946), pp. 761-62. Used by permission.

White's *History of the Warfare Between Science and Theology,* but to subtler misgivings and apprehensions concerning the development of moods and climates of opinion, and the challenges that the different outlooks on life offer to each other. To H. J. Paton, psychology—representing science—is a "great wave threatening religion." [9] Arnold Toynbee quotes the first secretary of the Royal Society in England, Thomas Sprat, who recorded the following observations:

> It is apparent to all that the influence which Christianity once obtain'd on mens minds is prodigiously decay'd. The generality of Christendom is now well-nigh arriv'd at that fatal condition which did immediately precede the destruction of the worships of the Ancient World, when the face of Religion in their public assemblies was quite different from that apprehension which men had concerning it in privat. . . . But this is certain, that the spiritual vices of this age have well-nigh contributed as much towards it as the carnal.[10]

In the same volume, Toynbee himself says,

> The opening of the seventeenth century had found the Western Christian Wars of Religion in full swing and Western Christian fanaticism still at its height. Before the close of the same century, Religion had been replaced by Technology, applying the findings of Experimental Science, as the paramount interest and pursuit of the leading spirits in the Western Society.[11]
>
> Since Technology has replaced Religion as the pursuit in which Western Man has put his treasure in the Late Modern Age, it is natural that he should have expected his new idol to reward him for his worship by enabling him to fill the spiritual vacuum which he had created by discarding his ancestral religion.[12]

Toynbee designates Sprat's observations as "Seventeenth-century forebodings of the spiritual price of the seventeenth-century revulsion from religious fanaticism" [13] and his own comments as description of the "secularization of western life," largely through the "apotheosis of Technology," a handmaid of science.

Sigmund Freud sees in religion and science a contrast, with misgivings only about the former:

[9] *The Modern Predicament* (London: George Allen & Unwin, 1955), p. 110.

[10] *An Historian's Approach to Religion* (New York: Oxford University Press, 1956), p. 156. Used by permission.

[11] *Ibid.,* p. 184.

[12] *Ibid.,* p. 216.

[13] *Ibid.,* p. 155.

Of the three forces which can dispute the position of science, religion alone is a really serious enemy. Art is almost always harmless and beneficent, it does not seek to be anything else but an illusion. . . . Philosophy is not opposed to science, it behaves itself as if it were a science.[14]

This contrasts somewhat with an earlier, more tolerant attitude toward religion. Some allowance must be made for special connotation that he employs when he uses the word "religion":

The reader need not fear that psychoanalysis, which first revealed the regular over-determination of psychic acts and formations, will be tempted to derive anything so complicated as religion from a single source. If it necessarily seeks, as in duty bound, to gain recognition for one of the sources of this institution, it by no means claims exclusiveness for this source or even first rank among the concurring factors. Only a synthesis from various fields of research can decide what relative importance in the genesis of religion is to be assigned to the mechanism which we are to discuss; but such a task exceeds the means as well as the intentions of the psychoanalyst.[15]

Of course the spirit and the achievement of modern science are too widely influential and too firmly entrenched for misgivings yet to achieve the dimensions of a movement or a climate of opinion.

The new scientific spirit was not confined to a philosophical class, but spread to all classes. We are still living in the age which (the) seventeenth-century movement introduced, and the scientific spirit is still waging war to hold the frontiers which it has occupied against irruptions of irrationalism. We may see the potentialities of such irruption, perhaps, in the unnoticed but extensive circulation of the literature of occultism, astrology and magic.[16]

Science seems secure for a long time to come, in spite of any and all misgivings of the present. While risks are freely mentioned and occasionally feared, no science worthy of the name interprets itself in other than favorable terms—its aims as lofty and worthy, its projects as constructive (even engines of destruction are always said to be for self-defense), its achievements as important already but to be even greater in the future. Even those proponents of pure science

[14] *New Introductory Lectures on Psycho-analysis* by Sigmund Freud, translated by W. J. H. Sprott, Copyright 1933 by Sigmund Freud, and published with the permission of the publisher W. W. Norton & Company, Inc., New York. Page 884.

[15] From *The Basic Writings of Sigmund Freud,* trans. and ed. by Dr. A. A. Brill, Copyright 1938 by Random House, Inc. Reprinted by permission of the Brill Trust.

[16] Michael B. Foster, *Mystery and Philosophy* (London: Student Christian Movement Press, 1957), p. 45.

who may have disavowed any ethical responsibilities would speak of the pursuit of knowledge as a good in itself, but also as a potential source of untold benefits.

It would seem appropriate to do the same for other enterprises. Music should not be defined and dismissed, in terms of the harrowing performances of a tone-deaf person or the vocalizations of a monotone. It would be an arbitrary limitation imposed on art to condemn it because a technically gifted rascal did obscenities in oils. Is logic to be despaired of because a demagogue may use the forms of logic to put across a nefarious conclusion? Shall religion be defined by deceits and cruelties and stupidities upheld and practiced in its name?

Shall an enterprise be defined by its exemplified best? Scientists do that regularly for science. Aristotle tended to define man in terms of fulfillment of potential, rather than origins or kinship with simpler orders. As for science, any destructiveness carried out by means of the products of science are conveniently called the misuse or misapplication of science. Of course it is possible to think of any number of enterprises which have no exemplified best since they are destructive and wrong in principle—murder, witch burning, superstition, human sacrifice, idolatry.

The clamor and push of powerful needs can induce or seduce mankind into a variety of perverted and even destructive modes of satisfaction, which turn out not to be satisfactions but palliatives, bromides, and the like. Thus, many acts and attitudes which attempt to serve as the meeting of needs do not do so. This may take place below the level of consciousness in some cases. But once initiated, such modes of satisfaction can become crystallized into rites and customs that are passed on from generation to generation. We are thus at a point where we may introduce two problems or questions that involve science and religion and relate them in new and surprising ways. Put for the moment into question form, they are: (1) Does religion develop from energies and compulsions below the level of conscious awareness? (2) Can we now speak of scientific inquiry that has at last mapped this territory? Freud has said in his *New Introductory Lectures on Psychoanalysis,*

> If we add to science the investigation of the intellectual and emotional functions of men (and animals), we find that nothing has been altered as regards the general position of science, that there are no new sources of knowledge or methods of research. Intuition and inspiration would be such, if they existed; but they can safely be counted as illusions, as fulfillments

of wishes. It is easy to see, moreover, that the qualities which, as we have shown, are expected of a Weltanschauung have a purely emotional basis.[17]

Then commenting on what he considers unusual features of religion that help to account for its power—not a constructive power in his estimation—he goes on to tell what he considers the proper way to make a scientific analysis of religious phenomena, "One can only understand this remarkable combination of teaching, consolation and precept in religion, if one subjects it to *genetic analysis.*" [18]

It is to a later work that we would refer at this juncture, one by Theodor Reik. This work represents an extension of method from exclusive concern with neuroses and psychoses, and the treatment of nervous diseases, to a study of and inquiry into such matters as "the history of civilization, . . . the science of the religions, and to mythology, as well as to the theory of neuroses." Reik says that this work "constitutes a first attempt to ascertain the position of dogma in the evolution of religion, to demonstrate its nature, and to describe the unconscious instinctual impulses and psychic mechanisms which govern the formation of dogmas." [19] The result is what may be called a "devastating exposure" of religion. Moreover, the author confidently envisions the "end of religions":

The history of all religions shows that they begin with vague and wavering beliefs, and then move onwards toward their dissolution, when they have sacrificed to reason and reality too much of their mystical content. Finally religious emotion is succeeded by historical interest, by religious research. The evolution of humanity is extraordinarily slow, and yet one may venture to prophesy this end for all religions. In this gradual process, this conflict between the beliefs emerging from the depths of the unconscious, and the conscious findings of religious research, dogma plays an important part, and its culmination marks the destined hour of the change.[20]

We have here an example, therefore, of what professes to be a new enterprise, involving science, religion, and personality. It is a scientific inquiry. It studies religion—more specifically dogma, in the work referred to. It does this through investigation into the depths of personality, into the unconscious life with its dynamisms and influences.

[17] *Op. cit.*, p. 218.
[18] *Ibid.*, p. 222. Italics added.
[19] *Dogma and Compulsion*, tr. Bernard Miall (New York: International Universities Press. 1951), pp. 7, 11. Used by permission.
[20] *Ibid.*, pp. 152-53.

There is no need, for present purposes, to present Reik's argument in full, to enter into any extended attempts at criticizing and evaluating it, or to ascertain to what extent and in what precise sense he is dealing adequately with science and scientific method or religion. That an extensive critical task lies ahead goes without saying. We can be fairly sure that some important revisions of interpretation are due. We can say, concerning our two questions, that the relation of religion to life below the level of the consciousness is something of a modern discovery, and that we live in an age when scientific inquiry is coming to grips with the problem of religion as never before. It is in such an era that facile and hasty conclusions abound. Some of these are extremely general and very sweeping. Also, under the aegis of science it seems easy to resort to judgments of value concerning "constructive" and "right" and "destructive" and "wrong" without being too careful to consider whether science really supports these or not. Religion, therefore, has been characterized as destructive or wrong more often than as constructive or right. We could quote official representatives of science, but one is more likely to hear these adverse judgments among the laity who seem to feel that science has made this clear.

Calling anything destructive and wrong suggests norms and standards. Ascertaining precisely the nature, source, and sanction of norms has been one of the most difficult of all theoretical problems for mankind. The difficulty of the problem is both illustrated and complicated by the proliferation of claims in behalf of a great variety of norms. This becomes particularly ironical when controversy between representatives of conflicting norms—both claiming concern for human well-being—erupts into violence that destroys. The causes operating in the particular instances may vary widely—all the way from the various forms of sincerity to deliberately tyrannical oppression. In some of these, the language of norms, standards, and ideals can be used to cloak the nakedness of tyranny. In others there will be the assertions of self-defense, the protections of interests, or the cumulative destruction by originally innocent bonfires.

What are the norms that science appeals to and professes to espouse? It should be obvious that there is no pat or official answer to this question. It is wide open to the virtuosity, idealism, and good will of committed scientists and friends of science. It gives critics of science a chance to say that science has no norms of its own, or that if it pretends to have any they are really borrowed from something that science probably disavows "officially." A more "neutral" point of view would say that science has no way of discovering or validating norms, values, ideals. This neutralism may in some instances be pro-science, in others con-science. Discussion of the subject of relationships between values and science has been extensive and difficult to classify and catalogue. Bertrand Russell says quite simply, "The sphere of values lies outside science, except in so far as science consists in the pursuit of knowledge." [21] Of course this is not all he says, but this sentence seems unequivocal. Everett W. Hall wrote an able and learned book, *Modern Science and Human Values,* in which he affirms the disparateness of science and values.[22] Later his position was subjected to vigorous attack by Robert Hartman in *The Philosophy of Science.*[23]

For present purposes an attempt will be made to open up some general questions with regard to the interpretation of science and to the problem of the relation of science to value. To aid in this we make use of an interesting and spirited paragraph by Harold E. McCarthy, which appeared in *The Humanist:*

> Science, in the last analysis, is something more than method and something more than neutral knowledge. It is a way of life, demanding respect for truth, honesty, and rational evaluation, demanding the profound recognition of human capability, fallibility, and individuality. That science *is* a way of life is testified to by the vigor with which free science has always been attacked by totalitarian regimes, be they communistic, fascistic, or ecclesiastical.[24]

This brief paragraph contains many suggestions and implications —especially numerous for so brief a paragraph. An examination of these can be helpful.

First, and somewhat generally, this paragraph seems to be a disavowal of the too severely constructed definitions of science that would detach it from values, confine it to the laboratory, neutralize it, or imply that it is not relevant to life. This is good, but it is dangerous, not that the danger is avoidable in this world. The danger is that when science is not neutralized, it will be inevitable that the powers and people that seek to "line it up on their side" will include many who do not have a beneficent way of life in their intentions or their

[21] *The Scientific Outlook* (New York: W. W. Norton and Company 1931), p. 266.

[22] Princeton, N. J.: D. Van Nostrand Company, 1956.

[23] 25, No. 2 (April, 1958), 97-108.

[24] "Science and Its Critics," XII, No. 2 (1952). Italics in the text.

plans. What is it that a totalitarian regime uses to fabricate plans and instruments for extending its power if it is not science? Is it a debauched science? It certainly would not be a science defined as the quoted paragraph suggests. Is totalitarianism a "way of life"? Or is "way of life" only to be defined as good? Will the totalitarian also be able to use the term "good"? Or is his use of good an example of the debauching of language as well as of science? How will the world in the long future convince the totalitarian that he is in error? Can we hope that his operating with a corrupted notion of what science is—as properly defined—will eventually prove self-destructive?

Second, our author says that this "way of life"—the scientific—"demands" certain things. Just who or what, we may ask, is doing this demanding? What is the subject of the dynamic verb "demand"? It can only be one or the other—or both—of two things, (1) the rules of science—as defined, or (2) the human beings who espouse and practice science. The first would be a somewhat figurative use of the word "demand." What is demanded? The list is impressive: respect for truth, honesty, rational evaluation, recognition of certain human states. Let us take these up in order. Science as a way of life demands respect for truth. What truth and how much? Of course it means, to begin with, truth in the particular efforts in which science is involved. This is a must in regard to a particular problem in science. A scientist working on a rocket is compelled to take account of true conditions if the thing is to work. But to what extent is this a guarantee that the scientist, respecting truth in this particular problem, will respect truth in general and truth in all other particular problems? It hardly seems possible that the author of the quoted paragraph was implying any such transfer of training. The crucial problem is this: Is it possible to be respectful of truth in a special area—to be scientific, that is—and use the results of these scientific efforts to violate truth in some other area? Apparently it is.

Science as a way of life also demands honesty, so our author says. Was it a nonscientist who perpetrated the Piltdown hoax? To be sure, if dishonesty is practiced in hypothesis formation and experimentation, there will not be scientific procedure, and results will not be conformable to nature. This is almost a tautology, something like saying that science demands honesty because if it isn't honest, then it isn't science. The problem would be, Can a person who is dishonest about *X* be a scientist in regard to *Y?* The honesty that science demands is honesty in scientific activity. It is particular. If it is being said that the honesty practiced by science and in scientific activity will develop a general condition of honesty, it would be good to have the psychology of this process explained. It certainly has an exciting idealistic sound. So far, however, it seems quite possible for people who are dishonest in some ways to make use of something which, if not science, is a result or product of science. In so far as this can happen, it multiplies the risks and hazards that can develop in a world where science has opened so many new doors to knowledge and power, and where it is theoretically possible for the totalitarians to subject the scientists to invidious control.

Furthermore, McCarthy says that science demands "rational evaluation." In a world where rational evaluation is possible, there are also extensive possibilities for "rationalization." Of course there is a sense in which we can say that it was science that exposed this *modus operandi* of human deception. But to make a point with a particular example of rational evaluation is possible only when the operations of reason alone are functioning. It is difficult for the voice of rational evaluation to make itself heard by stubborn and malignant irrationality. Aside from that, there are serious and sincere points of view that raise the question of whether this very combination of the terms "rational" and "evaluation" is not something of an incongruity. There probably is some incongruity, but the two sides are surely not mutually exclusive in all instances. Perhaps it might have seemed a bit more scientific to say empirical evaluation, since some representatives of science are a bit touchy concerning rationalism.

Science, he says further, demands a "profound recognition of human capability, fallibility, and individuality." The first two tend to be facts and the third a value. The word "profound" may be slightly question-begging. Does it suggest here a good sort of profundity? Demagogues sometimes have a profound recognition of human fallibilities and capabilities—or at least susceptibilities. In recent generations a certain mode of investigation into human nature has developed a profound recognition of human fallibilities that is almost frightening—the whole jungle land of the Id. In fact, there are those who go so far as to say that not only are the works and ideas of representatives of religion, art, and politics determined by deep and often hidden motivations, but of representatives of science also, so that it is unrealistic to talk of pure objectivity.

In the third place, we take account of a word that is crucial in the quoted paragraph. It is the word "free." We are told that totalitarian regimes vigorously attack free science. Is the science so much attacked as the freedom? Suppose the word "free" were to be omitted from the paragraph—the sentence would lose much of its punch and point. Suppose that for the word "science" we were to substitute the word "religion." We could say that free religion was being attacked by totalitarianism, or similar tyranny, long before the enterprise of science got going. Are we to say that totalitarians—for example, those of today—are averse to science? Who would answer yes to that? If anyone should answer yes, he would do so in the name of some very favorable definition of science. Has totalitarianism ever made use of religion or religions? They have created them! But what kinds? The kind that makes use of the same psychological and emotional raw material used by good religion. Here we encounter a tremendously interesting problem. We may state it in terms of a question, What is the difference between a totalitarian use of science and a totalitarian use of religion? This is a large question and will need to be given attention.

The first point in the attempt to deal with this question is that it is easier to formulate a definition of science that would be agreed upon generally than of religion. This is partly due to the fact that it is possible to isolate specific aspects of the scientific enterprise so that they can be named and investigated fairly directly. Also, there is presumably only one kind of science, one kind of scientific method, one ultimate context—nature—for the operations that science investigates, one intrinsic aim—knowledge, and certain specific instrumental aims—prediction, control. It is well known that many differences of opinion and many controversies can and do develop within this framework, which, incidentally, is not so simple as it may seem in the brief form stated here. There are controversies as to what are the best examples of science, whether science can verify values, whether there are data not accessible to science, and so on, but there is a high degree of uniformity in the summary discussions of what science is—as one may find in the ordinary textbooks dealing with science. Also there are some controversies concerning certain fundamentals—for example the disputes regarding Lysenko's claims in the field of biology and of science generally; the theories advanced in some of the claims made at the 1936 celebrations of the founding of the University of Heidelberg; and some of the recent discussions concerning causation, teleology, and cosmology generally. There has been a tendency, however, to think fairly univocally of science and to distinguish it from the nonscientific, the antiscientific, and the unscientific.

The second point: there has long been a tendency to distinguish between religions, as though there might be different religions and even different kinds of religions. There has also been a frequent effort to distinguish between true and false religion. It is not difficult to suppose that this is the way it ought to be, if there is such a thing as religion at all. Those who envision the eventual disappearance of religion may feel they can point to the superior example of science in its search for truth, with its well-defined method of discovery, formulation, and verification. As far as the present work is concerned it is agreed to begin with that there are many religions, but this is based on a very broad preliminary first step toward defining religion. At this stage of the discussion, therefore, the difference between totalitarian use of science and of religion is that there is only one science but—potentially—many religions. Totalitarian uses, which might be called science, are either (1) the results of science, or (2) those neutral aspects of science which can be turned to good or evil, depending entirely on the agent. Thus we can say, apparently contrary to the quoted paragraph, that there is a sense in which science is neutral knowledge. Our author however says that it is something more. Therefore, the only point at issue is whether evil people can be scientists. There is no hint in our quoted paragraph of evil in the uses to which science may be put. There is a reference to evil (totalitarianism) and to its resistance to science. In other words, as suggested earlier, our author defines science in terms of its good qualities and its good uses.

A third point, a continuation of matters included in the second, is that while we may speak of bad religions in a sense in which we cannot speak of bad sciences, may we not eventually claim that bad religions are not really religion? It is surely just as allowable and important and valid to define religion in terms of its exemplified best, in terms of truth, in terms of good, as to define science or anything else that way. The fact that it may be difficult to ascertain precisely what this best, this truth, and this good may be does not cancel the point. It is easy today to saddle religion rather indiscriminately with all manner of evils perpetrated in its name. But there is scant tendency to do the same for science.

Thus, our author, in his references to "something more," has opened wide doors to the extension of definition of science, and to the important problem of relationships. This takes something away from the emphasis on precision that has been one of the hallmarks of science. The more narrow the definition—whether of science or of anything else—the easier it is to formulate it, and the more definite it can be. With the indicating of relationships, one runs the risk of introducing other things which are probably not strictly science but rather are qualities of the scientist or of his aims and purposes—qualities having a moral or normative aspect. The statement just barely, but certainly, touches on the tremendous problem of the context, or contexts, in which science will be permitted to operate—particularly the context of freedom. What is there in science, narrowly interpreted, to keep it from operating according to the dictates of some political or social power? If there is anything to prevent this, it will not so much be something in science as something in the scientist. This is the "something more" that our author says belongs to the definition and the understanding of science. A widespread tendency in modern times has been to blame people for what they do to science when it is misunderstood, or misused, or neglected. On the other hand, there is an equally widespread tendency to blame religion for what it does to people. There is irony in this. It gives us the appearance of being quicker to "take sides" than to try to understand.

CHAPTER VII

Approach and Method

A CHARACTERISTIC MODERN PHRASE IS "THE SCIENTIFIC APPROACH." Its use often implies that its meaning is generally understood and that there are no limits to this approach. In other words, it is widely felt, rather than precisely assumed, that the abilities of science are or will be adequate for the discovery and formulation of the "truth about things," and that all areas of nature will eventually yield to this approach. This assumes (a) the "approach-ability" on the part of the scientist, and (b) the approachability of the data, of the objects of scientific inquiry. It has become easy to assume that the scientific approach will reveal the "secrets of the universe."

There are certain definable procedures and identifiable aspects of the scientific approach. It is necessary to be careful of the lengths to which we attempt to push the terms "definable" and "identifiable." What I shall do here is elementary. The main problem will not be of adequacy but of direction, which is fundamental to the understanding and practice of anything.

My task here, then, is to present these limited comments on certain procedures and aspects of the scientific approach. This will be basic to questions that will arise concerning the aims of the whole work. The divisions of this discussion are data, method, aims, and agent. These may also be stated in the form of questions. What are the data for science or for a particular science and what accessibility may be expected of these data? That is, are they accessible to the scientific approach? To what extent is there an understandable and fruitful method for this approach? Is it possible to ascertain the basic impulse —origin in human nature and experience—for this approach and to state understandable reasons for it? What is the ability of the agent to understand and to practice this approach? Since an agent—scientist—is indispensable for the defining and practicing of this approach, what specific questions may arise as to his place in and effect upon this enterprise? To a consideration of these questions we now turn.

The Data

In order to study anything, science must be able to get at it so as to measure it; to observe, test, and classify it; to analyze it; to ascertain its *modus operandi.* To investigate something, science must be able to maneuver this something into an observable, experimental, measurable position—under a microscope, into a cage or chemical solution; or, pending that, compile a statistical record of its maneuvers and venture a hypothesis of checkable sorts concerning its existence and operations. It is even felt to be unsatisfactory if one must infer a causal agent when he can observe only effects.

It hardly makes sense to speak of science without data—without something to concentrate upon, talk about, and work with; something to be the object of investigation. It hardly makes sense to speak of something which is "simply science" but does not work on or with anything. There may be and no doubt are certain common denominators of method and technique, but such a free-floating mode must eventually attach itself to some kind of data. If it doesn't, there is no achievement, unless it would be some improvement of spirit or attitude in minds able to conceptualize it. A characteristic question at science meetings is, "What is your field?" If one said poetry, or friendship, or mythology he would seem odd or out of place. On the other hand, such answers as foraminifera or tomato blight would be understandable. Even the answer, "Just a scientist, not of anything in particular" might seem unintelligible, unless it was supposed to mean that the speaker professed to make use of the scientific approach in all areas of life. It would be hard to imagine a bolder claim, yet it has a pleasantly idealistic sound!

Some areas of data are pretty thoroughly obvious—rocks, for example. The obviousness of rock strata and earth formations might induce in a geologist an unscientific disdain for a discipline whose data are much less obvious and presumably more doubtful—psychology, for example. Also, attitudes have sometimes changed as to whether certain data are proper material for scientific inquiry. It used to be thought that dreams were occurrences with no discernible rationale or significance. To be sure, there have long been notions of dreams as "messages" or as predictions. In the present age, steering a course between these extremes, scientific investigators have written treatises on dreams and their psychological significance.

There are new data and previously known data, which often need redefinition or redescription—"unconscious," for example, and "atom." It is understandable, therefore, that many scientists tend to suppose that nothing is ultimately beyond the purview of science. It may be permissible, however, to speak of this for the time being as a vision or article of faith rather than something demonstrable.

The data of a specific science will be homogeneous in the sense of having common characteristics and of conforming to the same law or laws. Presumably all data in the entire universe behave according to specific principles of operation. This rules out magic, caprice, arbitrary action, demons, and jinni. It must be possible to perform experiments. This means more than simple observation. There has been an increasing refinement of distinction between "experience" and "experiment" since the eighteenth century when these terms were used with a too casual interchange.

To what extent, we may ask, is religion an area accessible to science? That is, when science, in the form of a science or collection of sciences, decides to approach religion, what and whence are the data? This type of question has been answered with conspicuous success and unanimity in many areas—chemistry, geology, and physics, for example. But there is nothing classifiable as the "science of religion" which is comparable. It is often taken for granted that it is entirely appropriate or even essential to use the scientific approach in the study of religion. This would assume the existence and availability of data. The eminent Ernest Jones said:

> About the end of the last century a number of noteworthy studies were published on the psychology of religion. They were for the most part contributed by American authors. . . . A great number of valuable observations were recorded, but of the general conclusions tentatively put forward the only one of outstanding importance was the claim, ably argued in particular by Coe and Leuba, that religious phenomena come within the orbit of scientific investigation.[1]

A theologian put it this way,

> Our problems are personal and social; they therefore need to be approached on this level. The only reliable method we have, however, is science;

[1] *Psychoanalysis Today,* ed. Sandor Lorand (New York: International Universities Press, 1944), p. 315.

all other knowledge is hit or miss. Religious knowledge is usually arbitrary and subjective; philosophic knowledge is generally speculative, or evasive of the more exact issues of fact.[2]

What "religious phenomena" are has not been decided with the precision and unanimity needed in a scientific enterprise. If Jones believes he has succeeded with this, we certainly need not begrudge him his conviction. It remains only to persuade others that he has identified the data of religion and defined them. It is a question of whether he has made it clear how these phenomena "come within the orbit of scientific investigation." He certainly could not be held responsible for any difficulty that would result from the intractability of these phenomena. Data do not "come" into the scientific orbit. They are brought in. That there is no science of religion means first of all that there are as yet no data which we can identify with precision and know how to subject to scientific investigation. The scientific method may be the "only reliable method we have," as the second quotation has it, but the application of the method is at the mercy of the data, their approachability and responsiveness.

What might conceivably be the data of religion? The question is easy enough to answer in general—conversion, prayer, ritual, belief, certain types of behavior, certain types of statements and institutions. If, however, prayer is to be a datum, there are limits to scientific approach. If science can study man praying, can it study prayer being answered? Science has several alternatives to choose from. It may agree that some data are beyond the reach of science—God's answering prayer; deny the validity of all notions that anything is out of the reach of scientific inquiry; or be agnostic. There may be others. It would not be agreed that these are in every instance real alternatives. If religion insists on saying that God answers prayer, science will have to deny God's activity if prayer is to become a manageable datum, or give a negative answer to the famous question from Job, "Canst thou by searching find out God?" (11:7 K.J.V.) There is a sense in which science may tell religion how not to define certain data, but it is not an absolute right applying to all data. Part of the problem, therefore, is a jurisdictional question: Who may define religion? Religion—in the form of people representing religion—has certainly made many mistakes, and science—in the form of people speaking in

[2] Nels Ferré, *Christian Faith and Higher Education* (New York: Harper & Brothers, 1954), p. 180.

the name of science—is certainly not agreed as to what religion is or how, precisely, it operates in life experiences.

In regard to religious data, there is a question as to how far science needs to or could be permitted to tamper with the data. For some science to study some data, it is necessary to kill them so to speak. A cat in a biological laboratory has to be killed in order to be studied in a certain way, but then it has ceased to be a cat. It is easy to say that killing a cat is not the only way science studies it, and that laboratories are just as much concerned with live cats. This is true enough up to a point. They are best studied, however, when subjected to controls; the more complete the control, the more amenable to scientific study. The creatures are caged, dieted, put to sleep, et cetera. The more completely controlled, the less free they are. Is a controlled creature different in some respects from a free creature? If freedom is a valid concept, if it is a reality in any sense, it would be difficult to answer this question with anything other than an affirmative. The phrase "control group" is important in science. In the case of laboratory animals the extent of the control can be great. With human beings, however, the control-group principle has limited use, though it may give users the same "scientific feel" as its use with laboratory creatures. No member of a control group is ever a complete creature. They are in a specified and limited context, and this of course is good scientific procedure. There is no such thing as a scientific study of man in a total context, although that is where he is all the time.

An area now being explored is especially significant for religion—that "inside" personality. Depth psychology is almost as much a figure of speech as a technical term. But to say it is significant for religion should not obscure the swarm of varying and even opposed judgments that gather about the problem. Psychology is seen as a threat to religion, and religion, as an enemy of science. There are charges from experimental psychologists that depth psychology is not science; charges from stricter sciences that psychology in general is not science; claims that religion will be replaced by something else, and so on. In the midst of all this it may seem amazingly naïve to express the conviction that the deeper psychological researches give promise of being a genuine resource for religion—as do personality studies.

The Method of Science

There must be a method for the approach to and investigation of data. Hardly any modern phrase has enjoyed such prestige as "scientific method." Textbooks abound in salutes to and at least minimal expositions of this method. It is often explained as a series of steps, with special emphasis on such terms as empirical, experimental, observation, and verification. There are other factors such as attitude of mind, emotional neutrality, respect for evidence, readiness to admit error, formulation of hypotheses, and measurement.

In a sense the scientific method is a modern development, though we may indicate piecemeal examples of the use of the method in former times. A spectacular example in ancient times was the calculation by Eratosthenes in the third century B.C. of the size and shape of the earth, based on a study of shadows at two places in Egypt. This is conveniently described, with illustrations, in Lancelot Hogben's *Mathematics for the Million.*[3]

Today the practice of the scientific method is piecemeal also. There is no such thing as a person who practices this method in all the activities of his life. This brings no discredit on the idea of scientific method. As a matter of fact, it enhances it.

If anyone employs the scientific method to any extent, he does so within at least two important contexts: the context of the particular data with which he is using the method, and the context of his own life with its outlook, emotional condition, beliefs, and way of life. From the point of view of the scientific method it is reprehensible for anyone to tamper with the data to try to control the outcome. This is a profounder, subtler, and more complex problem than we may have supposed. If one's wishes can be a distorting factor, could it be true that one's whole philosophy of life could be a distorting factor in some subtle and possibly undetected manner?

Also, there is the distinction to be made between scientific method as interpreted and used by a true scientist and by a technologist who simply learns some of the many rules in some of the many provinces of science. The latter person may never contribute any new knowledge. He may never adopt those strict attitudes appropriate to the use of the scientific method. So many things have been learned, so many rules of procedure set up, so much material assembled that it is possible for a person to work within the household of science and yet never be a scientist in any special sense—in terms of originality, understanding, and creativity.

There is also a difference between scientific method in the purely intellectual realm, the realm of theory, and scientific method in actual

[3] London: George Allen & Unwin (1936), pp. 234-35, 344; issued in America as *Man and Mathematics* (New York: W. W. Norton & Company).

practice, in dealing with materials. Of course these are related, but it is possible to be a scientist in the former sense, leaving it to others to carry out the details and to apply theory to materials. We hear or read about the geniuses who formulate spectacular new theories. Attempts to explain them have never been successful because it is not known just how they accomplished these feats. The operations of the mind of a genius elude understanding. In the history of science there have been romantic "accidents" providing new knowledge. It may seem, indeed, that the development of science and the full use of scientific method involve some things not strictly scientific, but it is part of the importance and genius of the method that even what is revealed by accidents is seen, appreciated, made use of, incorporated.

We are all acquainted with comments that cast some doubt on the scientific method. Some will say you cannot use the method in writing poetry, in making love, or in verifying values. But this is not to say that science and the method of science are irrelevant.

Perhaps it would be simpler to refer readers to some excellent treatments of the subject. I mention a few items here because of their relevance to the latter part of the chapter. One important aspect of the method is the formulating and testing of hypotheses, which are important so that we may "get going" in the practice of science. There is always something tentative about them. Strictly speaking the hypothesis is forever tentative. If it is tested and found to be sufficiently dependable to be taken as true, it becomes something other than hypothesis. This involves one of the subtle aspects of scientific procedure—ascertaining when a hypothesis is ready to become law. The real puzzle is this: Do we know how to formulate a good hypothesis? Some of the most famous of them have seemed to spring Minerva-like into maturity from the fertile brain of an individual person. To put it in other terms, it seems that the vision of an individual sometimes clarifies to such an extent that, all of a sudden, he sees clearly in an area where neither he nor anyone else had ever done so before. But the "rule book" on how and when to formulate good hypotheses remains to be written. This is not to assume that it will be. A note by Bertrand Russell may be relevant: "As a rule, the framing of hypotheses is the most difficult part of scientific work, and the part where great ability is indispensable. So far, no method has been found which would make it possible to invent hypotheses by rule." [4]

A second feature of the method is the discovering, selecting, sort-

[4] *A History of Western Philosophy* (New York: Simon and Schuster, 1945), pp. 544-45.

ing, and classifying of facts. The ideal is to assemble a great many facts and to detect the pattern or principle of operation which is common to all of them, which puts us on the way to the formulation of a law or principle. Again, this does not mean that just anyone can assemble a great many facts and be sure of coming up with the proper theory or principle.

A third concern of scientific method involves proof. So much has this taken hold of the mind of modern man that he stands ready to apply the question, What is the proof? to almost anything that anyone says. People who feel their cherished beliefs threatened by science have sometimes taken refuge in the notion that, after all, some of their beliefs are "out of the reach" of science with its penchant for "proving." Sometimes insistence upon the necessity of proof may seem to take a dogmatic turn:

> It is wrong always, everywhere, and for anyone, to believe anything upon insufficient evidence. If a man, holding a belief which he was taught in childhood or persuaded of afterwards, keeps down and pushes away any doubts which arise about it in his mind, purposely avoids the reading of books and the company of men that call in question or discuss it, and regards as impious those questions which cannot easily be asked without disturbing it—the life of that man is one long sin against mankind.[5]

Another feature involves attitude. To say, "I hope the experiment turns out my way" is unscientific, how ever natural it might be as a human tendency. Attitudes considered proper would include respect for evidence, a desire to get the facts, a willingness to admit error, desire for truth, and holding wishes in check. We note the psychological terminology in some of these. This suggests that a basic problem in the understanding and use of the scientific method is a psychological problem. That is, the scientific method has to be practiced by *whole* human beings. This wholeness includes some things which are threats to the understanding and use of the scientific method—desires, wishes, biases, emotions. When a human being becomes a scientist and uses scientific method, he must be ready to restrain and discipline some of the potential of his own nature.

Another important ingredient in scientific method is theory. Originally this word meant "to see"—but a special kind of seeing. Obviously theory is related to some things said in preceding paragraphs, but

[5] W. K. Clifford, *The Ethics of Belief* (London: C. A. Watts & Company, 1947), p. 77.

here we add the figurative expression that theory means to see with the mind, and with understanding, to see patterns, to see things in relationship.

Another feature in scientific procedure is, or should be, self-criticism. The importance of self-criticism has been urged in circles other than scientific, but this simply suggests that self-criticism is an example of a point of co-operation between science and the non-scientific. Self-criticism is important in religion as well as in science. It is sometimes said of the Bible that it exhibits a self-correcting quality. A simple example is the criticism found in Hos. 1, leveled against something given approval in II Kings 10—namely the bloody policy of King Jehu. This, of course, does not represent an individual self, but the self of a community and a tradition.

Every enterprise has its own particular assumptions. Back of scientific procedures are such assumptions as the orderliness of nature, of reality as a process, of the universality of causal sequences. There are other assumptions, held by many, that the scientific method would not accept, or would find unnecessary, or disturbing—for example the assumption that there is providential purpose back of or involved in the universe. An individual scientist may say he assumes this. He may even say it is very important to him, but it would be easy to find other scientists denying it. Sigmund Freud and George Washington Carver present a striking contrast in this regard. It might even be said that Carver's assumptions would have been more appropriate to Freud's area of inquiry—the human person—and Freud's more deterministic presuppositions to Carver's area of inquiry—the peanut. Carver's work with his assumptions makes the peanut seem elevated to a status comprehended in a divine plan. Freud's work often makes the human person seem reduced to the earthiness and ephemerality of the peanut. It is intriguing, if futile, to wonder what might have been the outcome had each operated with the initial outlook of the other. In the terminology of Chapter II, What if . . . ?

Aims, Goals, Tasks

The briefest statement of the aim of science is "to know." The Latin word *scio* means simply "I know," except that the linguistic transition from the first person, singular *scio* to "science" in the modern sense and usage is involved and complex. But it is still the case that a dominant aim of science is to know. And, it is thought, it is good to know.

A goal of science is to be of help. A child can specify some of the helpful achievements of science and particular sciences. The province of operation for the achievement of such a goal is nature—mastering nature and turning her resources to human benefits. By now it may seem trite or obvious to call attention to the distinction between a purely theoretical goal—satisfaction of curiosity—and a practical one—providing benefits.

The task of science is mastering the methodology and the accumulated knowledge already known and developed—not without seeking to improve and add to—then applying it. If there are certain ancillary tasks, they also become part of the main task—for instance, to communicate aims and results and to see that these do not die out.

Before we become too idealistic we should take account of some stark reminders that the aims and goals of science are not necessarily fixed attributes of some natural substance. Such aims and goals as truth seeking and knowledge accumulation are beneficent only if man wishes this to be the case. J. Robert Oppenheimer says that "science is reason." [6] We could say too that religion is love. Yet, neither science defined as reason nor religion defined as love means guaranteed performance. It is still possible for man to decide against rational or loving behavior, even while offering a rationalizing argument that his behavior *is* rational or *is* loving. It is quite possible to practice irrationality in the name of reason, tyranny in the name of justice, and cruelty in the name of love.

In other words it is naïve, to say the least, to heap fulsome praise upon science because of its lofty aims and beneficent goals if we take no account of fearsome potentialities that threaten not only its good work, but also its very existence.

Thus the task of science is slowly coming to be something more than a free and untrammeled search for truth in a free and charitable environment. The tasks of science will therefore include some obligations that are not strictly part of the definition of science as science. We are coming to see that in this world science, and especially pure science cannot always be guaranteed a pure context for its operations. It should be obvious we have here two uses of pure. As it modifies science it means disinterested, theoretical, or intellectual procedure. Its aims are not primarily practical, if at all. The second use of pure has a strongly ethical flavor. It suggests that the context in which science tries to function may sometimes impose demands upon science that create psychological, ethical, or religious problems which cannot

[6] *Scientific Foundations for World Order* (Denver: The University of Denver Press, 1949).

be resolved with the ethical neutrality that presumably prevails in pure science.

Likewise it is naïve to heap fulsome acclaim upon religion for its hopes and dreams and ideals if we fail to become aware of the forces of corruptibility. Natural loyalties have been diverted to idols. Invidious compulsions have threatened competing loyalties without any attempt to understand, appreciate, or seek common grounds of psychological principles. It is interesting to note that there has been much less tendency to differentiate between pure and applied religion than between modes of science designated by these same adjectives. The most famous—in terms of frequency of quotation—statement concerning pure religion is really a reference to applied religion. "Pure religion and undefiled before God and the Father is this, To visit the fatherless and widows in their affliction, and to keep himself unspotted from the world." (Jas. 1:27 K.J.V.) This contrasts somewhat with the connotation of pure as applied to science, and in another way with concepts of religion that emphasize one's relation to God. For example, the statement from James emphasizes the second division of the Ten Commandments rather than the first—though it means to imply the first.

If we consider a subject such as health, we may say that the aim of science is to know about health, the goal to urge health as a general condition, and the task actually to promote it. This opens doors to all kinds of concerns. In other words it now seems not only fitting, but also essential, to probe more deeply than ever into questions about relations of science to world order, to ethics, to value, to responsibility. The picture of a pure science at work in an unthreatened, respected, and amply supported laboratory begins to take on a dreamlike quality. One is reminded of a graphic comment by a distinguished scholar in his discussion of a dramatic moment in Plato's *Symposium*. Socrates had transported his hearers with a speech on love when suddenly the drunken Alcibiades noisily rapped on the door. Commenting on this, our author said, "The world has a way of breaking in upon the philosophies by which we leave it." [7] This turns out to be much more than a homiletical generalization. Since these words were written a series of events has transpired to place in curious and ominous juxtaposition three concepts which, taken singly, all seem to have a good sound. They are health, science, and defense. These are related now in new and unsuspected ways.

[7] F. J. E. Woodbridge, *The Son of Apollo* (Boston: Houghton Mifflin Company, 1929), p. 198.

A goal and task of science may be the promoting of health, and science has always been at the service of defense. But now it transpires that if science is to be called upon to be at the service of defense, in ways that are by now general knowledge, then the health of the majority of mankind may be placed in jeopardy of a type hardly calculable in former ages. In other words, a sufficient amount of nuclear fission and fusion placed at the disposal of political defense can conceivably release enough damaging radiation to endanger the physical well-being of not only the present generation, but of future ones also. This both reveals and compels relationships of science as science to other questions not heretofore thought of as science—for example, responsibility, ethical obligation, religious significance.

Another aspect of the aims, goals, and tasks of science faces us. To what extent or in what sense is there a difference between objective study and participation? Again we may consider health to illustrate. How differently do we define or interpret science when we say that science should acquire knowledge about health, and when we ask whether science has obligations concerning promotion and participation? It is not the same when we say that science is applicable to human welfare as when we say that the individual scientist has obligations of a highly personal and individual sort and that he has responsibilities concerning his own health.

Is there any sense in which we could and should say that a scientist is obligated not to use the knowledge he provides for destructive purposes? The question is of course ambiguous. If not ambiguous verbally, we make it so by our conflicts, tensions, and divided loyalties. Tartaglia's experience illustrates this.[8] But even his experience is simple compared with the more subtle involvements in conflict and tension revealed by modern investigations in the area of personality.

The relevance of the foregoing for our understanding of and obligations to persons should be, to some extent at least, obvious.

The Scientist

There is a serpent in the garden of science; a subtle tempter who lures the scientific Adams and Eves into entertaining the notion that they will eventually be able to sprinkle salt on the tail of the owl of omniscience. This induces the notion that not only are there no other paths to truth and certainty, but that science is a complete and sufficient path or method. The following quotation is from one profes-

[8] Cf. pp. 96 ff., *supra*.

sionally classified as scientist. It is a mild example of this temptation's taking hold. It appeared at the end of a laudatory review which was being sent out to advertise the book under review: "I am by profession a research physiologist, so *that* (my favorable review) is not gush." (Italics added.) Any student of elementary logic could put this into syllogistic form: Research physiologists are not guilty of gush; I am a research physiologist; ergo, I am not guilty of gush. Formally, the logic is impeccable. Materially the major premise is valid only ideally. The meaning of "gush" need not concern us.

It is hoped that no one will interpret the foregoing as an attempt to downgrade science. For example, in the immediately preceding quotation—and all like it—science is not speaking; a human being is—the question is whether the speaker is accurately or adequately representing science. Such remarks present a dreamlike vision of what science and its methods may be or may become. They are not science, however much they may be inspired by it.

So long as science is in the hands of human beings, it is in the hands of creatures subject now and then to temptation. Of course it might be said that the enterprise of science is not subject to corruption if the operators are true scientists. Agreed, but the "if" is troublesome. While true scientists are proceeding apace, there will be others who are not "true," who succumb to some kind of temptation, and who destructively misapply science or naïvely dream of omniscience. There may be representatives of science who are subjected to political and social pressures and compelled by dictatorships to put their scientific capabilities at the service of invidious tyrannies. Some of the speeches at the 550th anniversary celebration at the University of Heidelberg in 1936 vividly illustrate this.

This points up a distinction difficult to make and perhaps more difficult to accept—the distinction between science and scientist, or to state it more fully, a distinction between what can be analyzed and defined in laudatory terms under the heading of science, and the human beings who are to practice and speak for the enterprise. It seems that our ultimate problem is not so much the control of nature as the control of the controller of nature.

This implies a second suggestion from the tempter. It gathers about or centers in the notion of control. This term looms large, and not usually ominously, in discussions of science. The temptation involved here is not peculiar to science and is not a temptation to control which issues in overt maneuvers, in attempts to gain undue power. What I refer to is a temptation that entices the mind and that induces euphoric notions about what we could do if only . . . "Science has placed in our hands opportunities and techniques for making this world a veritable paradise if only . . ."

There are numerous examples of this kind of dreaming, some of which are classic. Some are from so-called prescientific ages, and some are recent. Plato's *Republic* leads the list. Then there are others such as Francis Bacon's *The New Atlantis* and Thomas More's *Utopia.* Two recent examples are B. F. Skinner's *Walden Two* and John B. Watson's *Behaviorism.* Perhaps all these authors, if pressed, would confess to a monumental "if" as a stumbling block. Plato specifically said at the end of Book IX that the ideal republic cannot be realized on any national scale, but that the general pattern could be adopted and lived in the life of the individual good man.

Some features of these dreams merit consideration. One of these, seldom discussed directly, is what might be called the ubiquitous "we." This is particularly noticeable in Plato's *Republic* and Skinner's *Walden Two.* We could do this or that—we would know what should be done—we would initiate and control et cetera. In Plato's work the "we" are presumably philosophers functioning as monarchs. In Skinner's work the philosopher is a whipping boy, as he is for so many scientists today. So, in this work, the "we" are scientists of man and society, human engineers. It is assumed to be a thoroughly dependable board of control, and all would be for the good.

Apparently we are to assume that these boards of control would always act wisely and constructively. This assumes they would be trained for such responsibilities, even to the development of beneficent attitudes and purposes. By whom? And how would they all become so flawless?

It is possible of course to draw the outlines of a controlled future that would not be so beneficent. Consider Aldous Huxley's *Brave New World* and George Orwell's *1984.* Orwell's book may not be intended to lack seriousness, but there may be a note of melancholy levity in Huxley's. It would take much faith to say unreservedly and without qualification that the writings mentioned in preceding paragraphs are more credible than these two. This is the kind of faith that has usually been associated with religion. Now it is being associated with science.

Most of the visions seem easily to assume that this control will always be for the good—Huxley's and Orwell's are exceptions to the usual pattern—a thoroughly gratuitous assumption. Consider the following:

> Science occupies a rather unique position in society. It has so proved itself, by the repeated verification of its conclusions, by the integration of seemingly unrelated observations, and by the practical control of nature, that no informed person presumes to challenge its pronouncements within the limitations which the scientist properly imposes upon his own conclusions. Society recognizes this fact without exactly understanding how science has come to occupy such a pre-eminent position.[9]

These spirited words from an eminent physiologist are quite exciting. Our dominant problem today, however, is not "the practical control of nature." Moreover, nature is highly ambiguous. It cannot mean, in the use here, the movements of the stellar bodies which we hardly control, although they are conspicuous manifestations of nature. It could refer to the type of work Luther Burbank did, but the nature with which Burbank worked was pretty completely tractable, and his plants gave him no back talk and did not get out of hand. Is hit-and-run driving nature? It needs practical controlling. Surely we could not exclude man from nature, and if not, then practical control would be in order here. Our author pays special tribute to freedom in the same article, to its value and importance. Therefore, any practical control of man would presumably have to be conducted without destroying his freedom.

The only point being pushed here concerns romantic and idealistic connotations of control. Other kinds of controls are plentiful enough—demagogues, dictators, tyrants, exploiters—these have come to haunt us in our century more than many people, fifty years ago, would have dreamed possible. An example of the latter:

> Nowadays we . . . disallow the right of the State to interfere with free expression of opinion. So deeply is the doctrine of liberty seated in our minds that we find it difficult to make allowances for the coercive practices of our misguided ancestors. . . . The struggle of reason against authority has ended in what appears now to be a decisive and permanent victory for liberty. . . . Is it not conceivable that . . . some new force, emerging from the unknown, may surprise the world and cause a . . . set-back? The possibility cannot be denied, but there are some considerations which render it improbable (apart from a catastrophe sweeping away European culture).[10]

[9] Homer W. Smith, "Objectives and Objectivity in Science," *The Yale Scientific Magazine*, XXIII, No. 5 (February, 1949).

[10] J. B. Bury, *A History of Freedom of Thought* (New York: Henry Holt and Company, 1913), pp. 234-45, 247, 249. Used by permission.

Of all creatures, it would seem that scientists and representatives of science would be the least romantic and utopian, but science itself does not have the say. Presumably when a human being enters the mansion of science, he parks something at the door—his prejudices, romanticism, utopianism, and partisan tendencies. If he does all this, he is a new creature. This is such a large scale requirement that he would need to be "born again"—some new, nontraumatic birth, without resultant complexes and crippling influences which distort and impede.

Over and above being a scientist, the subject-object of our present attention is inescapably and obviously a person, with all the implications of that mighty term. He is by now in a double relation to science: as specialist in a particular science and as the area of data of one of the newer sciences. As person he is in a whole complex of relationships. According to some religious claims his status as person relates him to something outside an impersonal, naturalistic context. The naturalistic scientist does not admit there is an "outside" to the universe or the natural order. On another level and in another sense, however, he does insist on a certain type of "outsideness"—which is not usually called by this name. The scientist must stay outside of the data of scientific investigation. This is called objectivity. When considering data such as religion and person, however, we are constrained to stretch the objective method of science and even go on to raise the question of whether or not there are kinds of understanding other than the strictly scientific—for example, the appreciative. There are many objects of attention that cannot be understood, much less appreciated, from the outside as well as from the inside. Two of these are religion and person.

CHAPTER VIII

Psychology

PSYCHOLOGY IS A MOST USABLE WORD, AND IT IS WIDELY USED. Attitudes toward the subject vary greatly. Some regard it as a farrago of nonsense. Others regard it as the "new truth." Both attitudes are of course wide of the mark. A fragment of incidental conversation from an Academy of Science meeting demonstrates the first:

> "What is your field?"
> "I have just come from the psychology meetings."
> "Psychology! A lot of words and no sense."
> "What is your field?"
> "Geology. Now that deals with facts."

The first speaker was a distinguished geologist, but it would be a mistake to forget that he was inescapably a human being. Here he happened to be illustrating this in a way not particularly relevant to or expressive of his science. He was affirming—in the name of science—that psychology was not a science.

An illustration of the second point of view comes from an informal conversation concerning the subject of an article in *The Saturday Evening Post*.[1] The subject was a man who had originated and carried forward a unique project in a rural community. A member of the group considering the article suddenly asked, "What would a psychologist say about him?" Such a question has numerous potential implications such as:

"Are you suggesting that 'a psychologist' could give us the truth about Ted?"

"Are you assuming that all psychologists would agree?"

"Do you mean there would be no questions or criticisms, once the 'psychologist' has spoken?"

"Would just any psychologist be qualified to explain him?"

[1] Hartzell Spence, "Modern Shepherd of the Hills" (November 8, 1952), p. 26.

"Would 'the psychologist' be able to provide an explanation of Ted that you could depend upon from simply reading the article?"

The original questioner said he did not have any of these thoughts in mind when he asked his question.

Let us consider his question further in terms of implications. Suppose a cauldron were brought in containing what was alleged to be a witch's brew. We might ask, What would a chemist say about this? We have reached a stage of development and achievement in chemistry wherein we could repose trust in what the chemist would say, and we would believe that chemists generally would agree on their analysis. They would also agree on discrediting claims concerning witches and their brews. But in the case of a psychologist's explanation of a personality, we could not expect the neat and tidy sort of answer that a chemist would give in his field, nor could we expect as much agreement among psychologists as there would be among chemists. This is partly due to the complexity of the material with which psychologists work, and partly to the fact that psychology is a younger science—though as an art, it is much older than chemistry. We can say, however, that psychology is much nearer to being a science than our geologist was willing to allow. We do not need to consider here the question of whether psychology can expect to achieve the type of precision chemistry has achieved, or whether it will eventually prove to be more normative than descriptive.

Before the nineteenth century, such psychology as there was, in the scientific or philosophical sense, was highly selective. It was not thought inadequate to give attention chiefly, or even exclusively, to the higher processes such as reasoning and consciousness. That which was automatic—reflexes—or meaningless—dreaming—or considered to be so, was not considered. Thus, the present century presents the phenomenon of showing the rationale of dreams and of revealing the significance for psychology of automatic and physiological processes.

Modern psychological studies are selective also, in a different way:

> Some of our explorers are fascinated by one, some by another of the many phases of individual activity; and the schools can to a certain extent be distinguished simply by the activity which they prefer to investigate. More than that, each school believes that hidden in its own field is the true key to a unified understanding of human activity as a whole. For one school the illuminating fact is that man perceives the environment; for another, that he learns by experience; for another, that he feels and desires; and for

another, that he acts by use of his muscles and so does something in the world.[2]

Among psychologists there are sometimes sharp differences as to which investigations are and which are not scientific. Dunlap's criticicisms of Freud, and Freud's of Jung may be mentioned, though no attempt is here made to adjudicate these claims.

The following remark made by a psychologist in an informal conversation illustrates a form of selectivity: "I'm a physiological psychologist. When I think of work with people, I thank God for my white rats." The remark was no doubt facetious, but it is not entirely illogical. People present most of the major problems of existence. Immediately relevant is the following:

> To the outsider it may seem odd that psychologists should approach the problem of personality in such devious ways. There are people all around about, millions of them. . . . Why not approach the problem more directly? . . . Partly our trouble is the restless fluidity of raw facts. People will not stay still in stained-glass attitudes to be studied. . . . Partly also our trouble is due to the excessive timidity of psychologists. Many psychologists are academics who chose their career because it seemed to involve nothing more disturbing that the harmless pedantries of the laboratory, the peaceful revolutions of the calculating machine. To be faced with real people having real emotions was more than they bargained for. . . . Many psychologists felt safer when personal relations were restricted to the formalities of a test situation, and were not allowed to become tiresomely human. The problem is an awkward one, and does not arise to the same extent in other sciences.[3]

If this author is positively recommending that psychology as science must study the whole person, personality in its completeness and unity, he is no doubt aware of what he is saying, and of what protests this would evoke from many quarters. In fact it comes near to recommending, if not a return to, at least a revival of the kind of psychology that is older than the science of psychology, namely, the art. Those who envision making psychology a natural science have increasingly felt that they needed to get away from the prescientific psychology which is referred to in the well-known comment that psychology has a long past but a short history. Suppose that for the time being we call the psychology of the long past natural psychology and consider

[2] Robert S. Woodworth: *Contemporary Schools of Psychology,* Revised Edition. Copyright 1948 The Ronald Press Company. Page 4.

[3] Bernard Notcutt, *The Psychology of Personality* (New York: Philosophical Library, Inc., 1953), pp. 185-86. Used by permission.

it. It was uniformly concerned with the whole person, though not bothering to make a precise distinction.

"Natural" Psychology

No brief is offered here for the use of the word "natural." The use is nontechnical. It is conceivable that some other word would serve better. Here it simply refers to the fact that for thousands of years man has been making generalized statements about human nature, about man, about human relationships, about what should be done in dealing with people. At the same time man has for countless centuries exhibited everything from profound wisdom to vicious ignorance in his behavior, in efforts for and against neighbor, in attempts to develop his own personal life as well as his relatedness. In so far as man has recorded his notions and insights concerning himself and his neighbor, these records are a treasure house of material for inspiration and study. Modern man believes he has been able to find important psychological materials in the myths, insights, and judgments of ancient natural psychologists.

In this relatively vast collection there is much wisdom. These writings exhibit much maturity and astuteness of insight. There are also prophetic anticipations of future developments. Ancient works of creative literature contain much that is sometimes called psychological realism.

Some of this wisdom was comparatively conscious. How possessors came by it cannot be clearly understood. Attempts at explanation are often afterthought or hindsight. This wisdom was not usually, if ever, the result of slow, methodical investigation, of assembling a fund of knowledge and subjecting it to systematic classification and study. Rather it was often an inductive leap reached by flashes of insight, or quick mental transitions from observations of separate instances to a perception of patterns or relationships and to mature understanding. The suddenness was no doubt more apparent than real. When Socrates is called a "good psychologist" by modern readers, they usually mean that he was skillful in dealing with people. When others laughed at him, he knew not to flare up, grieve, sulk, or challenge a duel—he laughed with them. He was usually more aware of what was transpiring psychologically than other people were. He simply "knew."

Some of this wisdom was not conscious. Much behavior that was psychologically beneficial was not thought of as deliberate technique. There was often scant awareness of doing the "right thing." Much was done naturally without any knowledge of laws and principles.

For example, it is entirely likely that many infants in ancient times were loved adequately and wisely by parents, and thus they developed stability and integration that would not have been the case if these same children had been subjected to rejection, neglect, and hostility during infant years.

Another feature of natural psychology was the chance of error. Many mistakes, some tragic, were committed—often in sheer ignorance. We cannot smuggle any consolation into our deliberations by the use of the past tense. The same situation obtains today. We are not yet living in the Golden Age in which the prevailing question is, What can we do for the psychological welfare of people everywhere? The last place this question will be understood and significantly practiced will be at the level of international relationships.

Another feature of natural psychology is, and has always been, the dearth of self-correcting techniques. This is a double problem—moral and psychological. Scientific psychology had adopted the self-correcting techniques of scientific method, presumably. If an investigator deliberately falsifies procedure in science, he may be an immoral person, but he is also being, in the particular experiments, a bad scientist. He knows he is transgressing. But the natural psychologist who does not know that he may have exercised bad judgment, who does not know that the results could have been misleading, who does not suspect that what he has said or done may be wrong or bad—needs a new kind of intellectual orientation wherein he begins to operate with new presuppositions and general awareness. Therefore, we eventually have to consider both moral quality and procedural validity. The need for constructive criticism never becomes obsolete.

The older natural psychology rarely ever had a clear vision of a distinction between moral judgment and psychological insight. When psychology became science, however, some large-scale distinctions began to clamor for attention: pure and applied science, normative and descriptive science, intrinsic and instrumental values, moral and immoral uses of science's achievements.

Today the prevailing critical evaluation of natural psychology and all similar types—such as literary—is that they were not and are not scientific. This is important. Yet, by itself it is a too simplified view of the situation. This is the easy thing to say. A much more difficult problem is to ascertain how the aforementioned wisdom was possible and whether there can be any guidance for it. Lest we forget, this natural psychology is not simply a thing of the past; it is the prevailing kind practiced in the world today, and probably will be for a long time to come. While they may not intend to do so, many people talk about the unscientific psychology of the past as though we are or could be freed from it by casual decision. There is a place for commending the efforts of the prescientific psychologist, as he blazed away with his quick and subtle inductions without knowing quite what he was doing or how such vision was possible. Had he not done so, we probably would never have had scientific psychology.

Therefore, two incongruous situations prevail. One, already alluded to, is that natural psychology is the prevailing kind today. There is not much evidence that people generally are becoming or will soon become "scientific psychologists," either in their own personalities or in their relationships with other people. The other is that scientific psychology must both abandon and preserve something in the natural variety. We consider these in order.

To introduce the first I quote the following: "The modern tendency to psychologize at random . . . is dangerous, pathetic, and often laughable, and the time has come to curb it and to teach the serious minded among us its proper meaning and its rightful place in our lives." [4] Random psychologizing is certainly not modern. Recent misuse of modern psychology is one of the hazards of every enterprise known to man. If it is "dangerous and pathetic," it is less so than modern physics or chemistry. Moreover, curbing this tendency will require conscious and positive effort on somebody's part. Who will this be? Will it be the "serious minded among us"? "Proper meaning" is question-begging, though theoretically there is a proper way for any enterprise. The author would probably say we are pushing the implications of the quotation beyond reasonable limits. On the other hand it is a very proper dream and aim that seeks to throw light on the meaning and place of such a spectacular development as the modern psychological sciences.

The second incongruity suggests that scientific psychology must both abandon and preserve something in natural psychology. It must abandon unscientific and overly speculative procedures of the past, but it must preserve the wisdom and adventuresomeness of the past, though we cannot define the methodology of that wisdom. It is commonplace to say that, strictly speaking, science as science can neither originally discern nor subsequently validate any of the values usually known as moral and spiritual. The psychological sciences,

[4] William A. O'Connor, *Psychology Without Tears* (London: Rider & Company, 1953).

however, cannot afford to become exclusively impersonal and objective. Man, the prime datum of the loftiest speculative insights for uncounted centuries, challenged the wisdom of the natural psychologist, and now, as "personality," challenges the capabilities of scientific psychology. Hovering over and about both are many of the most significant of values.

To explore the problem a bit further, we borrow a term from music. "Improvisation" is something that some people seem to come by naturally. They perform "effortlessly," as their untalented friends are wont to say. It is far from simple and not fully amenable to control. We "teach" it in music, but not very much in personal relationships. From the standpoint of strict science, improvisation is one of those "fuzzy" and unmanageable notions, tolerated but not studied directly. Speaking of its elusiveness and subtlety is another way of confessing our limitations. We include it under natural psychology instead of a stricter type.

Many celebrated examples of the alleged use of a specified method have really been the work of skillful improvisators who used their own methods, which they could never have spelled out in precise detail. There has been much talk in recent generations about methods, particularly in the area of public education. Method-vs.-content controversies have been frequent. There has been a powerful claim that methods can be taught and learned, and there has been some recognition, but scant study of the "born teacher." He is extolled, even idolized after his demonstrations. In more than a few instances, the greatest among the scientists began as improvisators.

"Bad" Psychology

Another nontechnical distinction is that between good and bad psychology. "Bad psychology" has been a prominent phrase in modern times. This is not to say that it is always used with a specific connotation, nor does it mean it is always used the same way. It often designates something said to be characteristic of religion, or it is said that religion itself is a product of some unfavorable psychological condition. An example is the idea of God. It is sometimes said that this idea is not good for people because it teaches them dependence and that religion originated in fear, which is bad. The general theme of bad psychology and its exemplifications in religion has been dramatized in motion picture presentations such as *Jane Eyre* and *The Barretts of Wimpole Street.* These two pictures very dramatically presented religious people practicing bad psychology on others. This is not to say that producers intended to make a scapegoat of religion. We do not know if that was their intention. Certainly such conditions have prevailed in the name of religion.

In the history of religions there have been any number of examples of bad psychology—as there has been in the history of politics, family life, education, child care, jurisprudence, crime detection, international relations. It is more sensational, however, to speak of it in the history of religions than in any other area—unless it might be education. The more loosely the word "religion" is used, the more widespread is the notion that a characteristic component of religion is bad psychology. If we used the word "science" with a similar looseness and generality so that we could speak of bad science, we would have to include all the magical attempts at control within the fold of science. But if science is an achievement, a growing away from and beyond magical controls; even more so is religion an achievement, a growing away from and beyond idolatry, animism, and the like, and we should be just as highly selective in the way we define it. Bad psychology in the name of religion betokens bad religion.

Some of the more obvious examples of bad psychology have been ordeal by fire, burning "witches"; evoking confessions through torture, threatening children with spooky consequences if they did not behave, using of fear as an educational technique, wearing hairshirts to subdue the body, subjecting students to a curriculum they hate, rather than one they like, because of the greater "disciplinary" value; employing sarcasm and ridicule to "strengthen character." It cannot be assumed there will be perfect agreement on how to classify all the foregoing examples, but this is not the point just now. We will give some attention to the problem of how the concept of bad psychology may have developed.

The more conspicuous examples of bad psychology have been perceptible to many people through many centuries. It is only from the perceptions of mankind that we could arrive at the concept of this kind of judgment. True, there have been many customs in the past that no one would have thought of regarding as bad. If customs develop within a society, are accepted and transmitted from generation to generation, there may be no tendency to question them for a long time. The judgment that they are bad—whether as psychology or what—will be the work of, and will be possible only to, later generations. The badness could vary—indicating limitation of knowledge, moral violation, or sensitivity. What might be called bad psychology today is that which hinders personality growth, promotes disintegration, fractures human relationships, induces abnormal fears, and encourages hostility. We believe we understand the causal relations better than would have been possible in the past. Thus, many things of the past are denounced as bad psychology irrespective of what they were called then.

Yet, in the minds of perpetrators, "badness" often retains some moral and spiritual implications. This is often as it should be—considering the intentions—but it can become complicating. For example, it was often thought good to beat mental patients.The argument was that it would beat the "demons" out of them—the patients were demon-possessed, and demons did not like to be beaten, so they would leave. The slow lessons of experience and enlightenment often require ages to get across. It may be true, as utilitarians—such as Hume—have argued, that in the long run people generally will declare certain practices to be bad and others good because they eventually observe clearly that the former are obstructive to human welfare and the latter favorable. This is arguing on the basis of a presupposition concerning human nature: that human nature will eventually prefer that which is more conducive to its welfare and will disapprove of that which hinders or hurts. A similar line of reasoning results in the claim that what may have been called *vox Dei* is only *vox populi.*

There is a different suggestion, more complex and less readily classifiable as naturalistic. It might be said that these decisions concerning the badness of certain acts or attitudes have often had their origins in the insights of lone individuals. This does not mean these individuals were not prepared through being acquainted with some definite tradition. The biblical scholar George Adam Smith said, "Like every other Reformation, this one [that of the prophet Amos] in Israel began with the conscience and protest of a lone individual." [5] Earlier the author had said that the originality of the book of Amos was "due to a few simple ideas propelled into religion with an almost unrelieved abruptness, but the ideas have flesh and blood behind them." [6] Conceivably we could argue that this is simply a dramatic example of an individual's learning first what mankind generally will learn eventually, though if this is the case the race would learn it without prophets and teachers. Against this it could be urged that without the prophets and teachers, the race might never learn.

It has been customary to speak of people such as these prophets

[5] *The Book of the Twelve Prophets* (New York: A. C. Armstrong, 1906), p. 73.
[6] *Ibid.*

as "inspired." This would mean that what was spoken of above as *vox populi* was really *vox Dei.* This introduces a suggestion that departs from the usual naturalistic explanations. To put this in the form of a question, Are there people—like Amos—who are instruments of some kind of divine initiative? Many would dismiss this today, and for various reasons. The usual answer from the area of science commends to us the test of experiment and the various procedures for experimental verification. Assumption of divine initiative, however, is not the kind of hypothesis that yields itself to current testing procedures or to the normal kinds of experimental verification which have been developed in our day, and which have been so fruitful for certain other kinds of inquiries.

So far we have suggested two guides for classifying something as bad psychology: the naturalistic source in human nature and its eventual choices over long periods of experience, and the revealing of some kinds of norms through divine initiative. In the case of Amos it may be more widely popular today to say that he was simply manifesting a clear-sighted understanding of ancient ethical codes because he had lived a simple and uncomplex life and had no occasion to become involved in the luxuries and perversions of a Bethel. It could be said with equal confidence, however, that his life and interests had prepared the psychological soil for the reception of finer perceptions—revelations so that he was able to say that the people at Bethel had violated God's will in that they had "never a single thought for the bleeding wounds of the nation" (6:6 Moffatt).

Another possible usage of the term "bad" is much more controversial on a deeper level. It refers not to methods by which people deal with or relate to each other, but to the underlying theory or school of psychology, to basic assumptions, to modes of study and research. Of course the words "bad" or "badness" are not essential here, and no brief is made for them. But the controversies to which we shall refer are certainly real enough.

Our first example is Knight Dunlap's recurring criticisms of Freudian psychoanalysis. I need not quote from Dunlap, since many readers will be acquainted with his works. Much of the criticism, which I shall not pretend to evaluate here, questions the scientific basis and validity of psychoanalysis. We have here a case of one distinguished worker in the household of the psychological sciences calling the work —theory and all—of another distinguished worker "bad." One striking feature of the difference is that, whereas Freud gave much attention in his writings to the subject of religion, Dunlap writes a significant book on the same subject without referring to Freud and with only one fleeting reference to psychoanalysis: "Psychoanalysis, which is really a praxis varying from common sense to sheer magic, with no scientific foundation whatever, has had a great and profitable vogue." [7] At the risk of identifying ourselves with Pollyanna, we could say we have an obligation to learn from both.

The second example of controversial material on the deeper level is presented through the following excerpt:

> It is safe to say, though, that nothing in our data contradicts man's *reasoned conviction that certain ultimate standards of truth and goodness exist;* and that at least the most fundamental of them can be discovered by the ordinary thinking man. As we remarked just now, the essential difference between "primitive" thought and that of civilized man seems to lie in the soundness of the knowledge upon which the thinking is based, and not in any fundamental distinctions in mentality. After all, human nature everywhere shares the same essential faculties.[8]

We call attention to three features of this quotation: (a) the philosophical presuppositions back of it, involving as they do the rational psychology of Thomas Aquinas, (b) the affirmation of the ultimacy of certain standards of truth and goodness, and (c) the universality of human faculties. Thus, some of the sharpest controversy that could gather about this quotation would be on the philosophical level, but would eventually raise the question of whether psychology in the scientific sense could be rendered bad or misguided by the presuppositions on which it would draw. Our author would no doubt make a strong case for Thomistic psychology. Also, he would try to make a vigorous criticism of the secular and ultra-naturalistic psychology that is abroad today. He also tries to show what contributions Freudian psychology can make.

The next reference is from *An Introduction to Psychology,* by Hildreth Cross:

> Even with proper training, the undesirable patterns sneak in, involving more work, more care, more discipline. I contend that there is something in human nature that has a *bent* downwards, something that makes it easier to gravitate toward the unlovely than to climb to heights of unselfishness, high thinking and noble deeds. This *something* eludes mere education.

[7] *Religion* (New York: McGraw-Hill Book Company, 1946), p. 39.

[8] Francis L. Harmon, *Understanding Personality* (Milwaukee: The Bruce Publishing Company, 1948), p. 197. Italics supplied.

Along with training and discipline, there is an added strength upon which the individual may call,—the Power of One who is able to change this tendency toward the undesirable, this bent downwards, and Who can deliver the sinner from his evil ways.[9]

We call attention to three special features in this reference: (a) the ascription of ontological status to the "something" that works against good, (b) the implication of a doctrine of sin—this overlaps somewhat with the first, and (c) the definite affirmation of the supernatural. Very few things have been called bad psychology any more frequently than a theological doctrine of sin. Yet, there is much less optimistic rejection of it nowadays than there was three or four generations ago. Cross does not represent the revival of interest in these topics, however. She represents a continuing theological orientation that has never let go any of the three items listed above. Now that she has written a textbook in psychology—and one that has won a prize—she makes clear that she is writing with an evangelical approach, as the subtitle of the book states.

Some questions are in order: How crucial is the effect on psychology proper of the philosophical or theological base? Is there some approach that is significantly superior to all others? Is a Thomistic approach *ipso facto* inferior or superior to an atheistic approach? Is there some purely scientific approach that is the indispensable requisite for scientific psychology and which can detach itself from all nonscientific presuppositions?

There are special reasons for raising these questions at the moment. First, we simply call attention to the fact that critical issues are involved. The examples given could be added to, and it would not be sufficient simply to compare the resultant psychologies bit by bit. Theoretically, if psychology attains the strict status of a science wherein all its teachings can be tested in laboratories, most of the now prevailing differences could be resolved. It would narrow the field of psychology down to matters objectively accessible and measurable, ignoring theological and philosophical presuppositions. All the foregoing works cited acknowledge some contributions from the nonevangelical, non-Thomistic, nontheistic Freud, but they also contain criticisms of his work and presuppositions.

Second, some of the questions listed above are unanswerable in an objective sense. The question of which is the one significantly superior

[9] Grand Rapids, Mich.: Zondervan Publishing House, 1952, p. 363. Italics in the text. Used by permission.

point of view is not, at the present stage of world history, answerable in the way that would objectively commend itself to all people and thus cancel opposition. Yet, such questions clamor for attention.

Two concluding reminders are offered as to what makes bad psychology bad. The first is that this means some law of human operations has been overlooked, ignored, or misinterpreted. It may have been misinterpretation, ignorance, or lack of ability that stultified efforts. All such badness is error of fact, at least. To have declared that the earth was flat was bad astronomy. Let us choose an example of this type of bad psychology one from a famous source, though we cannot imagine that even today there would be unanimity in declaring it bad. Our example comes from Boswell's *Life of Johnson:*

> Correction, in itself, is not cruel; children, being not reasonable, can be governed only by fear. To impress this fear, is therefore one of the first duties of those who have the care of children. . . . No severity is cruel which obstinacy makes necessary. . . . Locke, in his treatise of Education, mentions a mother, with applause, who whipped an infant eight times before she had subdued it; for had she stopped at the seventh act of correction, her daughter, says he, would have been ruined.[10]

The second is that badness means that harm was done where it may have been thought good would result. In other words, whether in ignorance or as a result of a combination of sadistic motivation and elaborate rationalization, harm has often been committed. The badness here is to be found in the destructive results of actions, even if we say the motives of the actors were impeccable.

We come to one sort of impasse. It is due to a conflict of basic assumptions. There is a limit to the amount of fruitful reasoning that controversialists can engage in when they do not agree on basic assumptions. If some people allow for the possibility and operation of Divine initiative and others completely reject such an assumption, attempted explanations of someone like Amos would proceed in different directions. All controversialists could be students of modern psychology—since modern psychology does not speak with one voice.

[10] A.D. 1772, Aetat. 63.

CHAPTER IX

Personality

SCIENCE—BRIGHT, ICONOCLASTIC CHILD OF HUMAN GENIUS—HAS FINALly come "home" after spectacular journeys which took him to far distant places—the study of the stars—and into ingenious abstractions—mathematics, and later into geological, chemical, and other fields "outside." At last, personality, a most intimate and immediately present datum, becomes the subject for one of the latest of the sciences. It seems utterly trite to say that we all are—or have—personalities, that we encounter them every day, and that we have been slow to realize how little we have known about personality. It is true that some people through the ages have been unusually discerning in some kind of analysis and appraisal of personality—not that they thought of themselves as precursors of a "science of personality." The very word "personality" is new. Such ancient approximations as there were have proved inadequate; as indeed "personality" may prove inadequate in the future. As for the valid insights through the centuries, it is not yet possible to distinguish them clearly from the invalid. Of course the scientific study of personality hopes both to correct past errors and to add materially to present knowledge. Let us very briefly meet a "modern" personality.

"When I'm not 'killing bears' I'm overwhelmed with anxiety." This striking statement is a lament. The speaker was attempting a bit of self-evaluation. The figurative "killing bears" suggests a yearning to achieve, to do something over and above the routine and the mediocre. It may even suggest some euphoric condition. The second half of the statement is a wet blanket to the yearnings of the first half. The anxiety stimulates the notion that the bears are a mirage and the killing a futile beating the air. Professional students of personality—psychologists, psychiatrists, psychoanalysts, psychotherapists—could say many things about this type of statement; about the possibilities of drives, needs, compulsions, and the like that provide unconscious promptings for this and other types of statements; about the dynamics of personal history; about needs and hungers.

Whatever else we say, we still recognize the statement as the work of a personality. Almost suddenly—in the span of history—the notion of personality has leapt into prominence in a variety of ways. In the first place, the word "personality" is found in advertising. We find readers promised enhancement of personality through the use of whatever is being advertised—a physical object such as a pair of eyeglasses; something more subtle such as perfume; some self-improvement that will show; or any of a number of other marketable commodities. Most of the guarantees of improvement seem to deal with what can be added on or added to; with that which meets the visual, aural, olfactory, tactile, and even gustatory susceptibilities of other people. Presumably other people more readily and appreciatively see, hear, smell, touch, and taste you when your personality is enhanced. It would be difficult to diagnose the various dimensions of this whole complex situation.

In the second place we are in the first period of history when personality study becomes a professional and scientific concern. The books published in this country on the subject of personality since the middle thirties—beginning with the 1937 appearance of G. W. Allport's notable volume, *Personality: A Psychological Interpretation*—present a formidable manifestation of professional inquiry, scientific research, and some speculative syntheses. In Europe an even greater outpouring of works on "characterology"—more or less an equivalent of personality—has signalized this century as one of unique exploration, especially in comparison and contrast with much work of the past. Henry P. David and Helmut von Bracken have brought together in *Perspectives in Personality Theory* a valuable collection of essays by both American and European contributors.

In the Foreword, Otto Klineberg said, "Except for the reports of the various psychological congresses held over the years, this is the first important venture in such cooperation (as previously referred to), with a truly international character both in its contents and in its contributors." [1] In the twenty years between these two publication dates, science has sought to come into its own in consolidating work thus far attempted. What does this signify?

These explorations are in a sense unique. The Columbuses and Magellans of the psyche are attempting to explore and chart the shores and thresholds of our interior "continents." In the dawn and

[1] New York: Basic Books, Inc., 1957, p. vii.

predawn of our modern era, the speculative geographers warned explorers of "dragon pits," of "jumping off" places, and of other threats in distant parts. Speculations of "interior geography" warned of "lusts that abound in the human soul like snakes in an old hedge." It is interesting to observe, as has already been noted, that the science of terrestrial geography preceded that of the "interior" by centuries. There is something novel, unexpected, and sensational in both areas of exploration and discovery. In the area of "interior geography," the discovery of the dimension of the unconscious has been both exciting and disturbing in its influence. On the one hand, it is seen almost as *the* explanation, or the sphere of origins of much thought, feeling, and action which had heretofore been explained rationally. Much of the irrational is now found to have its own peculiar rationale—this has been exciting. On the other hand, it is widely thought to be the source or area of operations of deceptions we did not know to be deceptions. It exerts pressures that often issue in behavior that man attempts to explain without realizing that his explanations are wide of the mark, if not downright erroneous. This has been disturbing. One premature result has been an increase of activity in leaping to a variety of conclusions classifiable under the comforting rubric "now we understand."

In the third place there is, in process, an extensive reviving and revising of attempts to understand the relatedness that does and should obtain between religion and personality. The reviving has also been marked by an intensive rereading of the innumerable classics of the human spirit that come to us from the distant past and distant places. Many of these writings are now seen in a new light, their many prescient intimations are read with a new appreciation of their wisdom and insight. Their errors are more clearly perceived. The psychological perceptiveness of some ancient thinkers, writers, and vital participants in the art of living are seen now to reach beyond the comprehension of these ancients themselves. Intimations and implications in their work often point directions accurately. Their perspectives are more often valid than not. Dorothy B. Phillips and a staff of editors brought together into a unique collection material from a variety of sources—ancient and modern, Eastern and Western, scientific and poetic.[2] Swami Akhilananda presents the West with comments and expositions of Hindu insights into human personality that both anticipate some of the modern developments and challenge

[2] *The Choice Is Always Ours* (New York: Richard R. Smith, 1948).

certain modern conclusions—largely from the psychological sciences.[3] Paul Johnson wrote *Personality and Religion* and shows how bridges of understanding may connect the continent of religion and the specialized islands of personality study.[4]

In the fourth place, the scientific study of personality will inevitably lead, as it is already doing, into more and more thought and planning concerning technologies—good and bad—for dealing with personality. Already we talk with favor and appreciation about improved techniques in therapy for afflicted, or even normal, personalities. Already we are hearing with an awesome horror talk about "improved" techniques for brainwashing. Between these extremes, attention is given to "objective" techniques and technicalities of the Pavlovian conditioned reflex. Furthermore, the psychology of learning tends of late to eclipse the psychology of teaching. Methods of education are pushed into the limelight, and content into the shadows. "Learning by doing" is extolled; "learning by hearing" is depreciated. Of late the experiments with "hidden persuaders" raise the spectre—when it is not promise—of inducing action by "perception intake" that transpires below or outside the circle of consciousness. This is put descriptively in the following:

> With the aid of a tachistoscope, Fisher has demonstrated that in the process of preconscious visual perception, an enormous amount of intricate visual material can be registered psychically with almost photographic accuracy in time intervals as short as 1/100 to 1/200 of a second. That the material has been registered can be demonstrated by various tests. . . . But, except under experimental conditions, this material is not accessible to awareness.[5]

In the fifth place, we are now having to wrestle with the concept, the "whole person," or the "total personality." Such a notion both arouses excitement and causes dismay—the first because it seems at first glance to be such an improved point of view, the latter because such a term is so wretchedly vague and incapable of being defined. It is, therefore, thought to be an uninviting prospect for scien-

[3] Swami Akhilananda, *Hindu Psychology: Its Meaning for the West* (New York: Harper & Brothers, 1946); and *Mental Health and Hindu Psychology* (New York: Harper & Brothers, 1951).

[4] Nashville: Abingdon Press, 1957.

[5] Edward S. Tauber and Maurice R. Green, *Prelogical Experience* (New York: Basic Books, Inc.), 1959, pp. 83-84. Reference to Charles Fisher "Dreams, Images, and Perception," Journal of American Psychoanalysis Association, IV (January, 1956), 15-27.

tific inquiry. We will give some attention first to this point, and it will be seen to involve some of the other points.

The Individual Person as a "Whole"

It is easier to accumulate and formulate specialized knowledge of people and human nature if they are treated analytically and in terms of specialities—easier to "divide up" the data and to confine our study to selected areas. When and if this is done, however, there is almost certain to develop a measure of dissatisfaction with such piecemeal and specialized work. Such has been the case with regard to the study of personality. Interest in the "whole person" has developed. Today there are attempts to employ scientific procedures in the study of the "total personality." Such study encounters charges of being "nebulous" and "fuzzy." It is insisted that the range and complexity of the data implied by such terms as "whole person" do not lend themselves to accurate measurement and description. This is partly true, but it is also possible that the demand that all data be measurable and describable is, though unintentionally, somewhat Procrustean. It would sound as though the mode of procedure is dictating to the data. On the other hand, what we have always encountered are whole persons whose wholeness may be intact or in some cases fractured. No personality has been dissected so that the parts could be seen separately. To be sure, there is a place in science for dissecting, for taking apart, for cutting up, but in the world of living things this requires that the subject be killed, and when this is done, some subtle component seems to depart. If you leave him in his wholeness he is very likely to show up as a problem, or as different kinds of problems. First, it is difficult to study him in his wholeness. Second, he may and often does become a problem to others because of some disorder which develops within to disturb his wholeness. Third, he can change in some respects, even while being studied. The use of one-way screens is an attempt to observe live objects—such as children and monkeys—so they won't know they are being observed and therefore "change" in some way. We have here a sort of uncertainty principle which is not completely solved by the screens.

Thus, if we do try to dissect this wholeness without destroying it, we do so only in theory. We dissect in our explanations and descriptions, or we try to arrange tests and diagnoses which will provide us with little indexes of the nature and performance of the various "parts." In the realm of biology and organic functioning we have developed marvelous systems for observing and diagnosing regular or irregular activities of parts, and as a result we are often able to cut out or replace parts without destroying organizational wholeness —in fact, some type of wholeness is often restored when the bad effect of the part on the whole has been removed. This partly explains why some psychologies are interested in staying as close as possible to biology.

If there is a psychic aspect to the life of personality, its elusiveness and invisibility are such a problem that if we can safely conclude that it is only a mode of the functioning of the organism, we can more profitably make our investigations by confining ourselves to these functionings. We would do so by studying the organism exclusively. All this raises one of the most difficult of all theoretical questions concerning investigation and inquiry. It is a double question—one part concerning the *area* of inquiry, and the other concerning the *mode*. Is the totality of existence homogeneous? Is it subject to one general type of principle or law? Is there essentially only one general type of investigation for all data? To state the questions differently: Is it possible that a word like nature can be used to include everything without any significant variations in definition or connotation? Can we and should we use the same method if we propose to investigate any aspect whatever of the whole business? The very fact that such questions are as yet unanswerable and unprovable does not make them irrelevant. In fact we are caught in something of a trap wherein we cannot completely ignore such questions, but whatever decision we make regarding them will affect all we do. Even though one becomes very sophisticated and attempts to be selective and to ignore insoluble problems his behavior may even more definitely imply some kind of decision with regard to ultimate questions.

This is particularly the case in attempts to study the human being. Consider the following: "If . . . psychology is to gain a complete understanding of human nature, it must take into account the findings of the science of biology." [6] We may assume that "complete understanding" in this quotation is not to be taken literally. Surely it is just a manner of speaking. Are there also other inquiries which must be taken into account as well as biology? No doubt the author would agree that there are. No understanding of man could possibly be complete without our knowing what is to happen to him eventually. This would still be the case even when we say that we have no way of

[6] Charles H. Judd: *Educational Psychology* (Boston: Houghton Mifflin Company, 1939), p. 15.

knowing what happens "eventually." Yet there are those who talk as though they knew that complete disintegration and utter oblivion will be man's only destiny. Others are as strongly persuaded that there is a meaningful destiny for man far beyond the confines of biology, and in no sense would this cast any reflection on the importance of biology as a specialized study or on the contributions that it can make.

In one of his very able treatises on the subject, Allport lists and classifies more than forty definitions of personality. There is a resemblance of a sort to Leuba's work in 1912, when he assembled and classified more than forty definitions of religion in a book that Ernest Jones singles out as a good example, as he sees it, of a psychology of religion. It may be that Allport's confidence in and respect for personality exceed Leuba's for religion, despite the acclaim of Jones, whose specific statement is: "the name of Leuba should be singled for special preeminence." [7]

Thus, using the term "psychology" in a broad sense for the moment, we find personality slighted in many psychological treatises but made the subject of special studies in others. A frequent theme in the latter is the importance of giving direct attention to the wholeness of the personality, even while granting its complexity, indefinability, and inaccessibility. We may ask, Is there a sense in which this "wholeness" is some kind of "oneness"? Is it clear whether the themes of *Dr. Jekyll and Mr. Hyde* and *The Three Faces of Eve* definitely cast doubt on any theory of oneness, or merely highlight in some spectacular way that complexity which is subordinate to a fundamental oneness?

The Whole Person as an Individual

It may be that the whole person is in some sense *one*, that he is a unit, even irreducible. He is not complete in himself, however, nor is he entirely self-dependent or self-made. Also he is in a sense fracturable. It may be that religion will say that he is ultimately dependent on God. Whatever science may think about that, science has tried to make clear that the individual owes his wholeness to the group. In other words, he could never become a human personality, in any intelligible sense, unless he had been trained, conditioned, and developed by the group. Without this influence, he would be in a parlous state indeed—not that he would know it, or have any connotation for "parlous." He would be without speech and many others of the so-called

[7] Jones, *op. cit.*, p. 315.

human accomplishments. Perhaps the most vivid description of such a condition ever to appear in a periodical was an article entitled "The Biography of a Wolf-Child," by Arnold Gesell.[8] Even if the author had invented the whole story about Kamala, it would be no less vivid as a description of what may be involved in the contribution that the group makes to the development of the individual.

In a sense one would be an individual no matter what his relation to any group. There have been some interesting developments in the use of the word "individual" and its derivatives. For example, there has been the persistent use of "individual" as a noun, much to the distress of grammatical purists—some of whom steadfastly refuse to use it as a substantive. Also, there have been many and varied discussions of the origin and nature of a social and political point of view called "individualism." Many attempts have been made to grapple with the problem of what the individual is and what his rights and responsibilities are—all the way from the statements in the Bill of Rights to the Hegelian concept of freedom, of the relation of the individual to the whole and on to the severer collectivities that allow the individual very few independent rights or privileges.

The individual is a unit, though "unit" as used here is not easy to define, or perhaps it is too easy to define variously—that is, there are many kinds of unity. Both the unity and the complexity of personality seem obvious to superficial observation. The individual as a complex unit has a humble origin—we do not know with certainty just what his origin ultimately was, or is—and he may have an imperial destiny, or none at all. He has been courted and cudgeled, developed and degraded, praised and preached at, bullied and babied, made up to and made into; he is the tetherball of his own slugging mass society; he is the occasional spiritual guide for faithful followers who do not always understand him; he can rise as a conspicuous unit in lonely grandeur or sink as an indistinguishable unit into a sea of his own kind.

He may indeed be the final citadel of the inquisitive, curious scientist. If it may now be assumed that he is a proper object for scientific inquiry, it is also true that for the first time the object of inquiry is also the subject, the inquirer. What do we expect these new scientific endeavors to tell us? Can they tell us what personality is, what it can do, what its worth is? To ask what personality is may sound like a continuation of Greek patterns of thought wherein we look for some underlying, attribute-bearing substance. To ask what it can do sounds

[8] *Harper's Magazine* (January, 1941), p. 183.

very much like a modern, pragmatic, functional emphasis—which at the same time tends to ridicule the substance-attribute type of inquiry. To ask what the individual personality is worth will sound to some people like an attempt to elude the rigors of science and escape into religion or something like that where poetic and figurative language may be acceptable.

The individual in his uniqueness may be called the special concern of two enterprises more than any others: religion and the psychology of personality, or the scientific study of personality. It of course may be that politics makes the individual its concern more than psychology, for it is often said that though you may let politics alone, it will not let you alone, no matter where you are. What is meant in the first sentence of this paragraph is that religion and psychology give specialized and extensive attention to the individual in a sense that no other enterprises do. The individual both in and out of the group is the datum par excellence of psychological inquiry. Religion has far more to say to and about the individual than any psychology could ever prove, or disprove by using the customary canons of proof employed in the sciences.

We need now to call attention to some features and dimensions of the nature and existence of the individual, the personality, the complex unit that we understand only partially. These must all be taken into account—and even this is only a partial list. Yet it is possible to select some of them for specialized study and investigation, even to the apparent exclusion of others.

In the first place, the individual personality is tied to "matter," but how firmly and indissolubly, it is difficult to say with confidence. Reckless confidence can of course speak with an arrogated competence and freely use such circumscribing and reductive terms and phrases as "merely," "it is simply," "nothing more than." To say that personality is tied to something else may have a dualistic sound, but such a premise is not inevitable. Many would welcome it. Others would not tolerate it. Efforts both to prove and to evade dualistic assumptions are many and varied. But from womb to tomb, the individual personality, as we are trying to understand it, has dealings with physiological structures. The inadequacy of the "body-only" concept is felt all the way from the notion of psychosomatic studies to the training of people for medical missions.

In the second place, the individual is not wholly free in his decisions and choices. Innumerable discussions of the so-called freedom-determinism controversy have been conducted in such a constricting way that the implication has been that we had to choose one or the other. This is not a strict dichotomy. Yet the extent to which the individual is free is not, and perhaps never will be, precisely specifiable —if we mean precisely. It differs with each individual according to the force and nature of a multiplicity of influencing factors.

In the third place, and this is related to the foregoing paragraph, the individual personality is always being motivated or propelled into action. To some extent this is a conscious process, and to some extent it is unconscious. Consciousness is a shifting dimension, and conscious awareness is a sliding scale of perception. The extent of conscious control may not be ultimately ascertainable, and the extent to which the semitechnical term "rationalization" has caught on indicates it is both a bane for those personalities who are exposed in using it, and a blessing for those who have sought to explain certain peculiarities in their behavior.

In the fourth place, the individual is never complete without the contributions of the group. This is said so much today that we might wonder how well we understand it after all. In some respects it seems too obvious. Yet, these contributions are not the whole story. In such a drastic experience as death, the individual participates alone, and his dying doesn't "kill" the group. The only way to kill the group is for all the individuals to die. Even then the group does not die in quite the same sense as the individual does. Also, it never seems quite the same kind of question to ask what happens to a civilization when it dies as to ask what happens to a person when he dies. It is hard enough to define death, and yet if we ever learn how to define it precisely in biological terms, the information may turn out to be anticlimactic and not sensational at all. If it is true that the individual is never complete without the contributions of the group, it is also true that he is never complete without some very non-group contributions such as vegetables, milk, water, et cetera. True, the contributions of the group belong more under the heading of personality, but are we to say that all the ingredients of personality are nonbiological?

"Personality" as a Common Concern

In the light of these considerations, a pressing question is, What are the relationships of personality to science and religion? Rather, we might ask, How much are we learning about these relationships? These questions are natural, but they are too large to be manageable by ordinary human beings. Inevitably we personalize them somewhat so that we could ask, of any individual person, "What is your understanding of these terms?" or, "How are these concerns related in your life?" No doubt there are answers in theory for these questions in the life of everyone, but the individual himself could not give adequate answers. His own answers might often be misleading. We cannot consider these subjects fully. Any full consideration of science, religion, and personality is out of the question for most people. This seems to say that we are "sentenced" to the limitation of necessarily considering these subjects inadequately, since we can neither comprehend them nor escape being involved in and related to them all. Of course for centuries man was "sentenced" to living his life in a condition of pathetically inadequate knowledge of infection, disease, and health generally. If he was fortunate enough to escape some of the standard ravages of infection and disease, he never understood why. If, on the other hand, he became ill, he did not know how or why, but he tried to know. For such efforts that set him apart from the rest of creation, we usually give scant credit. We find it easier to ridicule his ignorance and the misguided nature of some his attempted explanations, but without such "drive" we should never have learned anything.

Not only is there a limit to the extent of scientific achievement possible to the individual person in everyday life, but the expert is also limited. One hears him say, "I can't even keep up with the developments in my own field." "My own field" is usually one of the standard sciences, or perhaps only a subdivision of one of the major sciences. This kind of specialization and departmentalizing can lead to an increasing "technicalization" of language in each area and to a decrease of interdepartmental communication. If non-specialized areas of common interest and concern become fewer, there will indeed be less communication. Granted that the majority of people are nonspecialists, it sometimes is even more of a problem for any kind of communication to obtain between the specialist and the nonspecialist. The odd problem here is that it is possible to "divide up" personality study and center inquiry on parts. In human existence, however, we encounter whole persons. The quotation from Notcutt on a previous page illustrates this in one way.

As far as technical language is concerned, at least three observations are in order. In the first place, technical language at its best is precisely defined language. There is something ideal about this—up to a point. In the second place, it is true that there is an unfortunate amount of pseudotechnical language which, in this country, has been satirized by a famous word that is itself a brilliant example of a pseudotechnical term—gobbledygook.[9] In the third place, the uses and usability of language will probably never be confined solely to its use and functioning as a precision instrument. It is easy enough to say that we should always aim at precision in all that we say, that we ought never to use words for which we do not have a clear and precise definition. Also, it is true that this is pre-eminently an aim of science with respect to language. Furthermore, it now seems clearer than ever that there is a significant relationship between mental and emotional health and one's motivations and habits in language usage.

Already there is desperate need for recognition and development of nonspecialized and nontechnical interests and concerns which would be relatively free from being "reduced to a science" and from being "technicalized." This may sound as though it were an invitation to be prescientific or unscientific. Yet it only raises the question of what we should be and what we can be, in addition to being scientific and accepting and making use of science. It might be better to raise the question of what our aim, mission, and destiny truly are—and to which science can and should be constructively subsidiary. Are there norms, not strictly scientific, to which science, as well as all other enterprises, should yield allegiance? There is a general, and perhaps vague, assumption that the contributions of human genius should be beneficial, should promote well-being. What of the development of that which is obviously destructive? It is easy to rationalize its use or potential use—dynamite for use in construction, guns for defense, poisons for insecticides, whiskey for snakebite, opiates for relief from pain, and stilettos for letter-openers.

We are confronted by at least three major problems at this point. The first one is great need for a thoroughgoing conviction that the constructive use of the developments of human genius be increasingly guaranteed, and that this conviction take the form of desire, understanding, and deliberate practice. This problem has suddenly become more crucial than ever we thought it would. A graphic phrase which is new to the twentieth century and expressive of the crucial nature of our problem is "the use of nuclear energy for peaceful purposes." The personal well-being of scores of millions of people—and of life forms generally—depend on constructive rather than destructive uses of such an immeasurable development.

[9] See the discussion of this term, originating with the Hon. Maury Maverick, in the *New York Times Magazine*, May 21, 1944, page 11; and in H. L. Mencken, *The American Language* (Supplement I; New York: Alfred A. Knopf, Inc., 1945), p. 414.

The second can be represented by a question, Who can tell us why it is that there can be so much deliberate—if indeed it is deliberate—misuse of special forces, products of human inventive genius? Is there an answer that is definitive, conclusive, and ascertainable? We know only too well that dynamite can be used for vandalism, guns for shooting the defenseless, poisons for murder, whiskey for corruption, opiates for subverting human abilities, and stilettos for violent assault. Will the developing science of personality throw more light on this problem than has ever been done before? If so, will its contribution be more than simply adding to the sum total of knowledge? Will it also help to develop a common concern involving all personalities and inducing widening and deepening of this common concern? The guarantees are neither secure nor inviolable, but certainly the science of personality will be able to provide a fund of information and guidance.

In the third place, we are coming to see that the greatest of all our problems—to use an already over-worked word—is the problem of personality. It can be stated in various ways, each of which will emphasize some recognizable aspect of the nature and functioning of personality—its development and maturing, the understanding and appreciation of aims and goals of living, the deepening and heightening of mutual interest, and the moderating of destructive passions. Personality is our greatest problem in more ways than one: in the centrality of our concern for and with it, its potentiality both for good and for evil, and its peculiar susceptibilities to effects from varying types of influences—especially influences operating today. This may seem so obvious that an illustration would be superfluous, yet, a news item with a London date line of August 12, 1959 read:

> Even children in the cradle are feeling the strain of modern life, says Dr. C. F. Bramley, school medical officer for Gloucestershire. . . . Asthma and skin complaints—now recognized as anxiety diseases—are commoner among children under 5 than they were 20 years ago, Dr. Bramley said.[10]

G. M. Stratton, writing more or less in the role of a social philosopher, addressed himself to one of the aforementioned themes in his *Man, Creator or Destroyer:* "The creative powers in men have always contended with what is destructive in him. But in our present age this conflict has reached a magnitude our world has never known be-

[10] *St. Louis Post-Dispatch* (August 13, 1959), p. 1.

fore."[11] The co-operative volume of the Harvard Psychological Clinic, *Explorations in Personality,* by Henry A. Murray begins on a dour note:

"Man is to-day's great problem."[12]

How is this problem to be met? We could give many general answers: by indoctrination, by use of the arts of persuasion, by the institution of effective controls, by a program of conditioning, through inspiration, by elaborate programs of guided discussions and social participation. Some of these sound like religious answers; some sound like formal education; some like science. Some have an ominous sound to some people. Any of these answers can take an invidious turn when in the hands of those who would use other people for ulterior purposes. A distinguished theologian has remarked that civilizations have all too frequently evidenced the tendency of man to make use of his neighbor.[13] It seems, therefore, that our problem is not to be solved by one particular method, and there is no guarantee ahead of time that any combination of methods will work. In an age that has seen the rise of "-complex" as a combining form, it is tempting to speak of the "open sesame"-complex. A mother asks, "What should I say to my child who has been stealing?" She will not necessarily believe the famous story of the words that opened the door, but she seems to have a wistful longing for the right combination of words that will settle the stealing problem. It is not a fully conscious belief that the words of themselves will settle a personality problem that has confronted her. She has, by a process of "social osmosis," acquired a speech habit, and with it, some slight trace of its primitive connotation.

We should call attention to a phrase such as "science of human relationships." When we said above that there is crucial need for some common concerns that involve people generally, are not the specialized domains of experts and are not ringed about with formidable terminology requiring special training to understand, we were thinking of the stricter uses of the term science. Perhaps there is a certain inevitability in attempts to use the term "science" with sufficient generality that we envision the eventual incorporating of everything into a science, or a complex of sciences—in which event we could talk about the "science of friendship." An example of this use is found in the title of Chapter One, "The Problem: A Science of Human Relationships,"

[11] London: George Allen & Unwin, 1952, p. 3.
[12] New York: Oxford University Press, 1938, p. 3.
[13] H. Emil Brunner, *Theology of Crisis* (New York: Charles Scribner's Sons, 1929).

in the book *Living Without Hate,* by Alfred J. Marrow. The subtitle, *Scientific Approaches to Human Relations,* also indicates the general line of thinking. The first chapter opens with a quotation from the late President Roosevelt: "Today, we are faced with the preeminent fact that if civilization is to survive, we must cultivate the *science of human relationships.*" [14] Such a quotation and such a book confront man with imperatives, with invitations to the assumption of responsibilities that draw upon resources beyond the stricter borderlands of science.

In the same book, there is a discussion of religious training. In the midst of the discussion is this sentence, "That a person has received religious training does not influence him to be less prejudiced." [15] It would be to the point to ask, What went wrong in the supposed religious training? On what basis are we saying that religious training does not influence the trainee to be less prejudiced? If a person should say he had studied science and then was found to be glibly talking about phlogiston and his application for a patent on a perpetual motion machine which he developed, who would not want to raise some large questions about his scientific training? It would be simple to say that he had not had real scientific training. It would be extremely controversial to say of a person who had been, for example, a deacon in a church for fifteen years, that since he participated in a lynching, we can raise some serious questions about the adequacy of his religious training. But say it we must, if religious training is to have any meaning. It is a travesty on any significant use of the term "religion" to speak of a failure in religious training as a result of the training.

The "Sacredness" of Personality.

Some attention to this phrase is in order, if for no other reason than its widespread usage—irrespective of the fact that there may be no very clear notion as to what it is supposed to mean.

When we try to relate the phrase "sacredness of personality" to some theories and explanations of personality, odd developments transpire—at least linguistic oddities. For example, the phrase "split personality" is very much a part of today's language. It would sound odd, however, to speak of the "sacredness of split personalities." In fact the psychological investigations into the nature and functioning of personality have given us a large stock of adjectives for use with

[14] New York: Harper & Brothers, 1951, p. 1.
[15] *Ibid.,* p. 74.

the term "personality," and many of them are used by people who neither understand the adjectives nor have any particular appreciation of personality, with or without benefit of adjective. The phrase "sacredness of personality" is rather consistently used without an adjective, although the adjective "human" may be implied. If an adjective, such as "divine," is used, the whole idea is different. Years ago a speaker declared, " 'Divine personality' is the most stimulating and dynamic concept the human mind can hold." He was not trying to reinforce the idea of the "sacredness of personality," however.

If one wanted to make use of the phrase "sacredness of split personalities," he could probably develop an explanation, as he intended it, to equate it in some respects with the concept of the "worth of persons." This would involve a certain amount of arbitrariness in the use of terms. Still the "sacredness" would not apply to the "splitness" but to something that, by virtue of its sacredness, is entitled to be relieved of its splitness if possible. No doubt there have been instances in human history wherein certain pathological states were considered divine. In numerous instances something like ecstatic states have been regarded as evidences of spiritual visitation or possession. But "sacredness of personality" is not meant to apply to special and bizarre states and manifestations. The phrase "holy jumpers" may have been intended to say that the "jumping" is a positive manifestation of some kind of spiritual infusion. "Sacredness of split personality," however, would not mean that splitness is a positive evidence of the right to be regarded as sacred. In the modern scientific studies of personality the concept of sacredness falls by the wayside, or else it continues as an unspoken assumption which is the ultimate validation of therapeutic work with personalities whose sacredness is not to be found in the splitness, or whatever the pathological condition might be. The personality is to be regarded as something to be salvaged, in the name of science, or saved, in the name of religion.

Thus, the concern in this chapter has been with personality in its nature and function as revealed by science, and not its sacredness as might be affirmed by religion. In other words, the concern here is with personality as a datum in a new science, though this might involve some presuppositions as to worth. To be a datum for scientific investigation means to be accessible to inquiry, to certain kinds of measurement and experimentation, and to be an area wherein certain kinds of laws operate which can be reduced to some kind of formulation.

Personality, person, human being, human nature, man—using any or all of these terms, and more—could be said to have been the object, or objects, of much observation and inquiry in human history. Method and emphasis are not always the same, however. A few of the major examples will serve as preparation for later discussion. A characteristic type of consideration of and attention to man, or human being, or person has been to try to relate him to a norm. What ought man be? What should he do? To what should he conform or measure up? What should he stand for? Concern with these and similar questions can be maintained completely apart from any direct consideration of man himself or of personality. Far back in his history man was confronted with a list of obligations and imperatives, which, frequently, he was not allowed to question. Where they originated, how they were ultimately validated, or how they became related to him—such questions were beyond him, beyond his understanding, and beyond his right or ability to question or investigate. Often times they were sacred. He himself may not have been thought to be sacred, but he was confronted with the sacred in object, idea, imperative, and obligation.

CHAPTER X

Religion

TODAY, ONE IS TEMPTED TO BELIEVE HE CAN HEAR FAINTLY THE BUGLE call and drum roll of Armageddon in the distance. There is increase of the talk that contemplates Armageddon as the literal fulfillment of Rev. 16:16. This has been the case in the Western world in times of undue stress, such as the Black Death epidemic in the fourteenth century, and at special times on the calendar such as the year 1000, and as may be the case when the year 2000 approaches to stimulate chiliastic notions.

The ominous term also finds its way into speech as a figurative designation for a possible military holocaust of unprecedented and incalculable dimensions.

The former usage and interpretation have an advantage of a sort over the latter, based as they are on a presupposition that the apocalyptic catastrophe will be managed by Divine Power. This would guarantee ultimate victory. The other usage tends to see the catastrophe as either the ultimate manifestation of man's incapacity for social control, or of his inability to stem the tide of destruction. This would demonstrate that our legal and moral levees have been less effective than we had had the wit to contemplate or the foresight and will to strengthen. What it would demonstrate concerning religion is something of an open question.

Such a time as this virtually demands a reopening of the subject of religion and a reconsideration of its truth affirmations and its value claims—such as the reality of God and the worth and obligations of persons. This chapter and the next will reintroduce the subject, even to the extent of dealing in definition.

Assuming for the time being that we have some ideas as to what religion is, we consider in this chapter some other aspects of the subject. We may indicate some of the attempts to conduct organized inquiry into this universal and timeless area. Many of these inquiries have become highly specialized. They have assembled masses of data not yet fully assessed as to validity and use. We consider briefly such questions as the origins, history, progress, study, and exemplification of religion.

A perfectly natural question, and one asked a multitude of times, has become a concern of specialized studies. How did religion begin? What were its origins? To say that it had its origins in psychological impulses and promptings has, in the minds of many people today, assumed the status of scientific verification. To say that it ultimately made its appearance on the human scene as a result of divine initiative and of some inspiration or revelation from this source is to part company with scientific explanations—as these might be understood today. There are many examples to this day of the latter type of explanation, even among people wholeheartedly welcoming contributions of science. Controversies may obtain as to the generality of divine initiative. A striking example of a broadened interpretation of divine inspiration—how ever it might be interpreted today—is the comment of Clement of Alexandria on a passage in Plato. Clement noting the remark in the *Republic* to the effect that the lot of a "perfectly just man" appearing in society would be violent death, ventured to say, "Is it not similar to Scripture when . . . Plato, all but predicting the economy of salvation, says in . . . the *Republic* as follows: 'Thus he who is constituted just shall be scourged, shall be stretched on the rack, shall be bound, have his eyes put out; and at last, having suffered all evils, shall be crucified.' "[1] This expansive touch would be favorably received today by some who like to think in terms of a universal area of divine activity. That is to say, the spirit of the comment would be favorably received, irrespective of literal interpretation.

The phrase "religion's origins in human experience" has been fairly popular in this century, and not only among humanistically minded who have tried to detach the subject from any anchorings in transcendental havens. Sociological studies and all sorts of science-inspired inquiries have sought to identify, explain, and trace the developments of religious ideas, forms, customs, and aspirations. There has not been unanimity of results. Perhaps the widest differences are those involving the idea of God. In many of the problems dealing with religion in general, and not just in terms of origins, thought revolves around three themes: God, man, and nature. Did religion in human experience ultimately originate with God? Is religion exclusively a human concern with human origins and with, perforce, a human

[1] *Stromata,* V, xiv.

death? To what extent is religion a "natural" development that illustrates natural law at work in much the same manner as it works in the mating habits of scorpions or the actions of Betelgeuse? Or is a better explanation to be had in terms of some combination of the three?

There has been a veritable flood of books during the past few generations dealing with various aspects of the story of religion or religions. There have been the massive collections of data in such works as Sir James Frazer's *The Golden Bough* and A. B. Cook's *Zeus,* to name only two. There have been histories of particular religions and histories of all the religions. There have been numerous and often famous studies of primitive religion. But primitive tribes are not the only examples of the primitive as far as religion is concerned. Erich Fromm said:

> If we scratch the surface of modern man we discover any number of individualized primitive forms of religion. Many of these are called neuroses, but one might just as well call them by their respective religious names: ancestor worship, totemism, fetishism, ritualism, the cult of cleanliness, and so on.[2]

With such a mass of material to draw upon, it becomes very easy to use such a sentence as "Religion practices—and has practiced—ancestor worship," or "Religion developed fetishism," or "Religion urges submission." The supply of predicates seems limitless. If we proceed toward clarification of perspective, we must have some guide for avoiding undue selectivity. With a limitless supply of predication, would it make as much sense to pick out something good and say, for example, "Religion has improved the status of women"? If one were disposed to say, "Religion has practiced child-sacrifice," could another say, with equal appropriateness, "Religion abolished this ritualized slaughter"? The abundance of predicate supply makes it possible for this person to condemn religion right out of the record, and for that person to justify it. This ambiguous use of the term "religion" is not always a recognized ambiguity. Nor do we always bother to locate the "villian," or the "hero." We are left with the question, What is religion?

Studies of religion classifiable as history have some natural limitations. The very word "limitations" may have a reproachful sound. Here it is meant to be simply descriptive. In the first place, modern

[2] *Psychoanalysis and Religion* (New Haven: Yale University Press, 1950), p. 29.

histories of religion tend to follow the rules for historical writing and to hold back from trying to say anything about God or cosmic purpose. A prominent historian, whose religious orientation is Christian, evidenced this willingly assumed limitation when he said, in his monumental historical study of the missionary expansion of Christianity: "Into one field, it must be noted again, these volumes do not enter. They do not seek to discuss the cosmic significance of the events they record. . . . He has endeavoured to conform to that kind of objectivity extolled by the school of history in which he has been trained." [3]

Another limitation, usually considered salutary, is to hold back from the free use of judgments, to "let the chips fall where they may," to be guided by the balance of evidence. This is far from simple. There are certain requirements that are inevitable and which are oftentimes the result of covert judgments—they cannot escape being such. For example, what is to be selected from the mass of accessible materials for inquiry and discussion? What is to be presented as religion? Shall it be anything and everything that anyone has ever called religion? Shall there be any judgments as to what belongs in the category or under the rubric of religion? The questions are inescapable.

The most rigorously objective of historians or scientists cannot avoid the making of judgments, however much they try to keep them from showing. The historian of religion cannot avoid feeling distinctions between various manifestations of religion. He probably could avoid proceeding to the ultimate question, What is "true" religion? He will have many private feelings about good and bad in religion, and he will feel, and sometimes articulate, distinctions among the many data coming to his knowledge. He will "officially" avoid making distinction between the true and the false in such a field as religion, however.

The problem eventually shapes up as one or the other of the following possibilities: (1) Religion contains all these horrible ideas and practices, therefore religion is a bad thing; (2) Religion is a story of undue trafficking in superstitions, thus, religion is superstition; (3) The history of religion is the history of all that has been thought to be religion, and it is essential therefore to separate the good from the bad and the true from the false; (4) The history of religion should help us to rescue religion itself from the accretions of the nonreligious and the irreligious.

[3] Kenneth Scott Latourette, *A History of the Expansion of Christianity* (New York: Harper & Brothers, 1937), I, xxii-xxiii.

What is the task of the history of religion? Is it primarily the making of distinctions between that which is religion and that which is not? To do so would involve one's whole understanding of religion and one's own religion. The fundamental commitments of the individual historian will be potential influences on his professional work. Let us look at the problem in connection with the history of science. This has been a flourishing enterprise in our century, more than in any other century. It is commonplace in such works to make a distinction between that which is science and that which is not, between anticipations which we subtly consider wise and fruitful and those that have proceeded on false premises, and between the various uses of science. A basic premise is that science is good and capable of development. Moreover, science is not blamed for the mistakes, failures, blunders, and misuses that man's curiosity and tinkering perpetrated in his search for the true and the good in that particular form of his search issuing in what we now call science.

Our point here is not that religion and science must both be considered good, or that the parallel we have drawn is an exact one. We simply say that there are basic, often unspoken and sometimes hardly conscious, preferences that affect the direction of our efforts and the general pattern and details of our perspective. If we are incorrigibly antipathetic to religion—or to science for that matter—we are more alert to the unfavorable appearances that engage our attention when we investigate, whatever the subject. Also, there are many examples today of unfavorable attitudes toward "religion," which make some of us reluctant to exert any effort to fill in the credit side of the ledger. There is also some indication of a growing disfavor in attitudes toward science.

Yet, we are not inevitably and inescapably subject to the determining influence of fundamental preferences that are completely beyond our direction, or even our control on occasion. Both religion and science have their ideals, often violated by disciples of both. There are also ideals that, at least in their general form, are common to both enterprises—humility, dedication, respect for truth, commitment to the furthering of human welfare, fellowship of faith and functioning, subordination of private and self-centered interests, respect for the work of others, transcending inflexible orthodoxies that reject the new on principle.

Another aspect of the general problem of religion concerns the nature and possibility of progress in religion. What is progress in religion? Is it possible for people to understand, to further, and to accept such progress? Using the term "religion" in its broadest sense —as might be done in a comprehensive history of religion—we could say that a transition from the worship of mice and snakes to the worship appropriate to ethical monotheism would be progress. It might be less easy to gain general consent as to whether a transition from theism to humanism represents progress. Also, it would be difficult for many people to grasp clearly any distinctions between progress in terms of evolutionary development of potential in human beings and progress in a deepening appreciation of the idea of God. Three areas in which progress does and should take place in religion and in the understanding and practice of religion are the development of human potential, the maturing of both understanding and practice in human interrelatedness, and the refining and spiritualizing of human conceptualizing of the idea of God.

Has there been a development of human intellectual potential? Has there been a process of evolution wherein man has become more capable and more generously endowed with cranial area, brain-size, and increased cortical capabilities? Has this been an inevitable and completely natural process? Or has it been in part dependent on the way man has exercised his potential and brought it to periodic improvement, which eventually became inherent or "built-in"? These questions are natural and quite easy to ask. But there is less confidence in answering them now than in the first years of its reception, when Darwin's great book was completely and uncritically accepted by some people. Such acceptance, monitored by wish as much as by intellectual scrutiny, was perhaps no more substantiated than many hostile and equally uncritical rejections. The theory of natural and inevitable progress seems much less secure now than in the optimistic days of the nineteenth century.

Let us consider another aspect of progress, one that is less in the "directing hands" of nature than are the laws which we often call the universal and invariable laws which it is said we cannot disobey, but only illustrate. The kind of progress that is entertained as a possibility by a purely naturalistic and humanistic point of view sees man as doing the whole job himself, including the formulation of the aims, goals, and methods. To this outlook nature is of no help except in providing the raw materials and a set of principles of operation. God is of no help beyond the possible allurement provided by a stimulating idea. Thus, the kind of progress seen as a purely human achievement will depend upon education, learning, use of scientific procedures, universalizing of effort and aim, benevolent controls—in fact it would be an elaborate, universal, beneficent program of "human engineering." In such a point of view, it is easy to see that religion becomes divested of much of its supposed meaning—this is a "post-religious" point of view.

Yet at the center of much religious thinking there has long been an ideal of progress that conceivably could be achieved in the life of individuals and society. This central deposit has persisted. A common criticism against it has been that it centered more attention on the glory of the ideal and less on the details of methods for fulfillment. A correlative criticism has been that too much reliance was placed on the inevitable and unmerited assistance of God. This type of thinking has not limited itself to progress in this world. It was taken for granted that this world would not last. Thus, any notions of progress involving permanence would have to transcend the limitations of this world.

To none of these notions of progress has unanimous consent been given. There has not even been general understanding. The subject is too complex, and interest and effort are insufficient for detailed inquiry working toward general agreement. The actions of many people in many centuries, however, are an indication of notions of and hopes for progress. It is quite likely that many efforts that aim in a certain direction or at a certain goal may not be the right or effective efforts. Man has not yet learned to be assiduous in the critical appraisal of his prior efforts for the purpose of revising them. Yet, generation after generation expends time, effort, and money on the training of the young "for the future" and for ushering in better conditions. A belief in some kind of progress is persistent. A variety of effort manifests such a belief, but there is nothing on which man is hazier in his outlook and understanding than what, precisely, is the nature of religious progress and proper *modus operandi* for actualizing it.

What has man thought and done about the study of religion? There has of course been vastly more study of the doctrines and institutions of one's own religion, of how to incorporate them into life and transmit them, than there has been study of religion generally and objectively.

Why study religion in general? With the rise of modern science, it was inevitable that this new enterprise would give reasons for such a study. In so far as religion could become an area of data for scientific study or for a new specific science, the aim would be the seeking of knowledge, the formulation of such natural laws as this enterprise gave evidence of, and the attainment of newer and more adequate understanding of something figuring so prominently in human experience. This would include giving attention to measurements, controls, and study of origins—steps in the scientific study of any area.

Would scientific study of religion be supposed to lead to any further and more extensive practice? This may be a serious gap. Subtle temptations operate to induce people to think that since they possess new knowledge they are practicing it. This could result in the study which subtly avoids the transition to actual performance. This would be more the case with religion than anything else.

Modern studies of religion have had some curious results. Two of the most prominent and spectacular have been the developing conviction that religion is not definable, and the notion that religion is an illusion and a continuance of infantile concerns. Thus the study reveals why we should not wish to exemplify religion. Both types of study lead away from religion.

There is another type of study that seeks to show that world religions are supplemental rather than antagonistic or opposed. This is not the same type of study as those previously named. The former types, represented by Sir James Frazer and by Sigmund Freud, more or less profess to lead away from religion, presumably having shown its relation to magic or its prolonged involvement in continuing infantile feelings. On the other hand, studies initiated and edited by Kenneth Morgan seek the establishing of some rapprochement between representatives of diverse religious professions.[4]

If the study of religion is supposed to lead to some kind of exemplification, some improved manifestation, and some more earnest commitments and dedication, trouble develops if study seems to make it less clear as to what there is that should be exemplified. It has been a persistent claim that religion cannot be defined—presumably one type of result from some kinds of study—that people cannot agree on what the proper *designata* are for the word "religion"—if it is to be a word with denotable referends.

Something else has developed in recent generations which has curiously affected the whole picture. This is the study of the religious personality, or the study of religion in the personality—all of which is a part of the larger enterprise of the study of personality. We call attention here to one type of result. What a person says about him-

[4] *The Religion of the Hindus; The Path of Buddha; Islam: The Straight Path* (New York: The Ronald Press, 1953, 1956, 1958).

self may or may not provide a valid clue as to what he is. The investigation of human depths makes this reasonably clear. Thus, we can go further with a very special aspect of this development: what a person says about his own religion may or may not be accurate. This does not necessarily mean that he has the deliberate intention to deceive. What he says may be subtly and unconsciously motivated by influences from the depths of personality. He may be involved in subtle and unsuspected self-deception. This is not to say that we all are always fooled.

Two dimensions of reality are suggested by the foregoing: the reality of our total context, and the reality within. Man has been looking, ever since he began to look with any degree of self-conscious awareness, for clues to reality of both kinds. In no area has this been a more complex task than in religion: the search for clues to the aspects of reality involved in such polarities as God and idols, true prophets and false, sincerity and hypocrisy, pure religion and defiled; divine authority and demonic; the spiritual and the carnal; knowledge and faith. Furthermore, he has always believed he has found some hints and even evidences of both realities in the "beyond" and the "within."

We remind ourselves that the intermediate stage of reality between the beyond and the within is the curiously ambiguous reality of everyday life and experience; the world of objects and events impinging on us with a now pleasant, now shocking, familiarity and immediacy; an endless round of the real but impermanent, the certain but misleading, the obvious but often too obvious, the inspiring but threatening, the accessible and measurable but inadequately accessible and measurable, the recurring but unexpected, the orderly but chaotic.

Man has often doubted the possibility of gaining knowledge of the full dimensions. "The heart is deceitful above all things, and desperately wicked: who can know it?" (Jer. 17:9 K.J.V.) Job 38 and 39 pose some questions about the nature and extent of reality that are presumed to be unanswerable. Today it would be possible to say with a measure of accuracy that both sets of questions from both Jeremiah and Job are more answerable than we have thought they would be. The psychological researches into personality depths have thrown some light on Jeremiah's question, and science generally has answered many of Job's questions—though not all of them. Does this suggest that we are definitely on the way to complete answers? It would be arbitrary and gratuitous to give too confident an affirmative to this question, though such extrapolation is certainly tempting. Yet the spectacular successes in acquiring knowledge and gaining controls in the intermediate area referred to above have encouraged many to believe that the other two dimensions are now definable and explainable in terms of our intermediate area. It is thought, therefore, that nature's ample maw has ingested both the eternal God and the immortal person, thus "naturalizing" them and changing the type of reality to be ascribed to them.

Now we turn to the question of a "credit rating" for religion. This is not an accountant's problem. Prior to any such task is some examination as to what kind of question it is that asks whether religion *has* any credit balance.

Religion has been charged with ineffectiveness and accused of failure. We may hear statements declaring that it has had centuries in which to prove itself and validate its claims. William James has quoted Morrison I. Swift to the effect that certain facts adduced now prove:

> religion a nullity. Man will not give religion two thousand centuries or twenty centuries more to try itself and waste human time. Its time is up; its probation is ended; its own record ends it. Mankind has not aeons and eternities to spare for trying out discredited systems.[5]

In other words, religion is considered ineffective or a failure in that there still are problems, and that there have not been sufficient improvements of religious techniques and religious methods for the solutions of these problems. Moreover, the problems themselves are scarcely any better understood as a result of religion, since the analyses attempted by religion are often wide of the mark—if not downright erroneous. For example, it will be said that religion's attempts to explain illness and disease have long dealt in such things as demons, punishments, judgments, and kindred themes which would never have discovered the lowly and unromantic germ and the facts of contagion and antisepsis.

It is further said that religion, the defendant, can be accused of numerous inadequacies, errors, and bad guesses. Such general charges as these are made: religion has too long evinced a lack of knowledge, or has acted on the wrong kind of knowledge; its methods have

[5] *Human Submission* (Philadelphia: Liberty Press, 1905), Part Second pp. 4-10. Quoted in *Pragmatism* (New York: Longmans, Green and Company, 1907), pp. 31-32.

too often been futile, if indeed they have not sometimes been the wrong kinds of methods in that they hindered rather than helped; it has lacked sufficient controls, or has too often exercised invidious controls; it appeals all too readily to the nonrational and the irrational, or when it appeals to the rational it does so in defense and support of some doctrine of the suprarational or the supernatural; it threatens, cajoles, or coddles instead of reasoning with or attempting to convince through proofs; it has too long carried a cargo of myth, miracle, superstition, magic, notions of the ineffable, the mystical, and the otherworldly.

That there has not been unqualified success would be admitted on all sides. But would there be equal admission of some successes? No one would deny that the conditions listed in the preceding paragraph have often obtained. But to explain them is by no means a simple task. If all these charges can be leveled against something called religion and if they can be substantiated, there is not much point trying to make a case for it. When adequate proof is submitted, then comes the time for judgment and sentence, provided we can locate the defendant. All I shall try to do here is to specify two types of explanation for the failures and inadequacies, one made by religion and one by science. For linguistic convenience I shall speak of religion and science as though they were individual, articulate beings. Also I believe it is obvious that not all representatives of either religion or science will be in complete agreement on these explanations. I offer simply what is thought to be a fairly representative summary of certain types of explanation that bear more resemblance to each other than we may have thought.

What explanations have been offered by religion for its failures and inadequacies? We shall be concerned only with an explanation that is widespread and general. In so far as there has been a failure it has been, according to this explanation, a human failure. Ultimately it involves a whole theory of human nature, an attempt to say what man is and an assessment of human potentialities and liabilities. Examples of this explanation vary widely. They involve language that is sometimes figurative, poetical, or mythical. One type of explanation has said that man is a sinner, which means, variously, that he is infected with sin, that he has a prepossession to sinfulness, or that he is more often sinful than righteous. We need not go into all the definitions and attempts at definition of sin. It also has been said that man is a disobedient creature. Whether this is synonymous with sinful we need not say. Again, it will be said that man is a creature of pride, and that when he becomes a battleground for the contest between his obligations and responsibilities and his haughty, self-centered pride, pride often wins. It may be said that in the majority of cases, judging by past history, man is more often likely to take up with some form of idolatry than with substantial and valid religion. It is pointed out that the majority of mankind are idolaters, even when there is no specifically designated idol before which they regularly genuflect.

In other words, this type of explanation specifies that there is something in man's nature that gives ample explanation of any and all failures charged to religion. Yet it will be insisted at the same time that there is a potentiality in man that not only makes achievement in religion possible, but also makes it possible to see that there is a problem and to see some basis for criticism. Religious literature is replete with examples of criticisms by religion against religion. In a sense this is self-criticism, and it has been more extensive and searching than criticism from the outside. It is this self-correcting process that accounts for many of the successes that can be attributed to religion.

This type of explanation seems to affirm some sort of polarity deep in the texture of human nature, in the inner man, or in the depths of man. Two contrary, diverse, and often warring propensities seem to be contending for supremacy on the battlefield of person or personality. Since religion has wrestled with this problem, both theoretically and practically, for so long, it has been inevitable that some representatives of religion conceive of this dual problem in nonhuman form and superhuman contexts. In some religious circles these elaborations have pictured two disparate and contrary world forces, far beyond and above the mere human domain—good and bad, light and dark, right and evil, or whatever terminology might seem acceptable to users. This is a thoroughgoing, cosmic dualism. Other religious circles, however, have denied such a far-reaching or total dualism. True, there may be God and devil, but this devil is not a coordinate, opposite world force. He is perhaps a fallen angel with a propensity for disobedience, or he may have been created by the very God who is the ultimate and sole power. Therefore, the explanation, thus "elevated," seems quite similar to explanations given in purely human terms—disobedience, rebellion, pride, and kindred propensities. In the religious history of the Western world, the former is represented by the Gnostic theories of early days, and the latter by the more definitely biblically inspired theories of a supreme God and—as in the writings of John Calvin—the theory of a created devil.

What sorts of explanations have been offered by science for the ineffectiveness or failure of religion? A first example and one of the commonest types of disputes that science has had with religion deals with certain affirmations or claims that religion is supposed to have made. With the increase of knowledge that science has accumulated about the world of nature and with development of refined techniques for checking the truth of statements about the world, science has had only to take a few examples of such statements that it has checked by its objective methods. Did religion say something about the "four corners of the earth"? Did it also say that the world is six thousand years old? Or that the stellar bodies were divinities dwelling in a purer type of environment than earth? Or that Galileo was some kind of transgressor? Or that some people develop unusual powers by trafficking with the devil? If so, then science has only to do some objective checking to ascertain what sort of validity may or may not be ascribed to such claims. Thus, a first type of explanation by science of religion's ineffectiveness or failure is the exposing of errors of fact to which it has subscribed.

A more recent type of explanation attempted by science has been the tracing of origins of numerous religious doctrines and dogmas to psychological conditions in man himself. In other words, an attempt has been made to show that many of these doctrines and dogmas are the results of illusions, wishful thinking, or projecting inner conflicts and frustrations into world dramas. It is said that people have personified wishes, attachments, and dreams. In other words, religion is often said to be a development from delusions, obsessions, compulsions, and other irrational or abnormal conditions transpiring deep in man's own turbulent inner life. A whole new type of interpretation of religious doctrines and dogmas attempts to explain the irrelevance of any effort to prove the objective validity of these doctrines and dogmas. Instead of considering whether the statement "God is real" is objectively true, such a statement is said to mean that *belief* in God is real, thus indicating a psychological condition that can be studied without any reference to whether there is a God—the assumption being that there isn't. "Praying to God" means that the subject has hoped there might be a God to whom to pray and the hope has sired the belief that there is. Again it is a psychological condition and process that explains the whole thing. This type of explanation has shifted attention to the genesis in the psychic life of the affirmations of religion. Thus it becomes unnecessary to examine the alleged objective truth of the affirmations, or so this explanation would have it.

Both types of explanation attempted by science, find the trouble to be in man himself; in his susceptibility to illusion, deception, error, mistaken judgments, wishes, dreams, frustrations; in his incapacity for self-criticism and his capacity for quick generalizations, hatreds, aggressiveness, moodiness, depression—in short, the root of the trouble and the explanation for religion's ineffectiveness and failure is to be found in man. If he is not a sinner he is at least a creature of passion and illusory notions. Yet, he has potentiality for integration or reintegration and some degree of rational behavior.

All these explanations find the causes of the trouble in man, in human nature, in frailties and foibles of personality. It is people who have fallen short, fallen from grace, or fallen by the wayside. It is no nonhuman or abstract entity, religion, that has failed. Nor is it any nonhuman or abstract entity, science, that will succeed, that will "make man good," that will prove effective. If science in the modern sense has been here such a short time, it might be argued that it will take it a much shorter time than religion ever had to fail, and even to cancel the whole human story. Today many people are talking in these terms. There is much discussion about the "destruction of the human race." But surely no scientist would agree for a minute that it will be science that fails. Even those apprehensive scientists who raise the question of whether after all science is good will hasten to an affirmation of its intrinsic goodness. If the world is destroyed by nuclear fission and fusion, by lethal radiation, or by any other horrendous discoveries and developments, it will not be done by science, but by irresponsible, fearful, frustrated, and perhaps wicked people —this will be the argument.

In the explanations attempted—whether by religion or by science —man shows up as a creature of polar conflicts. It may be said that man can be saved by religion or salvaged by science, but these are qualified by a very large "if." If it is questionable to say, without qualification, that religion has failed and that science will succeed, then what is it that has failed, and what is it that will succeed? Tucked away in all attempted explanations of past failures and future successes is the irreducible implication that the failures on the one hand and the successes on the other have been and will be due to man. Is this by any chance what Herman J. Muller said? [6]

If there are promises of success, but also mortal threats, as far as the future is concerned, are the explanations for each to be found in man? Apparently so. Thus, there is another form of the discussion to be noted. If it be granted that it is not linguistically accurate to say that religion has failed, it could still be argued that the real meaning comes to focus in this: man failed when he tried to be religious or to uphold and propagate religion. This would make it very doubtful that we could blandly assume that science will succeed, for by the same token there is no guarantee that man will succeed any more surely with science than he has already done with religion.

It would be an over-simplification to say that religion has failed and that science will succeed. It would be an over-simplification because it tends to build on a dubious connotation of religion. It would define the subject by concentrating on and emphasizing its failure, errors, and misdeeds that do not belong in a strict definition of religion. One of the most difficult things in the whole of human linguistic experience is to ascertain a strict, proper, adequate, and unadulterated connotation for religion. This would take us to the very limits of our capabilities. Also it would be an oversimplification because of the tendency to think of science primarily or even only in terms of its demonstrated best, its successes, its beneficent accomplishments and possibilities, and not of its dangers, threats, and temptations. Science is rarely depreciated by being traced to illusory and frustrated experiences in man's psychological history. The most likely effort at a psychological explanation is to cite its origin in curiosity, and curiosity is cited as good. It would be easy, however, to indicate aspects of unwholesomeness and intemperance in the history of curiosity if we were disposed to enter into polemics, but such is not the present intention.

If we want to locate some causal area of ineffectiveness and to assign responsibility for failure, we may say that man has failed religion. This suggests also that he seems to be demonstrating capacities for failing science. Representatives of religion have had their golden dreams about what could be and what, in the fullness of time, would be. Representatives of science are not without their own dreams and roseate prognostications. In both cases the outcomes will depend to a great extent on the decisions and choices of man.

[6] See quotation on p. 38.

It has always been known that man, the individual, can destroy himself and can harm his neighbor, and nowadays there is occasional lugubrious talk about universal destruction.

If we want to account for the successes of science, could not man be given the credit? Individual successes, group achievements, wise and inspiring anticipations—are these not significant evidence of man's potentialities? Have some of us been intimating that in the future man must decide to have done with religion and become scientific, that man must cease being "tender-minded" and become "tough-minded," that with the knowledge already accumulated man can establish a civilization of order and plenty if . . . ? The "if" vaguely indicates the ill-defined and inadequately blueprinted interval between potentiality and realization. Into this interval we have hopefully poured a significant linguistic composite of remarkable nature and variety—choice, inspiration, genius, "call," planning, control, knowledge, reason, foresight, guidance, sanity, education, wisdom, pioneering, and many others.

The reference to "tough-minded" and "tender-minded" in the preceding paragraph is simply another instance of the influence of the terminology in the writings of William James. We raise a question as to whether these flexible terms are sometimes used in ways that turn them into mutually exclusive value terms. Certainly William James, in *Pragmatism* did not do so in such a way as to designate the former as unqualifiedly good and the latter bad. His own position was not wholly on either side. Yet, S. S. Stevens seems to sharpen the disjunction. Of course no one is necessarily obligated to employ the connotations James had in mind. Stevens said: "The scientist has always been proud of his hard head and his tough mind. When William James sat in judgment and divided the universe of temperaments into the tough and tender-minded, the scientist knew where he belonged." [7] Stevens uses these terms to distinguish between empiricists—the tough-minded, the scientists—and rationalists—the tender-minded, usually found, as he says, in philosophy departments.

An even sharper disjunction is found in a quotation included in an article by the anthropologist, Loren Eiseley. He said:

> Some time ago I had a letter from a professional friend of mine comment-

[7] "Psychology and the Science of Science," *Psychological Bulletin* (1939), *36*, 221-263. Quoted in *Readings in Philosophy of Science*, ed. Philip P. Wiener (New York: Charles Scribner's Sons, 1953), p. 158.

ing upon the education his daughter was receiving at a polite finishing school. "She has been taught," he wrote to me a little sadly, "that there are two kinds of people, the tough- and the tender-minded. Her professor, whose science I will not name, informed her that the tough-minded would survive."

This archaic remark shook me. I knew it was not the product of the great selfless masters of the field, but it betrayed an attitude which demanded an answer. In that answer is contained the whole uniqueness of man. Man has not really survived by toughness in any major sense—even the great evolutionists Darwin and Wallace had had trouble with that aspect of man —instead, he has survived through tenderness. Man in his arrogance may boast that the battle is to the strong, that pity and affection are signs of weakness. Nevertheless . . . the truth is that if man at heart were not a tender creature toward his kind, a loving creature in a peculiarly special way, he would long since have left his bones to the wild dogs.[8]

The quotation does not indicate precisely what the disjunction intended by the girl's teacher really was, but it sounds as though it may have been science-religion. The qualities of personality and outlook that Eiseley considers significant are more readily associated with religion than with anything else. Yet we are not saying that Eiseley was primarily attempting to make a case for religious tender-mindedness. As a matter of fact, if we wish to make these sharp distinctions and to use the popular terminology of William James, we can say that even within the ample folds of religious profession there have been the tender-minded and the tough-minded. This distinction could be as sharp as any obtaining between religion and science or anything else. We turn now to some introductory attempts at definition.

[8] "An Evolutionist Looks at Modern Man," *Adventures of the Mind* Series. Number 1. *Saturday Evening Post* (April 26, 1958), p. 120. Used by permission.

CHAPTER XI

What Is Religion?

THIS CHAPTER'S TITLE IS NOT SO MUCH A PROMISE OF ENLIGHTENMENT as a recognition and a confession that the question is unavoidable. Even those who are against it often seem unable to leave religion alone—indirectly testifying, by their strictures, to its universal presence and its perennial challenge. Those most committed are often unable to say just what it is. They may demonstrate it magnificently, but this is no guarantee they will be understood; they may even be punished. There are those less dedicated who often prefer to make their demonstrations largely verbal, endlessly professing their affinity and equally endlessly condemning sin and sinner. Moreover the fervid commitments of idolaters are properly parts of the total picture of religion, perhaps even more so than the lukewarmness of Laodiceans. The varieties of idolatry go far beyond those obvious examples formally classified as such. Also, lukewarmness has a way of invading the human heart at any level of human achievement and status. The degree of truth exemplified by religious commitment is not always in equal balance with the degree of commitment. It often seems possible to espouse truth indifferently and to be wholeheartedly committed to error. Strangely enough there is real danger in turning over to any particular human being or group the final authority to pass on what is to be accepted as truth and what rejected as error. Particularly is this a danger if these "authorities" are to be free from question and criticism, and if they are privileged to demand the commitments of others.

Who may answer the question? As many make the attempt as for any question ever asked. The proper question would seem to be, Who is qualified to answer? This question seems easy enough to answer if the crucial word is something like chemistry, deep-sea diving, philately, surgery, or any one of scores of enterprises. Ask a chemist or a philatelist, for example, or read a book on the subject. For our question shall we ask a "religionist," or read a book entitled *What Is Religion?* Religionists are not as clearly defined as geologists, physicists, and many other "-ists." Shall we ask St. Francis of Assisi or Torquemada? Elijah the prophet or Jezebel the daughter of a priest-king and herself a queen with many prophets? Moses on the remote mountain or Aaron close to the people? Joan of Arc or the English bishops? Saul of Tarsus or Paul the Apostle? As for books, which is better, *What Is Religion* by Mr. X or *What Is Religion* by Mr. Y? George Fox's *Journal* or Mencken's *Treatise on the Gods?* Wesley's *Sermons* or Calvin's *Institutes?*

If there is something obvious about how such questions are variously dealt with, there is far less obviousness about how they ought to be answered. One reason for the *variety* of attempted replies is that two people can discuss religion yet not talk about the same thing. Even if they did talk about the same thing, they conceivably could feel differently about it. Thus, anyone trying to take a cue from science and attempting objective description would forthwith encounter two sizable problems: (1) what to choose for description and (2) how to assess evidences of the dimensions of feeling in religion that are both inevitable and vital—but also complicating.

To define religion, or to answer the question of this chapter, presumably it would be essential to find it or locate it. If that were sufficient, we would need only to point and say "There it is. That is what religion is." Thus our task would indeed be simple. If it becomes necessary to proceed further, however, and add connotation to denotation, the task is more difficult. Thus we have difficulties that transpire as we approach the task of answering our question—such difficulties as locating religion (denotation) and choosing, from the numerous possibilities, that which is to be described and explained (connotation). What are these numerous possibilities? Is religion a set of statements about reality? Sometimes people will say that Mr. *A* is a religious man, and they will base this statement on the fact that he makes certain types of statements. Is religion a set of judgments about special types of values? Certainly judgments of this type are essential ingredients of religion. Is religion a concern with certain kinds of relationships? We hear it said, "She is sort of religious. She is always talking about what God does for her." Is religion a certain mode of activity? Though there is a tendency to class as religious people who pray, who worship, who attend divine service, there are at the same time frequent judgments that some of these are deluded or hypocritical. Is religion a certain type of sentiment? Many are inclined to say of Abraham Lincoln that he was not "officially" a religious person, but that he was a person of profound religious sentiment. Is religion a type of moral behavior? A devotee of ethical culture will see religion as ethics primarily. Is religion primarily belief in God? The standard demurrer offered to this identification of religion is Buddhism, and yet some kind of theism is probably a more nearly universal component of religion than anything else.

There is, however, a subtler problem confronting us in the attempt to deal with the question of this chapter. There has been a strong tendency to define religion primarily in terms of truth, or reality, or of that which is right. The following pages represent a departure from this procedure. As everyone knows—though the explanation is not obvious—there has been a widespread tendency for people to think and feel—primarily to feel—that "my religion is the true religion and the others are false," thus pitting "true religion" against "false religion." There was no tendency therefore to use the term religion in any over-arching sense to refer both to "mine" and "the others." This was vividly illustrated by some of the early reactions to the academic phrase "comparative religions." This enterprise seemed to be directed toward defining religion so as to include them all, as well as toward trying to discern kindred and supplementing values in all religions. Yet some people acidly commented, "The very idea, talking about comparative religions. There is no comparison!" This reaction represents a disinclination to admit that the worship of Thor is religion. Yet it may go without saying that there have been many, many "false gods." It would be allowed in this work that the idea of the one, true God is probably the most germinal and significant development in all human history. Yet, is it not possible for a person to say, "I believe in the one, true God" and yet not be religious in any mature sense? On the other hand, are we to deny the title "religious" to the sincere and committed idolater who never knew anything else? Lord Lindsay, formerly principal of Balliol College, Oxford, in a public address once gave an ingenious connotation of pagan—a pagan is one who "takes his religion as he finds it." In other words pagan is not simply the term that religion *X* applies to the "benighted" devotees of religion *Y*, but it can be applied to the nominal membership of any religion if they have no other reason for their religion than the accident of birth and their own social conditioning. Had these been otherwise, the religion would have been different. Lindsay's remark is a judgment of a sort on immaturity found in all religions, or rather in much of human experience.

It is here readily granted that eventually and ultimately religion must be defined in terms of truth and right. But the temptations to control the interpretations of truth and right are very great, and these temptations will involve many violations of truth and right. For religion to be a meaningful and continuing concern, it must not too long carry a cargo of error. Error is often treated as though it were perversity, deserving of punitive action, when it is actually, in some of its forms, normal immaturity. Therefore, allowance needs to be made for the inevitability of types of error characteristic of certain stages of growth—for example, the fancies of children.

If religion is to be defined as truth and right, would this imply that infants and children are not religious? Also, might it seem to imply that religion is a collection of valid statements? Could a liar then speak the truth? Could a nonreligious person affirm religion? A child is certainly an object of religious concern. Also a child is equipped with potential that can and should flower into religious fulfillment. As for the liar and the nonreligious person, their vocal and verbal performances are not the norms for the appraisal of religion, although it is true that anyone can spin a linguistic web that can snare the unwary. This is not limited to the liar and the nonreligious, however, but applies to anyone trafficking in the intricacies of language.

Though an attempt is herein made to point out something basic, something that ought to be included in answers to the question, no dogmatic or doctrinal stand is taken. If, as I believe, religion and psychology must eventually "make sense" to each other, then the subject matter of this chapter is believed to be stated in a form that makes psychological sense without doing violence to religion. Violence has been done to religion from every quarter, even from within religion itself, and by professed representatives of religion. This should be so evident that it should not even be necessary to mention it. There are two major complications in tackling the question of this chapter: basic assumptions concerning religion can differ greatly—for example, as to whether it is good or bad—to put it very generally—and as to how far we can, or should, go in defining religion. Actually, there is no precise limit to dealing with religion. We can, and should, go as far as we have the wit, faith, knowledge, and wisdom to go.

Insofar as God is fundamental to religion this makes for a sort of limitless dimension.

For the present work two things should be said concerning these complications. In the first place, my basic assumption is that religion is good. This assumption seems to rest on at least two important convictions. The first is that most of the things people profess to object to in religion—superstition, authoritarianism, illusions, dogmatism, and the like—are not religion, but distortions of one sort or another. They are due to "tampering hands" that ignorantly or willfully obstruct man's realization of his true destiny—physical health, spiritual wholeness, and righteousness. These distortions are not religion any more than primitive attempts at control of nature, such as magic, are science. They are weeds in the same soil out of which religion grows. Thus, the second conviction is that religion is an achievement, a development, a fruition, and to attempt to define it in terms of its embryonic forms and states is to leave out that which is most important and conspicuous. To try to speak of religion in terms of its maturity rather than its infancy makes our task more difficult, but none the less essential.

1. Religion is loyalty. Whatever one is most loyal to is his religion. It is not too much to say that everyone is loyal to something, that for everyone there is a highest loyalty. This does not mean that a person can always be sure what his highest loyalty is. It may require a test case to prove where one's chief loyalty is to be found. How many hit-and-run drivers have known thoroughly beforehand that they would make such melancholy choices? How many have clearly known that they would be more loyal to their own skins than to the general welfare? Stories of faithful devotees of high loyalties who have been cruelly tested are numerous. Most people escape such drastic testing. Someone says frankly, "I don't have the stuff of martyrdom in me; it's a good thing the situation doesn't depend on what I'd do when the going gets too rough." This does not necessarily prove that the speaker would be a coward, or would fail the test if it should come. People can underestimate as well as overestimate the strength of their loyalty. And people can mistake the identity of their chief loyalty. Self-knowledge is far from a precise and perfected enterprise.

Of course such a definition is too broad, but it is not a definition yet, and it is not supposed to be. It is a necessary starting point. Religion without loyalty is unthinkable. When one contemplates the "things" to which people can be, and have been, loyal—even unto death—what would be omitted? If religion is loyalty, then haven't there been bad religions? Yes, many of them. With the coming of greater and greater understanding many of us will be able to say, "How could I ever have been so misled as to give my chief loyalty to such a false god?" The parade of false gods is a procession whose variety and length are enough to torment the imagination. Through the whole story there has lingered the dream of our being able some day to draw a sharp line between the true and the false. But there has been a persistent tendency to draw such a line too quickly, too sharply, too recklessly.

This part of our definition is too broad in another way. There is no one certain way in which loyalties take hold. It would be worse than naïve to say that every loyalty represents a clear and conscious choice. It would seem almost natural to ask if any loyalty is a thoroughgoing choice made after considering all the facts. Loyalties are the results of a variety of determinants. There are processes of conditioning, loyalties suddenly formed, slow-growing loyalties due to the whole context in which a person lives, deliberately taught loyalties, and unconsciously acquired loyalties. But whatever the object of loyalty, how ever acquired or developed, it becomes a force in one's life.

Two important aspects of this force need to be indicated. One is the psychological process that goes into the formation of one's loyalties. That is to say, all the influences operating upon the individual come together to unite or to do battle within the personality. In other words, the manner of the teaching, conditioning, educating, and influencing will have something to do with the kind of loyalty and its direction. A young man says, "They tried to make me love the Bible, but they only made me despise it." Another says, "My dad loved old Mother Earth, and it burns me up to see things like soil erosion." Still another says, "They always taught me to respect the flag, and I'll be hanged if I stand around and watch you drag it in the dirt." Whether all this vast area will ever be "reduced to a science," it is hard to say. It is not too much to say that we now know more than we ever did about the subject.

The other aspect is concerned with what the object of loyalty does to or for the person. A general question for the whole human race practically asks itself: What can your object of loyalty do for you? It is difficult to think of a larger or a more ambiguous question, but the question is inevitable. What may one expect from his object of loyalty? What does the object of loyalty expect from the subject? What type of loyalty does it demand—abject submission, or critical co-operation? The dramatic story of Elijah on Mount Carmel presents Elijah as asking the Baal worshipers what they think they can expect from their object, or objects, of loyalty. (I Kings 18.) The impressive thirty-sixth verse states Elijah's basic conviction, "Let it be known. . . ." Had a Baal-worshiper been living in the time indicated by chapter 19, could a thoughtful one of their number have asked Elijah as he ran south to escape from Jezebel, "Now what is your god able to do for you?" The biblical narrative records no such reflection on the part of a Baal-worshiper, though Job asks an even more pointed question (7-9), as does Jeremiah (12:1-2), as do countless thousands of other people throughout man's eventful history. The point is, objects of loyalty do something for their subjects. They inspire or destroy; they lead or mislead; they save or condemn. It is even more complicated sometimes. A nonentity in the form of a carved stick, exalted to the rank of a divinity, becomes a force. But the force is not where the worshiper thinks it is. On the other hand, a demagogic dictator may win the fanatical loyalty of willing subjects. He becomes a force. The subjects ascribe power of one kind to him, whereas his real power may be of a different sort—a combination of his own peculiar dynamic and the tragic susceptibilities of his slaves.

The mistakes of the experience of loyalty make all the more significant the whole immense subject of the propriety of any particular loyalty. The inevitability of loyalty of some kind makes the problem of high and highest loyalties a religious problem. Thus, to speak of religion as an illusion is inept and unrealistic. That human nature is subject to illusion is true enough. That false gods too often engage their attention is a wearisome and tragic story. That people give their lives in futile causes is part of the tragedy of history. But to say of religion that it is an illusion provokes two important questions. Is religion something outside human nature that deludes or misleads human nature so that we can point to it and say it is an illusion? Are all false loyalties illusions? If they are, then valid loyalties are not illusions. This would not justify calling loyalty an illusion, however, though it would make as much sense as calling religion an illusion. To put it another way, if human nature is a victim of illusion, where, what, or who is the deceiver? Suppose we should answer, idolatry is the deceiver. Where is idolatry located—in stones, metals, or trees? It doesn't make sense to hold them responsible. So what is being said when religion is called an illusion is that human nature fools human nature. It is, then, purely arbitrary to say that in those instances in which human nature fools itself most extensively . . . *there* is religion.

2. Religion is acquiring or receiving the dynamic to "do." It is a commonplace of human experience: failing to see a difference between knowing what to do and being able to do it. This is a rather large scale generalization wherein a distinction is felt rather than clearly perceived. "Of course knowing what is right doesn't necessarily mean you will do right." Imposing phrases which seem to say a great deal are used to explain the actions of someone who "should have known better." For example, "he suffered a temporary dethronement of reason." This is ordinarily a vague allusion to the general fact that difficulties can develop in the emotional life. Since this is a subject opened up by depth psychology, it is frequently thought that the new science will explain all this.

One fascinating ancient notion of how some unusual people were able to do certain kinds of things was that they were "possessed." A poet for example, was temporarily under the control of a muse. Plato's *Ion* is a classic dealing with this notion. With the waning of notions as to the reality of muses, however, the problem of how to explain or simply to say something intelligible about the condition still remained. What is the ultimate explanation for or stimulus of the creative imagination—and all forms of genius?

Divine inspiration is probably the most significant religious formulation of the idea of receiving dynamic to do. Today, however, many of those concerned with the newer science of depth psychology, who are profoundly and significantly concerned with the dynamics of human doing, are often unfavorable to any such idea as "the Divine." They are likely to explain unusual examples of stimulation or inspiration in a "naturalistic" way. Many of them have an absolutely basic presupposition, presumably not requiring proof or even investigation, which explicitly denies the Divine. For them this is a closed question. Testimony to having received divine inspiration will be judged before being investigated.

At such a point what is it possible to say, conclusively, as to how religion and psychology are—or ought to be—related? Numerous statements are made which are conclusive in form: "Religion is outmoded," "Science is godless," and the like. But the world is not yet prepared to make statements on such large questions which are conclusive in essence. Strictly speaking, we do not yet have adequate evidence or authority. When a prophet says that the Lord took him away from his flocks and sent him to prophesy to a designated group (Amos 7:14-15), we are deeply divided on how to interpret such a claim. Is it a rationalized explanation of what was merely a psychological condition? Is it a report of an authentic experience of being divinely commissioned? To be sure, we know that a physiologist would have something to say about the man Amos, but his explanation would, and should, stay within certain limits. A chemist would have his say, also within limits. If a depth psychologist begins to discuss Amos's report, however, he may not stay within any limits. His explanations might show him to be making or implying some affirmations about the whole universe or the total context of things. For instance, he might assume or affirm that "of course there is no God inspiring or calling or commissioning Amos." Can we be reasonably sure that such an explanation is not double-edged? May not the same type of psychological device to explain Amos's God also be used to explain the modern interpreter's rejection? This is more of a question than a criticism. We may ask, Is the question concerning Amos's God closed? Is the rejection of Amos's God complete and adequately justified?

If some psychologists—not all of them—have tended to close the case with regard to Amos's God in the negative direction, many professed representatives of religion have tended to close the case in the other—the positive direction. It was said above that some scientists could discuss Amos quite satisfactorily and validly within certain limits. It was also pointed out that some psychologists in discussing his report observed no such limits; they make assumptions or affirmations about the total picture. This is not strictly scientific procedure. Amos's statement does have something of an unlimited quality. This has been characteristic of religion generally. We might even say that it is part of religion's "business" to make statements about the total picture. It is in this area that science has often been most critical of religion. It is true that professed representatives of religion have sometimes gone to extremes in not only affirming the reality of God, but also in threatening and coercing others into doctrinal conformity. Some have not, however. Many have in their own minds accepted this conviction, but have been willing to treat it as an open question in their discussions with other people. This brings us to the point of this section. Co-operation and communication are not possible between those who dogmatically close the case negatively and those who close it positively. In such a situation each tries to write the rules and make the assumptions for the "other side." Constructive co-operation is possible only if each allows the great questions to remain open, especially for others.

3. Religion is caring. Those in whom religion has taken hold cannot say, "I don't care." Sometimes people who profess to be religious are

really callous about those who ought to be objects of friendly concern. The book of Amos is a classic in this respect. The prophet attends a religious gathering to rebuke the people who "are not grieved for the affliction of Joseph" (6:6); or, as the Moffatt paraphrase has it, "with never a single thought, for the bleeding wounds of the nation." Caring is not a garment which can be doffed or donned at will. It is an achievement, and in its best form, it is an unlimited concern. Perhaps some people can more easily or readily achieve this condition than others. Just why that should be is no doubt due to many different factors—psychic and cultural. Those who are thoroughly taught hatred for any segment of the human family may find certain kinds of caring difficult to achieve. If by some process one ingests the curdled food of hatred, it will in time seem natural to discriminate, to make invidious distinctions. If we call them unnatural, this is a special use of the term. It is a value use, not a scientific one. In one sense, nothing that happens is unnatural. In this ultra-scientific sense, psychology as a science would not traffic in value judgments. On the other hand, religion is forever valuing. If it is said that Mr. *A's* hatred is natural because he was thoroughly taught and conditioned, then religion will say he should be "converted"—turned in another direction. If he has been taught this hatred in the name of religion, religion in this case ceases to be religion, except in the broad sense discussed earlier in the chapter.

4. Religion is a relationship. A young man was expressing his animosity for a certain other person. After he had made what from a literary point of view could be called a brilliant diatribe, it was suggested that he might try looking for some good quality, or at least a favorable bit of behavior in the other person. The suggestion was routine, a rather obvious thing to say. The following conversation resulted:

"I don't think I'd like to do that," the young man said.

"But maybe it would be a simple little project of getting all the facts. Isn't that a modern ideal made famous by science?"

"Yes, but I'm afraid of what would happen."

"What might happen?"

"Well, I'd probably find something good. . . . I suppose that is what you are hinting at."

"That's no hint. Every copybook in the country has quoted versification about 'a little bad in the best of us, a little good in the worst of us.'"

"But if I found that to be true of Jim, then I might be tempted to start liking him, and I can't stand the thought of that happening."

Perhaps, psychologically, there is some relationship between this simple illustration and the unending and sanguinary narrative of man's hostility toward man. Both are growths, rooted in the soil of human nature. Again we might introduce the term "unnatural." Is hate natural or instinctive, as Freud seems to suggest, or is it unnatural, as Suttie insists? Is hate a normal resident or an alien intruder in human life? At the risk of juggling words we might say that hate is natural but bad. That hate is natural could be interpreted to mean that any specific instance of hate is an inevitable result of some causal sequence. That it is bad means that it is destructive.

Hate is a general name for a virulent type of infection which disturbs human relationships. It can be taught in a variety of ways; it can be acquired in another variety of ways; and it can sometimes be dissolved. It is not the only disruptive force which makes for cleavage and strife. Even hate is sometimes recommended under specific circumstances. A distinguished leader in the field of religious education once said in a conference that it is perhaps a mistake to speak of hate as an unmixed evil, that as a matter of fact we should hate war and other excessive forms of destruction. A prominent American general said, some years ago, that American soldiers did not hate enough. There is not the slightest chance that the two people just quoted would agree on the importance of hate. "Hate the evil" urges Amos, somewhat in the spirit of the first person quoted above. (5:15.) The case of the Jebusites' being "hated of David's soul," however, is a situation closer to the point made by the general. (II Sam. 5:8.)

Relationship is indispensable for adequate communication. Communication is a unique development among human beings. The invention—if it is an invention—of language has multiplied the possibilities of communcation. "Let's talk it over" has far greater possibilities than we may suppose. When communication breaks down, human associations are riven as with an axe. Many things can cause it to break down. Rapport, in the sense of the ability to communicate in the fullest sense, is a high and holy achievement. A religious relationship between human beings can hardly exist without communication. Suppose two people are in hopeless disagreement on some question. *A* says it is thus and so. *B* flatly disagrees. Thus far it does not necessarily mean that communication has broken down or that rapport is rendered impossible. It is still possible for at least one side to leave open some door of possible agreement. For instance, one person might see that the radical disagreement of the other person is due to psychological causes—emotional blocks or frustrations.

Thus, it might be possible to shift the attempt at communication to a consideration of some of the things that really bother the other person.

5. Religion is the perceiving of distinctions. To be sure, all of education of whatever sort involves learning to perceive some kinds of distinctions. An American young person sometime ago was mildly shocked and also amused to be told by a young person from the Orient, "You people over here all look alike." But she had not thought it unusual or shocking or amusing when she had said, "Chinese people all look alike to me." The significance of "to me" in her statement had escaped her—it seemed not to disturb the supposed generality of her statement. Religion in the sense of perceiving distinctions would, or should, tend to concentrate on certain types of distinctions. Basic types of distinctions include those between the true and the false, the good and the bad. One can hear an immense rustling of protest at the very mention of such terms, particularly when they are introduced in connection with religion. In a day when the term "relative" has been put to such a fantastic variety of uses—including the use of the term to denominate a "true view"—one knows that all the rustling is preparation for battle. The problem of the true and the false, and the good and the bad, is one that man must face up to. Sometimes it is a negligible matter. Which is best for me, a brown hat or one not quite so brown? Sometimes it is a life and death matter. Were the Nazi racist theories true? Sometimes the issue hangs in the balance. What is the proper ratio of liberty to authority in government? That people will make distinctions is true enough, but also they often try to escape making distinctions. Suspended judgment, neutrality, deferred decisions, seeing good in both sides, keeping quiet—these are only some of the otherwise useful methods that are employed to try to do what can't be done. All these efforts involve the making of some kinds of distinctions. All are choices of a sort. All are examples of perceiving or of refusal or inability to perceive. To do nothing is to do something. To make no choice is a choice.

Religious distinctions concerning man involve something much more ultimate than distinctions of race, size, appearance, or any of the many measurable distinctions that man is able to record with precision. As measurable and ponderable distinctions become more and more possible, it is quite easy, even natural, to concentrate action and interest on these and to assume that we may safely neglect the others, or even that they do not deserve attention because they do not submit to measurement and precise description generally. "God hath made of one all nations of men" is, in form, a religious distinction and as such is a denial of many of the arbitrary distinctions man makes which seem to have a measurable or ponderable basis. To insist that God placed a curse on Ham and all his descendants is an afterthought that attempts to accord one of man's arbitrary distinctions the high status of a religious distinction. To say that nature has made of one blood all nations of men is to attempt to preserve the essence of a religious distinction without allowing the idea of God to be a religious concern. To wear a new hat to church on Easter Sunday is not a religious enterprise. To worship together without arbitrary and peripheral distinctions of race or social position is a religious enterprise. But some people who would refrain from the latter perform the first almost as an obligation.

It should be fairly obvious that making distinctions concerns every thing that has so far been said in this chapter. In the first place, it is difficult to overemphasize the importance of making distinctions between objects of loyalty. In the terminology associated with religion, this ultimately concerns the distinction between the true God and all false gods, between the eternal God and all cases of created gods, and of imputing divinity. On the latter point Eugene Lyons' article entitled "Dictators into Gods" is as vivid an example of this kind of process as it is possible to find.[1] In the article he assembles examples of poetry-like compositions that refer to certain modern dictators in language normally used to refer to divinity. This is by no means a modern phenomenon. It does suggest, pessimistically, that the world has not matured beyond this naïve or primitive practice. Even the great Roman Senate voted divine status for an emperor. We may believe we know better than this. Indeed we thought, early in the present century, that we were civilized and matured beyond all that. Loyalty to the divine is presumably the highest of loyalties. For those who do not believe in the divine, a substitution is made—some ideal, goal, or worthy cause. These may seem nebulous compared with the idea of reality as applied to God. It is sometimes thought to be more mature to develop loyalty to an ideal goal rather than to any kind of object. Much of the training and indoctrination of the young today is in the interest of loyalty to ideals and causes rather than to objects, such as nations, groups, cults, emblems, or even God. The theory seems to be that we should save whatever idealism that is worthy out

[1] *The American Mercury* (March, 1939), pp. 265-72.

of affirmations concerning the will or purpose of a Divinity, and let the notion of a Being die out.

Distinctions between gods and God, between false gods and true, and between God and non-God are fundamentally religious distinctions. Traffic in a multiplicity of gods raises two very large questions: is the whole idea wrong, or is there some ultimate distinction between the true and the false? This whole subject has been approached from every conceivable angle. Now, long after the events, some distinctions may seem easy to make. A good example is Isa. 44, in which the prophet satirizes the inconsistency of a man who makes an idol to worship from one end of a log, and firewood from the other. Such an arbitrary handling of a log may now seem clearly misguided, how ever much we salute the man's sincerity, although the writer does not. If there is some kind of psychological justification of the man's actions and attitudes, it would be only at an elemental level. It still is a matter of importance as to what one worships. As long as there is a tendency or urge to worship, there will be vital problems of distinctions between the objects of worship, and these are religious problems. We know, or we should know, that it is possible for someone to worship something—whether he would allow the term or not—who, at the same time, might decry and disavow religion.

This introduces a very important distinction—that between different conditions and dispositions in the act of loyalty. If the psychological sciences in dealing with depths of personality have thrown light on this—and they have—there still have been anticipations in the past. It should not be very difficult to see that the condition of the loyalty to God of the three friends of Job leaves much to be desired in their own lives. An interesting addition to the book of Job would have been a bill of particulars appended to the disavowal directed against the three in the final chapter of the book. In the Middle Ages, one interpretation of the seven deadly sins sees them as sins of "disposition." Presumably people guilty of these are nominally and doctrinally loyal to God before they enter purgatory, but their dispositions need extensive renovation. These seven sins were described as sins against love. That is to say, love, fundamentally a supreme condition of loyalty, can, in individual lives, be distorted (pride, envy, anger) defective (sloth) or excessive (avarice, gluttony, lust). This is Dante's arrangement in his "Purgatorio."

Since people need to learn something about loyalty, about the proper objects and the mature conditions, it is a matter of vital importance how all this should be induced. At no point has professional and formal religion erred more variously and extensively than in the modes of inducing proper conditions of loyalty within the personality and in identifying the proper objects of loyalty. The questions of what to teach and how to teach it have directly or indirectly engaged the attention of all societies everywhere. In recent years the highly specialized and professional investigations into the psychology of learning have centered attention on some aspects of why there are failures with certain methods and success with others.

There is still the problem of distinguishing between different types of exemplifying the obligations put on us by the specific loyalties we profess. Putting the problem in religious terms, we ask, How shall we exemplify the purposes of the God in our faith? The standard complaint about this sort of question is, How would you or could you know what those purposes are? On that score it is easier to assume there are not such things as purposes of God. On the other hand, it is also easier to avoid the problem of exemplification of purposes by simply professing a belief and not bothering too much about practicing. This is where much of religious profession breaks down.

The major distinctions concerning the "dynamic to do" are the kinds of dynamic there are and the developing of dynamic. There is a third feature of the whole problem that often presents difficulties: the presence of some powerful and destructive dynamic that has become unmanageable, such as a mania. This is a special form of the first two. At least two aspects of the question have received much attention in the Western world. One has to do with the absence of dynamic—"the good that I would do, I do not"; the other concerns the infusion of power "from on high." The Apostle Paul, psychologist that he was—of the natural sort—discussed and exemplified both of these, whatever interpretations we make concerning them. A modern naturalistic interpretation of "holy spirit" is illustrated in F. A. Spencer's *Beyond Damascus,*[2] in which it is spoken of as "enthusiasm." Whatever we might say of the terminology of, for example, Rom. 7, such a chapter is riddled with references to problems and conditions deep in personality that today will challenge the wit of the best of us to deal with analytically and therapeutically. Perhaps when the enterprises of psychology and religion join hands in co-operative effort, no chapter from ancient writings will be more fruitful with suggestion and hint than Rom. 7.

A young man said, "I was embarrassed and my pride was hurt

[2] New York: Harper & Brothers, 1934.

when I found that I could not stop a habit I had—when at last I wanted to." Whence will he get or how will he develop the dynamic to do? Another young man said, "I could stop that habit anytime I wanted to, but I don't want to." He is probably more naïve than he suspects. So thought the first young man. "Have a smoke?" another was asked. "No," he replied. "Have you sworn off?" "No, I've stopped entirely." With three simple illustrations as a start, we could go on and on into a recital of examples of man's possession or lack of a dynamic to do, and of his varied misunderstandings of the subject. The loftiest religious maturity achieves for man increasing understanding of himself and of his relation to the highest of all possible sources of the dynamic to do—the inspiration that comes from God. That we get beyond the data of our immediate and arbitrary controls is obvious, for we have entered the realm of faith, of trust, and this operates when sight and sense generally fail. This is an area where fantastic failures and distortions are possible—especially if we subtly import into this vicinity of the "burning bush" our hankerings to control and to dominate.

Distinctions between modes and types of caring are important in any consideration of religion. The simplest distinction is that between selfish and unselfish caring. If we personify religion for the moment, we can say that religion knows very well that man's capacities for self-deception are unlimited and that he can very easily fail to make the distinction between a caring that is a subtle love of self, and caring that is nearer to the selfiess love that human beings do and can achieve as they more nearly comprehend and exemplify the truth of religion. It is less than realistic to pour scorn on all the self-regarding virtues, such as pride—not the same type as the first of the seven deadly sins—self-confidence, concern for one's development, self-improvement, and all the rest. But this is done sometimes in a surge of thin perfectionism. Religion is never properly regarded if thought of as a thin, sharp line which one crosses from a reprehensible "selfishness" to pure selflessness. Man is a sinful creature in need of redemption, and those who believe in God believe in his caring, mercy, and redemption. As for man himself, he sometimes cares about salvaging his fellow creature. If we wish to make a distinction in terminology here, we can speak of the higher conceptions of redemption by divine power as salvation, and of man's efforts to rehabilitate his more hapless brother as salvaging. We have a distinction here that is sharp only when it involves faith in a God who redeems. Otherwise, the only kind of redemption is the temporary efforts of human beings during lifetime.

Distinctions between various kinds of relationships can be an ever-present problem. Some of the varieties are fairly obvious, others wildly misinterpreted, and still others only dimly sensed. At least since the time of Plato, there have been discussions of relationships between different aspects of personality. Even Freud sticks to the number three. His discussions of the relationships between id, ego, and superego become far more sophisticated and complex than the Platonic type. The simplest designation of relationship between elements of the personality is that between "head" and "heart." This is given very creditable attention even today in *Ethics and Social Policy* by W. A. R. Leys.[3]

One of the most discredited attempts at a distinction, with all its affirmations and implications, has been that designated by the terms sacred and secular. That is to say, it has been discredited by many moderns who object to what they call this dualism or dichotomy. There is an ambiguity in the use of the terms secular and secularism. Some rejoice in the advance of the secular, and others think of secularism as one of our dominant modern problems. Some questions to be answered are: Is there a fundamental error in the type of thinking and interpretation issuing in a distinction between the sacred and the secular? We at least need to ascertain what people were originally trying to say when they develop this terminology. Was there an allowable distinction in the first place? There was, how ever inadequate it might be by standards available now but not then. We sympathize with human efforts to designate distinctions with the aid and instrumentality of language. There is not just one vast, homogeneous type of existence wherein all notions of value, significance, permanence are so much arbitrary cosmetic to apply to the gaunt face of reality to make it superficially acceptable. If we have already been offered supposedly conclusive explanations of the merely psychological origins of certain ideas, will we eventually be treated to merely psychological explanations of the explanations of our total context of the utterly bleak type? Will we eventually be served merely psychological explanations of merely psychological explanations?

We have interrupted our catalogue of ingredients in religion. What else is religion? Since there is—as there has always been in higher

[3] Englewood Cliffs, N.J.: Prentice-Hall, Inc., 1941.

religion—a strong suggestion of the inexhaustible, we shall limit ourselves to three more components in or of religion.

6. Religion is perfection. Such a concept as this is inevitable among poets, visionaries, dreamers, and in fact all who ponder the themes of change, defect, improvement, goals, aims, achievements. It even appears in the final pages of Darwin's *Origin of the Species*. But it can show up in verbal form at least among those who work with machines and talk of their being perfected. It can be taken for granted that ambiguity would obtain in these usages.

In religious contexts the term is as ambiguous as elsewhere, but just as surely employed. Usage ranges all the way from varied forms of depreciation of mundane perfection to an awed adoration of divine perfection.

Operating aside from and outside the control of received norms, poets like Walt Whitman and Oscar Wilde have had their say about perfection. What these two authors said generally is often a combination of literary genius and individualistic romanticism. The former said in "Song of the Universal" that "the seed of perfection" nestles within "the central heart" of "this broad earth of ours." The latter said in "The Critic as Artist" that it is only "through Art" that "we can realize our perfection." A less romantic note is articulated by Robert Browning in "Old Pictures in Florence": "What's come to perfection perishes."

As a component of religion, perfection tends to take three forms, or to point in three directions: toward eternity, to the divine, and to human life and experience in their variety.

In so far as religion affirms an eternal destiny for man, the notion of perfection is not limited to this world and this life. Beneath the struggle to arrive at a satisfactory connotation for the term, we detect the insistence that perfection refers more to fulfillment and achievement than to any notion of freedom from blemish or sinlessness. The religious emphasis on perfection is not incongruous with a conviction that man cannot be or become sinless. Thus, there is a persistent or recurring emphasis on eternity in religion's grappling with the concept of perfection.

The very existence of religion in human thought and experience is also a conviction of the divine. No concept of perfection makes too much sense without a concept of the Divine, without a source and sanction of perfection, without the support and gift of perfection itself. It is of course possible to think of perfection in purely naturalistic terms, especially if one also entertains a notion of teleology in nature, of potentiality at the heart of matter, or goal-seeking and freedom as capacities of creatures. It is an attenuated type of perfection, however. It would be the only kind we could have if the hypothesis of the Divine were invalid.

As to perfection in human life, one form of this has already been suggested in the preceding paragraph, but there are more advanced forms in the more theistic expressions of religion. In this third type of connotation, it is repeatedly affirmed that the religious mind and heart can never validly say that the limits of human achievement and performance have been reached or that man is ever able to say "I have arrived" or "Now perfection is realized." This is the upper limit of the concept of perfection in the human context. Herein perfection is the constant lure and norm, never the point of arrival. As for the lower limit, the religious component of perfection affirms the importance of dedication to the specific, individual, and lowly task. The religious mind can thus speak of the eternal in the present, of the perfect in the particular.

Also, in the human context, the notion of perfection provides the highest sanction for the individual's sense of unworthiness. This can immediately suggest the modern psychotherapist's struggles with the affliction of a sense of guilt. Those who take an exclusivist attitude toward guilt—namely, that it is simply bad—will take a dim view of relating a sense of unworthiness to any notions of "perfection." But a sense of unworthiness need not be thought of always as merely morbid. It is true that many human beings do become afflicted with morbid feelings which take the form of exaggerated self-recrimination. On the other hand, it would seem inevitable that a sense and intuition of the perfect would engender a sense of unworthiness in those most clearly understanding it.

7. Religion is love. It could be argued that love is the central, primary, and most significant ingredient in anything that is to be called religion. In fact, so much has been said on this theme that it would seem hopeless even to try summarizing the main points.

Today the theme of love has engaged a heretofore unexpected amount of scientific attention—as evidenced by books on the subject written by professionals, particularly in the psychological sciences, to say nothing of discussions, in other professional writings, such as anthropological.

Some particularly complicating features hampering understanding of love are extreme ambiguity of the word, some close associations with biological functionings, intimate relations to emotional and emotionalized conditions, and the ease and subtlety of distortions.

We may list questions that are natural and easy to ask, but which defy facile answering: Is unselfish love possible for human beings? Is love always or primarily an emotion? Does spiritual love have identical psychological roots with carnal? Con love be deliberately and consciously cultivated? Can it be impartial and unemotional? Are there levels of maturity in love? Can love be dissociated from desire? What is the difference between "the love of God" and the "fear of the Lord"? What is involved in loving one's enemies? Can the emotion of hate and the works of love obtain at the same time in the same life? In what sense have we an obligation to love?

We may indicate four basic guides to a consideration of love as a component of religion: God loves, Man should love God, Man should love his neighbor, and Man does love himself. Two of these are simple affirmatives, and two are imperatives. Religion has always been challenged in various ways and by various types of critics, with reference both to its affirmations and its imperatives. A particularly acute form of criticism and challenge has come from competing religions or from within a particular religion. Ultimately these challenges and criticisms involve questions of the true and the good at the highest possible levels. Different periods of history and different critics will stress now questions of truth—the affirmations—and now questions of goodness—the imperatives. Some will borrow significant imperatives—Love thy neighbor—and dispute certain affirmations—God loves the world.

The four guides of the preceding paragraph are listed in what may be called a descending order. Religion at its most affirmative has tended to accept this order. Disagreement is most likely to begin with the first, but criticism rarely ever continues through to the fourth item—that is, criticism in the sense of disavowal. Thus, a development like science, beginning with the fourth item, can cooperatively meet religion coming from the other end of the series. At what point they meet cannot exactly be stated ahead of time. As of the present, it is interesting that both science and religion are using the same word, love.

8. Religion is exaltation. As an ingredient in religion exaltation has only a moderately definable status. In one sense only God is exalted, according to the voices of religion. (Cf. Isa. 2:11.) At the same time, however, the voices of religion have never been silent on the theme of the corruptibility of this notion, and how the exaltation of

baseness opens the doors of wickedness to the sons of men. (Cf. Isa. 12:8.) Sometimes warnings are issued, which have a perennial relevance: "[Beware lest] when thy herds and thy flocks multiply, and thy silver and thy gold is multiplied, and all that thou hast is multiplied; then thy heart be lifted up [exalted], and thou forget the Lord thy God." (Deut. 8:13-14.) Then somewhat between or aside from the foregoing we hear the injunction to "humble yourselves" that God "may exalt you in due time." (I Pet. 5:6.) The ability of man to distort this is too well-known to need reminders.

The foregoing are warnings more than they are promises, connotations, or definitions. Exaltation is first of all a verb and refers to what the mind and the affections do about attitudes toward something. Beyond that it refers to inherent status which may or may not be recognized for what it is. The Lord is exalted. Man exalts—lifts up. When man is exalted, however, through divine recognition or inspiration or through superiority of work or affections, then he is experiencing or participating in religious achievement.

At this point we should turn to a consideration of central facts and primary manifestations of religion. God and faith in God, as central facts, will always challenge the mind and heart of man, the "companion of [God's] eternity." Closely related to these facts are special manifestations of religion such as prayer, worship, and significant institutions and ethical imperatives. Development of these themes would require a volume in itself. We thus limit discussion herein to two themes, the idea of God and the worth of persons—to the first because of its centrality and to the latter because all the foregoing concerns are related to and supportive of such an affirmation.

CHAPTER XII

The Idea of God

WE CONSIDER AT LEAST ONE FORM OF THE QUESTION OF WHETHER and how God may be available to scientific inquiry. We leave aside all the attempts to present arguments, rational or otherwise, for the existence of God; the philosophical and theological attempts at definition and explanation; and the temptation to engage in high-level and large-scale theological polemic. We concentrate on the one question, How may God be or become a datum for scientific inquiry?

It may seem to many that the obvious answer is that God is out of reach of science, or, for that matter, of direct access for any human endeavor bent on direct inspection. Zophar's question-statement comes readily to mind—quite relevantly some will say—"Canst thou by searching find out God?" (Job 11:7.)

In another sense, it seems to have become very easy to introduce God into the orbit of scientific inquiry. When the realization dawns of what is transpiring, the results may be very exciting, or very devastating. On the one hand there is a sense of exhilaration at the prospect of having an age-old question settled so simply and apparently so conclusively. On the other hand, there is alarm and consternation as many people behold the maneuvers of a sophisticated "wrecking-crew" threatening to demolish some of the most revered of institutions.

There are three principal steps in this seemingly simple task of making God a datum for scientific inquiry:

1. Assume to begin with that there is no God.

2. Then change the question "Is God real?" to the question "Is *belief* in God real?" This would change the answer of the first, "God is real," to this answer for the second, "Belief in God is real."

3. The final step is the attempt to explain the genesis of the belief. This is a psychological inquiry.

This seems to simplify the task enormously! What might have appeared to be a futile theological or philosophical task—affirming and validating the objective reality of God—thus becomes, rather suddenly, a simple psychological task of tracing the formation and development of some human ideas and feelings. To put it somewhat technically, we have taken a quick journey from ontology to psychology. Thus, although science in general may often have been involved in complex and irresolvable controversies over the existence of God, now the task seems to be performed neatly and tidily by a particular science, or branch of a particular science, psychology—or some department of it.

According to this explanation, the whole problem of the idea of God becomes a problem of "interior dynamics." It seems to be a matter of relocating the question, of discovering the real locus of the problem. As one reflects on the efforts of creative scientists to address themselves to questions about God, and about what relationship there might be between their scientific innovations and this hallowed idea, their discussions often seem remarkably unproductive. The theological reflections of the great Newton are now respectfully ignored—not that *he* ignored them. Galileo insisted that his work on motion and the universe had no adverse effect on the validity of Scripture. Laplace abandoned the theistic hypothesis. In the twentieth century there has been a remarkable, high-level furore over what some front-rank scientists have done by way of interpretations of our world. For example, Sir Arthur Eddington gave a Swarthmore Lecture entitled *Science and the Unseen World*,[1] and Eric T. Bell in his *The Magic of Numbers* bewails the "return of Pythagoras" as illustrated in the interpretations and speculations of scientists like Eddington.[2]

It remained for a psychologist—not all of them, nor psychology generally—to "dispose of" God neatly and tidily, and to show that the idea was a bit of child's magic—a case of "putting papa in the sky." But there are some problems. The first step in the process, assuming there is no God, is more than ordinarily crucial. Without this first step, it would be difficult to proceed. This sets the stage for the inquiry, for now we have only to study the area of data limited to man. We do not need to try to encompass the whole universe in our inquiries. As we proceed to the third step, we find that we are en-

[1] New York: The Macmillan Company, 1930.
[2] New York: McGraw-Hill Book Company, 1946.

gaged in a genetic study, and the idea, heretofore thought to be so magnificent and awesome, now shows up as somewhat shabby and infantile.

The first step, strictly speaking, is a remarkable begging of the question. We assume to begin with the very thing that subsequent steps will seem to explain. How was the nonreality of God proved in the first place? None of the steps—here condensed into three—touches on this problem. All the while, it is the infantile idea that is being explained. What happens in the process to all the noble and elevated elements in the many attempted expositions of the idea of God? According to the three steps, all these must have been mere accretions that were arbitrarily and perhaps unconsciously added later. All the relationships between the idea of God and the moral and spiritual imperatives encumbent on persons would have to be classed as mere accretions also, added to the struggle of the child and of its continuing childishness, regardless of advancing chronological age, to cling to childhood securities and to entrap them in ideas beyond the reach of both mortal change and the challenge to mature.

It might be asked by our investigator taking these steps in his genetic study of an idea whether or not we have overlooked something. It may be asked whether the burden of proof for the validity of the idea of God does not rest on those who affirm the reality of God. This is a fair question. We hasten to remind ourselves that question-begging is not limited to any one group. It has been a notorious fallacy in the history of religious affirmations and religious arguments. Much time and effort have been spent in proving the existence of God after his reality had been assumed in the first place. Such "proofs" have often been sophisticated after-thoughts, and it is doubtful that very many of them have convinced anyone who had not already accepted the conclusion. The one-sidedness of many of these proofs is a fault in addition to the primary question-begging. Consider for example the famous "proof" stated in the first chapter of William Paley's *Natural Theology,* usually dignified by the title "cosmological argument."

> Suppose I had found a *watch* upon the ground, and it should be inquired how the watch happened to be in that place; I should hardly think of the answer which I had before given [to explain the presence of a stone]. . . . For this reason, and for no other, viz. that, when we come to inspect the

watch, we perceive (what we could not discover in the stone) that its several parts are framed and put together for a purpose.[3]

Of course the inference, as he understands it, is inevitable, "the watch must have had a maker." [4] The one-sidedness of the illustration may be suggested in this way: suppose that instead of a watch, our hypothetical finder comes upon a pair of brass knuckles, a saw-toothed bayonet, a time bomb, a crooked roulette wheel, or for that matter something more complex—an innocent person suffering incredible pain at the hands of malignant tyranny. In all these there would be evidence of some kind of "deliberate purpose." But with most of them, one could very well hope he would never be involved. Moreover there might be occasion in some of them for the kind of response we find in Job 3, 7, and 9.

If the watch implied the presence of a purposeful creator, or watchmaker, from materials supplied already by some previous "creator of the materials," the crooked roulette wheel would tend to imply the presence of someone with a sardonic sense of humor, if not something worse. Also, would the presence of a variety of purposeful arrangements suggest a multiplicity of creators or arrangers?

It seems simple, fair, and obvious enough to ask those who affirm the reality of God to assume the burden of proof. We may well ask how man comes by the idea in the first place. This is precisely the question our psychologist professed to answer in the three steps. If we are to assume he is arguing the ultimate origin of the idea, certainly we can think of a variety of secondary explanations. Most people who profess to believe in God have come by the idea through education, through some kind of influence exerted by the words, actions, or training of other people, or through some other type of associations with people. The idea is already established in the social world into which they are born. Moreover, they may even do some studying of the many available documents already in existence after they themselves have come upon the scene. This should seem fairly obvious. But we need to go further.

In the light of that, we may ask whether anyone could acquire the idea if not exposed to it somehow in human experience. There does not seem to be a society, so far as we know, without some idea of God, gods, or supernal spirits. Some people have tried to use this to support their contention that the idea of God is natural or instinctive.

[3] Boston: Lincoln, Edmands & Company, 1831, 1833 ed., p. 5. Italics in the text.
[4] Ibid., p. 6.

On the other hand, two exceptions to the claim that all societies have some kind of idea of God are the Buddhist religion and the Andaman Islanders. It would be better to say they are offered as exceptions, though they have been challenged as to whether they are genuine exceptions. Into this complex problem we need not go at the moment. More to the point we might ask whether someone like Kamala[5] would ever develop an idea of God. A definitive answer is probably out of the question. Such experiments are rare and what they have to offer is too inconclusive even to suggest the direction the evidence might eventually take. The question is natural, however. Would a whole society of Kamalas reenact what the race has already done? Would they develop the same kinds of ideas of God and gods as has been done through the past? Would the ultimate explanation be what our psychologist says? But would this explanation apply primarily, if not solely, to those who originated the idea? True, if the explanation is valid, the emotional experiences of the individual might be a support for the idea, until he grew up emotionally and intellectually.

We are omitting something, however. Our psychologist in his three steps makes use of some other presuppositions: there is no such thing as a spiritual experience that would confirm the reality of any divine presence; there is no such thing as revelation; there are no rational, philosophical, theological, or experiential arguments whatever that could confirm the reality of a divine dimension; mystical experience has no objective reference or contact that could be called the Divine Presence; any and all "flashes of spiritual insight," and "leaps of faith" have no validity whatever as support for a theistic hypothesis.

There have been alternative suggestions as to how the idea of God developed or originated. Moreover, it is a fair question, as suggested above, as to where the burden of proof for establishing the validity of the idea resides. This is by no means a clearly defined requirement, however. Put simply, it seems to ask whether there are other suggestions—beyond those of our psychologist—substantial enough to support a theistic affirmation. To put it crisply, What is the proof? Today the phrase "scientific proof" has a conclusive sound. But proof is not solely a scientific notion. Scientific proof, however, implies a most rigorous set of rules for certain kinds of procedure, and it may seem to imply that scientific proof ought to convince people. But this is exactly what it often fails to do. Proof of whatever kind often fails

[5] See page 145.

to do so. We therefore had better open up the problem more than is ordinarily done.

In the first place, there are various kinds of proof. Whether they can eventually be subsumed under one general category, it is hard to say. Some confusion obtains concerning the idea of proof when, for example, some people attempt to grapple with the famous quotation "The exception proves the rule." Some will ask, "How can an exception be proof for the rule?" Or they may say, "That doesn't make sense." The meaning of the statement presumably is obvious—that the exception confirms the rule. It escapes notice that for the statement to make sense it must be interpreted as saying that the exception puts the rule to test—probes. Thus, we might say that a common type of proof is consistent repetition, or rather it has the force of proof. It is easy enough to say no operation in the past proves, in necessary fashion, its recurrence in the future. This would not be called proof in any strict sense. It is rather like power to persuade or convince. Critical attention to the subject of proof regards only the objective processes that lead—conclusively if possible—to an allowable conclusion, irrespective of any psychological, emotional, or intellectual responses. Another sort of proof is provided by sense experience: "Take a look and you will see"—the question will be proved by the seeing. It has long been known that optical illusions, mirages, hallucinations, and similar eventualities make proof by sense experience something less than ideal. Yet, it provides a powerful appeal. Then there are intellectual and logical proofs—that there are at least two trees in the forest with exactly the same number of leaves on them. Certain authorities are accepted as proof, although how the authority became an authority will involve some prior kind of proof. Also it is well recognized, in general, that authorities may differ, and the individual authority may err.

Is there a special type or mode of proof that would be available to only a few people, or only to one? This is the type of question that modern science would resist, as far as it concerns such problems as proof, evidence, and verification. In science, the type of proof emphasized is the kind that can be repeated, that is accessible to anyone anywhere who wishes to re-enact the process, that can be communicated to others. Thus, the mystic who speaks of his experience of the "ineffable" is not taken seriously by science with its public, sharable rules for establishing proof. As is obvious, however, the emphasis is on the procedure, and not on the unique features of persons and personalities—their responsiveness, their resistance, their too-eager or their too-delayed acceptances. To be sure scientists are entirely agreeable to accepting the flash of insight that comes, he knows not how, to the creative scientist who formulates a new principle. Once it is formulated, the rules for proof will be applied. The suddenness of the flash of insight is much more apparent than real, however. Moreover, scientists would not recommend any method for the inducing flashes of insight, largely because they would not know what sort of method to recommend. Finally, the scientist's flash of insight is in a much more natural area than that with which the mystic is concerned. Any attempt to induce or conjure up mystical experiences is considered by all scientists and many representatives of religion to be very dubious procedure.

To put the question of the preceding paragraph differently, Is it conceivable that there may be special and austere types and modes of proof that involve the interior life in a way that scientific proof does not? It has long been thought that there are such experiences —inner experiences that have their own rationale of mode, method, and result. But the emphasis is often, if not always, on the power for conviction rather than the details of the procedure since these are too subtle for direct observation and description. Admittedly it is not easy to adduce sharply outlined and describable examples. This very admission could be taken as a point against entertaining such a notion. We have already noted that there are two very large considerations in the problem of proof: the method of proof and the capacity to apprehend and comprehend. Perhaps capacity and readiness for conviction—being conquered—may be classed as a third. There can be a distinction between being intellectually convinced and being convicted to the point of some kind of profound commitment that can even change a personality. We attempt to give one illustration.

This comes from the story of Elijah. It is offered more for purposes of discussion than as clearly illustrating anything that can be called proof in the strict sense. However, there is a sentence in the story that is at least linguistically related to the problem of proof. Elijah said, "let it be known this day that thou art God in Israel, and that I am thy servant." (I Kings 18:36.) Then, in the words of the story, Elijah gets all he asks for. When Jezebel is informed, however, she shows up as remarkably unconvinced. She threatens Elijah and he leaves the country. (19:1-3.) Then, as the account proceeds, Elijah himself shows up as either unconvinced, or subject to stronger powers. Yet, he eventually does return, in strength. The only explanation of this renewal is contained in the strange phrase "a still small voice." (19:12.) This whole account would raise numerous questions today, from various quarters. For instance, it would be stoutly asserted that this "experiment" could not be duplicated. This would rule it out as being something science would call an application of the rules of scientific proof. There are two realistic touches in the ancient document, however—resistance to conviction and susceptibility to conviction. These themes have long engaged the attention of innumerable people. We have sought for clarity on the modes and methods for the proof that carries its own convicting power—but we would need to add something extremely controversial here: power for the true and the good.

Thus, in the third place, there are two areas of convincingness. We may designate these, using colloquial language for the moment, as an "inside" area, and an "outside." The scientific method for proving has its convincingness outside, in the method itself. This is irrespective of the person. Anyone can apply it who has the minimum preparation for doing so. It is completely depersonalized, beyond its being something that must be operated by persons. It is even conceivable that a person might go through the process and not be convinced! The methodology for convincing, for presenting proof in the inside area, can be described only vaguely. There has long been a certain amount of practical knowledge on how to convince people of something, and any number of individual performers have worked at this. They cannot always be said to employ well-defined methods of proof, but they have worked successfully at the problem of convincing people. They know rough and ready, or sometimes very refined, methods for persuading. Today there is a tremendous volume of new material on processess of conditioning which can bypass the slower and less universally successful methods of proving or convincing, whether we speak of inside or outside. The pale, cool world of objective scientific proof, awaiting the capacity of persons to accept its deliverances seems lame and ineffectual as compared with the universal competence of a "brave new world" of built-in conclusions that do not need to go through a process of proof.

Is there, then, a method of proof that is appropriate to internal areas of experience and inquiry, that may operate in a world of experience that cannot be completely objectified, that is directly related to and operable in a condition that depends upon a capacity to be convinced or convicted? If science itself says that it cannot positively and objectively prove or disprove the reality of God, it would seem to open the question of whether there might be other methods. The scientific methodology for proving depends on certain human capacities both for operating it and for understanding its results. Is it conceivable that a conviction of the reality of God depends on both its own particular methodology and on the capacity and readiness of the subject to be convinced and convicted? If we say anything at all on the subject of the burden of proof and its resting on those who affirm the reality of God, we can start by pointing to a tremendous body of material of varied sorts testifying to the reality of God—all the way from reports of psalmists and prophets of ancient times to an able, sophisticated treatise such as William E. Hocking's *The Meaning of God in Human Experience.* It would be an extremely bold and reckless maneuver to write all this off in any peremptory fashion, whatever the reasons offered.

In the fourth place, with so ample a body of profession and testimony, it is at least allowable to open the question of whether there may be a possible relationship with a resource that participates in the relevant methods and in the experience of proof and conviction. If we complain that such a method is not within our control, we unwittingly assume that it ought to be. This may reveal our naïveté even more than it would testify to the supposed limitations of the method. There are limitations even to the most assured methods we now have. It is difficult enough to try to prove by the scientific method that our friends love us or that they ought to. Yet, we are sometimes persuaded and convinced by some other method that they do—though limitations may obtain here also. That some kinds of limitations attend all methods, we may assume. Particular methods of proof may be limited to restricted areas of data, or there may be limitations of response. The pendulum in the Peabody Museum at Yale University that proves something about the shape and motion of the earth is a sterile proof to a bevy of penguins. Many human beings profess not to understand the Pythagorean theorem. "Doubting Thomas" is a widely used term, extolled by one group, lamented by another. The will to do and the compulsion not to do present a conflict resolved by some kind of integration under more powerful auspices. It is commonplace to say that to know is not necessarily to do.

There are limitations in our conception of objective proof, but they are often concealed when we advance to an assumption that there are no such limitations. Thus, we demand that all suggestions submit to our limited rule, whereas it may be that the method is relevant only to a restricted area. We sometimes assume that proof leads to knowledge. But there are also proofs—granted that they may be of a different kind—that induce faith, belief, conviction, daring, or risk. These are far from the harnessing conditions laid down in W. K. Clifford's spirited dictum.[6]

We have been led unavoidably into a consideration of persons. Persons formulate principles and methods of proof, but persons are capable of such resistances that proofs will fail to prove. If in any sense "the heavens declare the glory of God" (Ps. 19:1), the only creatures to appreciate and be convinced are persons. If there is no God, then man is the only creature to have thought up the idea, and in its matured fullness, it is an idea of tremendous depth and scope. So if there is God, then a person is the only focus of realization and the only center for receiving the revelation of God. He is the only receptor capable of registering the proof and the only arena for the generation of conviction. He is the only creature to formulate whatever methodologies may validate the divine reality, and the only species to contemplate modes of proof too subtle for direct observation and formulation.

Our task is not to seek, as the *sine qua non* for the validation of the reality of God, some method of objective proof. Objective proof is scarcely more than an elementary step in the totality of human experience. The advancement of knowledge itself is secondary to the conviction of and participation in purpose. What purposes? Divine purposes if such there be. The most mature of human purposes if they are the only ones. In the latter, man becomes his own god, his own source of far-reaching and long-range purposes. Also he becomes the formulator of whatever methods he can discover or create and the agent and beneficiary of any fulfillment of these purposes. Again, it is the second of these two concerns that is crucial.

The two central and inclusive attributes of the divine, after we have dismissed or transcended the whimsical and arbitrary activities of the multitudes of mythological divinities, are power and purpose. In so far as God is related to the whole universe, through sheer creativity at least, any integral part of the universe is an exemplification of that power. It is only the human person that can be related to the divine through participation in conscious fulfillment of purposes. The story of mankind is the story of endless and grotesque fallibilities in man's evasions and errors. At the same time man has given occasional and luminous evidence of grasping and translating noble purposes into

[6] Cf. *supra* p. 116.

fulfillment in human life. What actually has man done with regard to the idea of God? We briefly consider three general types of answers to this question.

The first we may call distortions. Man has persistently represented God, or the gods, physically. He has claimed for himself or his group special favors and, conversely, special disfavors for enemies. He has exhausted the vocabulary of abuse in damning the enemies of his gods. He has checked over the entire furniture of heaven and earth in a search for gods or god surrogates. He has sought control of his gods, maneuvering or coercing them into the support of his desires. He has "created" gods in profusion. He has on occasion tried to be God. All this is elemental, primitive, and often obstructive. It is possible to grant certain kinds of concessions when we find him dedicating himself to his god. In so far as he, how ever mistakenly, thought of his god as a superior and beneficent force, his sincere dedication to his highest may have some elements of promise, some indication of serviceable potential—depending on eventual maturing in outlook and social vision.

The second we may call the more advanced conceptions of God. Here we find those examples, how ever rare they may have been, of God as "experienced," as "found" and responded to in some kind of "call." In so far as these are considered evidence of transcendent reality, it is not difficult today to speak of such examples as merely psychological experiences with no objective reference. The use of the term "merely" can be one of the most arbitrary of all reductive devices for demoting something. Usually its use is not supported, as though the appropriateness of its use were obvious to all concerned. It is a preliminary term of evaluation introducing a supposedly descriptive report. Thus, it could be designated figuratively as Occam's "battle axe."

Advanced examples of the idea of God include dedication and commitment that often carry persons beyond their normal power and status as human beings. If God is not real, these dedications and commitments are nevertheless thought to be responses to the holiest demands the mind is capable of understanding and responding to. Man has been challenged to the utmost by his idea of God. In God's name he has challenged and opposed the degenerate, the primitive, and the destructive.

The third type of answer presents the conflicts that can arise in man's thinking and wondering about God and about the instructions that have been given him by his predecessors, who may have been noted for their inconsistency and incompleteness. Thus we find man involved in some puzzles. God is said to be omnipresent, yes, but he is also hidden. He is declared to be omnipotent, but he cannot replace amputated arms, though he is often credited with physical miracles. He is severe in judgment, as well he might be; he is tender in mercy, and it is not always clear why he should be. He is repeatedly reported to have destroyed; yet we proclaim his redemptive power and purpose. He allows the whole of creation to be darkened by the shadow of death; yet we believe he saves unto eternal life. He is great in power and majesty, but *I* and *I* alone can shut him out.

Ever since beginning to wonder, speculate, experiment, and to articulate questions, answers, explanations, and formulations, man has occasionally been reasonably successful in some of these efforts. Eventually he has been able to clear up some supposed mysteries. We are now living in a time when he is caught between possibilities, or seeming possibilities, that on the one hand lure him toward achievements of a secularly millennial sort, or on the other hand threaten him with utter disaster. It is easier now, through improved means of reading the past and recording its story, to assess past performances. It is also easier to see greater and vaster possibilities of achievement that man can bring about himself, if. . . . Thus, we well may ask, what are some of man's more recent explanations? Has man at last explained energy? Has he solved the problem of space travel? Is life about to be explained, and perhaps synthesized? Is polio now controllable? Will we soon be able to "mine" the ocean? Need we no longer be apprehensive about our dwindling oil, gas, and coal reserves? Has science finally become able to analyze, define, and control personality and personal behavior? Do we see more clearly some prospects for dealing with the problem of justice? Are we getting ready to manage the population problem in our world of two centuries hence?

To single out one special question from the long list, Has science at last explained the idea of God adequately? Perhaps there are many who are ready to say yes—read Freud or Money-Kyrlie or any one of a number of authors to be found in almost any library. Yet, it is too early to assess the full and eventual force of this explanation, given more or less in the name of science. It has already been intimated that the process, condensed into a three-step description earlier in this chapter, is not conclusive, that the question is not closed in the sense that questions about Thor might be considered closed. Thus, we turn to a brief reconsideration.

For the moment we return to the pattern of Chapter II. If God is real, and real in the sense of supervening purpose, then we as persons are uniquely related to this purpose in the largest possible way. We are not only created things, we are participants in purposeful existence and activity, even in purposes beyond our immediate comprehension. We become involved in problems of drive and direction that meet us at the limits of our understanding and control, from the "fire shut up in [the] bones" of Jeremiah (20:7-9) to Francis Thompson's "Hound of Heaven." Problems of proof cannot possibly be limited to the usual and standard canons of objective demonstration available to any detached and uninvolved spectator. The results of these special modes of proof—if indeed we may call them that—are more than knowledge, yet not antagonistic to or different from knowledge.

It may even be pointless to say to Job, "If you say you know your Goel lives, tell me how you came by that knowledge, so that I may check it for its validity." He might say, "You will have to go through what I went through." Such an "experiment" could not be arranged at will, however, partly due to complexities. Further than that, we suspect that a large company of Jobs would not be in precise agreement as to the how and what of this knowledge. There would be undetectable variables. Thus, it may seem simpler to say that all such experiences as those of Jeremiah, Francis Thompson, and Job are merely something we can describe. Also, it is easier to do this if we assume to begin with that there couldn't be any external reference that has anything whatever to do with conscious purpose, divine initiative, or deliberate guidance and inspiration from "beyond," or from God. It seems easier to assign all these experiences to the same category—perhaps "rationalized verbalizings of compulsions, yearnings, and frustrations, which are projected onto some of our own ingenious creations in a supposed spirit world."

On the other hand, if God is not real, we still are uniquely involved in purpose and purposes. We still exemplify the development of conscious purpose, or the capacity for conscious purpose, in a universe or total context of purposelessness. In so far as we are capable of conscious purpose, we are the only creatures of whom that could be said, and we had to wait for the development of language for that to happen. If we were all to perish, the universe would have to "wait" a long time for this ever to happen again. Nature, so long thought of as purposeful, was eventually depersonalized and divested of the operations of final causes. Modern astronomy and kindred enterprises have ushered the once revered Host out of our cosmic "mansion" and in the process show this mansion to be, for the most part, notoriously unfit for habitation. The once revered "celestial spheres" are now seen as much less inviting than the formerly discounted terrestrial region. The latter also was demoted, however, from a location at the center to a spatially insignificant little orbit in a minor solar system in a small galaxy dwarfed by larger ones, and all more or less lost in the vaster reaches of illimitable space. Yet, an occasional astronomer can be found who will say, "In my Father's universe are many dwelling places," which is not meant to be an affirmation of heaven. It is a more secular speculation that there may be life on other "worlds." This might imply that wherever there are persons, there is capacity for conscious purpose.

The point is, that if God is not real, then we are alone in the exercise and fulfillment—if there is to be fulfillment—of conscious purposes. So far the conclusion has not been generally drawn that, on the assumption of our cosmic "loneliness," it doesn't matter what we do since we are only flickering lights of ephemeral reality between two immensities of oblivion. On the other hand, the very psychology that professes to have discovered the idea of God to be simply a construct with no objective reference has also pointed out the inadequacy of personality without purpose or direction, without participation in purposeful concerns. Man who, according to some, appears in this universe as an accident, and who, according to others, cannot depend upon any theistic hypothesis, is left as the sole agent and actualizer of conscious purpose. Today he is confronted with challenges and opportunities that are unparalleled, that are unique. He is faced with two dour prospects: (1) he could fail, and (2) he is an orphan in the cosmic scheme in a most radical sense. The human child in human society needs parentage, affection, help for development of a sense of meaning, and guidance in purpose. We lament the circumstances that make orphans of some of them. We offer training in work with the orphan problem. We have coined the term "orphanage," and we have established such institutions, looking forward to better solutions for these problems. But a cosmic orphan is in a natural orphanage—there is no other place for him. He must make it into a mansion through his own actualizing of conscious purpose. It will be the only mansion he will ever have—but of course he could make it into a shambles.

If there seems to be no basis for the idea of God, yet there is no escape from the problem of purpose—except in some drastic fashion: pathological, suicidal, or by insulation. However, the understanding of purpose as related to and integrated with the purposes of God is probably more difficult of apprehension and fulfillment than purely human purposes. In this connection let us try to see what point there may be in the idea of God.

We consider the phrase in three aspects: connotation, a referend for the term "God," and meanings.

The word "God" has had numerous connotations. A common accusation against many of these has been that they were anthropomorphic. Whether this is always thought to be discrediting we cannot say. If so, it would mean that representing God in human terms would cast doubt on the whole idea. But this would overlook the fact that much of the rejection of the idea of God can be even more definitely and rigorously anthropomorphic. Often God is assumed not to be real since he does not do what it is taken for granted that he will do. He is assumed not to be real because he does not do certain things that might be expected of a God—eliminate pain and suffering, establish justice, explain himself, et cetera. This says that if he existed as we think he ought to exist, he would do the things we think ought to be done. These are human standards with vengeance. It is hard to think of anything more anthropomorphic than such a line of thought.

There are certain limiting factors in the use and significance of the term "anthropomorphic." It is by no means clear yet as to what, precisely, the "morph" (form) of "anthropo" (man) is, either originally or ultimately. Also, it is much more anthropomorphic to say that God has "fists"—like a man's—as has sometimes been said on the basis of Prov. 30:4 (K.J.V.), than to say God's ultimate purposes are redemptive, that he struck someone with a bolt of lightning, than his mercy is from everlasting to everlasting. In the third place, the charge of anthropomorphism may imply a request for us to talk in terms we do not understand and have no direct access to—firsthand, objective acquaintance with the divine—rather than in terms we do understand at least partially and with which we have some direct experience—the human scene and human experiences.

The problem of the, or a, referend may seem the most crucial. The desire to see God, to locate him in a place, to catch him at work, to apprehend him directly in some kind of sense experience such as touch, hearing, or sight—all these lure man, even the skeptic, into statements of requirements that God must meet if he is to convince us. On the other hand, the affirmations that not any of these are possible or likely will affect people variously. That they are relevant requirements has never been made clear. Such proofs of God's existence could never guarantee resultant commitment to his purposes. Compared with this commitment, mere belief in his existence is a side issue, if an issue at all.

A more immediate question, in the light of Chapters III and IV, would be, What has man been trying to say when he has talked about God? Granted a large amount of the strange and fanciful, we still need to know what else man has been trying to say as he has endeavored to talk about God. It is not easy to give a thoroughly relevant and illuminating analogy. In general we may say man has been trying to give a name to something he identified as a type or dimension of reality. That he made innumerable mistakes we know—carving gods of wood or stone, locating a god in this grove or on that mountain, detecting a divine visitation in the informalities of inebriation, and so on. Did he make nothing but mistakes? Here we are "at the mercy" of our presuppositions and our convictions as to what questions are open and what questions closed. Ultimately this will involve our notions concerning the total context as well as understanding crucial parts, e.g., man. Superficially this may seem to put a damper on all conversation and questioning, as it is impossible to dispense with all presuppositions. As to the present theme we have two that are variously used and interpreted: the presupposition that all questions about God are closed, and the question of whether pre-suppositions about God are or can be fruitful. I would say no to the first, and yes to the second.

What are the meanings associable with the idea of God? Better yet, what is the meaning of this more than ordinarily unmanageable idea —what is the meaning of its persistent presence in human experience? Is there a single and simple explanation? Let us try to suggest some aspects of meaning that go beyond the simplicity of our psychologist's explanation, and through the door that he has closed as to allowable assumptions. In the first place, man, in grappling with the idea of God, often sees, how ever dimly, his own responsibilities. And with the idea of God these have a validity and comprehensiveness not otherwise possible. In the second place, man develops skills in evading or avoiding any identification with these responsibilities, and he often knows that he does. Again, in tracing out, as he can, the implications of the idea, he sees his own need of mercy, even as he is often reluctant to grant it to his fellow creatures. Furthermore, he needs, and may realize that he needs, the infusion of some supporting dynamic for the assumption of responsibilities. He cannot do the whole job himself. Finally, for present purposes, he sees in the idea the affirmation of an ultimate context for persons. This seems a thoroughly reasonable expectation, in spite of those who ridicule it and whatever their reasons.

There is some ingenuity in the explanation of the origins of the idea of God that has been offered under Freudian auspices or as a result of Freudian influence. That the Freudian influence has been powerful and extensive is well known. A small boy breezes into an office and says, "Well, Professor, shall I lie down and tell you my dreams?" thereby illustrating some of the far-reaching influence of Freudian terminology, whatever the measure and content of understanding. That Freud and Freudianism are neither entirely accepted nor entirely rejected is strikingly illustrated by discussions of the Freudian contributions such as Paul Johnson's *Personality and Religion* and Roy S. Lee's *Freud and Christianity,* to name only two from a host.[7]

The Freudian theory of the reality and dynamic functioning of the unconscious could turn out to be more important, more useful, better validated, and more lasting, than the Freudian notion of the illusory nature of the idea of God. The former stays within the general area of personality and psychology. The second either ventures into or blandly assumes something in cosmological and theological areas. It does seem a bit odd to base an explanation of a development within human experience, within personality, so confidently on a negative cosmological and theological premise. The former can claim some degree of scientific verification—not that this has not been challenged by many scientists. But the latter forever eludes scientific verification and is probably as much of a rationalization as any theistic presupposition. If, as Money-Kyrlie has said, there is no "empirical verification" for the idea of God, this is based on a bland assmption that there should be—a gratuitous assumption. Yet, the late Edgar Sheffield Brightman spoke of "empirical" arguments for the reality of God.[8]

[7] Johnson *op. cit.* Lee (New York: A. A. Wyn, Inc., 1949).

[8] R. Money-Kyrlie in *British Journal of Medical Psychology,* XI, Part 3, 173-93. "Empirical Approach to God," *Philosophical Review* (March, 1937), pp. 46, 147-69.

CHAPTER XIII

The Worth of Persons

Violation and Affirmation

THE 1924 EDITION OF WEBSTER'S NEW INTERNATIONAL DICTIONARY does not contain the word "genocide," but later editions do. The appearance in our language of this macabre term has been due to a series of plans and events violating the principle of the sanctity of persons. The extent to which these plans and events moved has probably established a record for the twentieth century.

To speak of establishing a record may be merely sensational language—pessimism reaching for a superlative. Yet, any catalogue of specific examples, any listing of names of notorious perpetrators of special violations, any recital of possible and probable reasons for such excesses would by their very volume and ghoulish quality challenge the mind's capacity for comprehension and credulity.

To single out specific countries and governments—and such large scale organizations have been involved—could provoke the most intense and explosive kind of controversy. Yet the very extent and ferocity of the violations are too vast for evoking righteous indignation. Beyond a certain point, perhaps never determinable, the very magnitude of horror reports exerts a numbing effect on the mind's capacity for critical response or emotional reaction. Thus, it needs to be pointed out that the intense controversy referred to above would be the work primarily of those adjudged most guilty, and no numbing process lessens the violence of their unrighteous indignation. Protestations of "non-guilt" come most explosively from the most guilty—though there may be exceptions to this strange state of affairs.

To list names of individual people as perpetrators of this special type of violence might be less controversial than to make cases against whole governments. This would be true particularly in the case of publications of "confessions" by key people in some of the genocide programs of this century. An example is the "autobiography" of Rudolf Hoess, *Commandant of Auschwitz,* translated from the German by Constantine FitzGibbon.[1] This work seems not to have occasioned any public furore, either for the magnitude of the offense or public determination to see to it that there be no recurrence. Some reviewers say "it should be read." If this suggestion has proceeded on the assumption that the knowledge gained will help prevent recurrences, one may well wonder. Since World War I there has been a series of attempts to build on this assumption, including the publication in the twenties of pictorial records to show what violence and destruction are possible in modern war, but especially the symposium entitled *What Would Be the Character of a New War?*[2] This latter was characterized by *The New Statesman* of January 2, 1932, as "the most terrible book which has ever been written." The publisher wrote that "no one could read . . . Dr. Woker's contributions on Chemical and Bacteriological Warfare without making a resolution . . . to prevent the coming of such abominations: and if people can be made to take this first step, they may be led on to the discovery of those economic and psychological factors which, in their inter-relation, are the cause of modern warfare." [3] Much—perhaps the worst—of the violence perpetrated against persons in this century has not been directly related to war—in the official and formal sense. It has been the results of willingness to violate the principle of the worth of persons, to deny any and all forms of human rights, to coerce, to desecrate, to slaughter people secretly or openly with or without justification, or pretended justification. It is easy to say, therefore, that the great need for our troubled world is the converting of the people of the world to loftier principles, deeper convictions, commitments to norms, standards, and ideals. It would be less easy to specify the methods or the procedures for implementation.

As for affirmations of our principle, we encounter a startling fact —the present century has not only been characterized by excessive violations of the principle of the worth of persons, but also by frequent affirmations of this principle. Occasionally the affirmation takes the form of extended argumentation. It would be difficult to envision a more striking contrast. The phrase "dignity of man" has, in fact,

[1] Cleveland, Ohio: The World Publishing Company, 1959.
[2] London: Victor Gollancz, Ltd., 1933.
[3] *Ibid.*, "Foreword."

been reiterated enough to lead at least one author to say that "stale repetition" of the phrase "seems a political commonplace, and useless to repeat again." [4] In succeeding pages we present examples of affirmations that transcend the charge of stale repetition and that illuminate and illustrate this most startling contrast of our century.

Some years ago I began to notice the extent to which the phrase "worth of persons" or some equivalent, such as "sacredness of personality," was showing up in a variety of places and in numerous contexts. The question arose as to what this signified. We shall assemble a limited number of representative quotations and advance some possible explanations.

Certain warnings are in order. The phrases differ here and there, but there is a sufficient similarity so that we may say they have a family resemblance. Even the few exceptions will have their place in our considerations. It is not always possible to know precisely what definitions the authors have in mind for terms like "sanctity" and "inherent." Usually, the crucial phrase is mentioned without discussion as to how it is to be validated, though it is no doubt assumed this could be done or had already been done. No references are made, however, to any definitive work that has performed this service of validation.

Because of severe space limitations, the following list is very short, so much so as not to be adequately representative. Many showed up in general reading. It is not always known where to look for them, even for some of the most significant. Occasionally a lone sentence in a book or article will contain the vital phrase as though it had already been generally agreed upon, not requiring discussion. Contents and indexes do not always furnish clues to whether respective volumes will contain or subscribe to this tremendous affirmation. There is some effort to classify examples. The guide to the classification is the context in which the author puts the statement or claim: ethical, political, religious, et cetera.

The first references link the concept of worth with religion: "On the primitive level . . . the individual is largely lost in the group. . . . Only on the higher levels, when genuine religious individuality has made its appearance, is he considered as having significant worth apart from his group." [5]

[4] Edward P. Cronan, *The Dignity of the Human Person* (New York: Philosophical Library, 1955), p. xv.

[5] Winston L. King, *Introduction to Religion* (New York: Harper & Brothers, 1954), p. 228.

Whatever may be said of specific religions and religious forms, it is difficult to imagine man without religion; for religion is the champion of personality in a seemingly impersonal world. . . . The sciences have greatly complicated the problem of maintaining the plausibility of the personalization of the universe by which religion guarantees the worth of human personality.[6]

The next quotation has special significance since it is part of an important document. Being such, it is the result therefore of much thought, deliberate group action, and of the consciousness of a weighty tradition. This tradition is Judaism and the document is the Columbus Platform, quoted in the symposium *The Jews, Their History, Culture, and Religion,* edited by Louis Finkelstein:

II. Ethics.

6. ETHICS AND RELIGION. In Judaism religion and morality blend into an indissoluble unity. Seeking God means to strive after holiness, righteousness and goodness. The love of God is incomplete without the love of one's fellowmen. Judaism emphasizes the kinship of the human race, the sanctity and worth of human life and personality and the right of the individual to freedom and to the pursuit of his chosen vocation.[7]

The next group identifies the principle with another world religion having, as it does, certain bonds of continuity with Judaism: "To be sure, when concrete problems present themselves Dewey actually employs the standards, ultimately derived from Christianity, of the worth of personality." [8]

The Christian faith is expressed in two great affirmations; that love is the ultimate principle of human relationships; and that the high worth of human personality which justifies the principle of love is in turn justified and supported by the character of reality itself.[9]

For the Platonic-Aristotelian aristocratic ideal Jesus substituted the supreme worth of every person before God and hence the obligation to regard all men as brothers and neighbors.[10]

[6] Reinhold Niebuhr, *Does Civilization Need Religion?* (New York: The Macmillan Company, 1927), pp. 4-5.

[7] P. 1344.

[8] Eugene W. Lyman, *The Kingdom of God and History,* ed. H. G. Wood (Chicago: Willett, Clark, 1938), p. 88, cf. p. 79.

[9] Reinhold Niebuhr, *Ventures in Belief,* ed. H. P. Van Dusen (New York: Charles Scribner's Sons, 1930), p. 12.

[10] Georgia Harkness, *The Sources of Western Morality* (New York: Charles Scribner's Sons, 1954), p. 220.

Jesus' ideal of the infinite worth of persons has lifted child life and womanhood wherever it has gone; it has abolished many forms of slavery; it lies at the root of democracy.[11]

That fact that man is God's creature gives dignity to every individual. No one who really accepts the Christian faith can ever look upon a fellow man without respect. . . . Such dignity is rooted in reality.[12]

Some quotations identify the concept as democratic. If it is not derived from democracy, it is considered as essential to the success of democracy. "Democracy is a doctrine standing for the ultimate worth of every human being." [13] "Basic to democratic education is the concept of the 'dignity and worth of every human being.' Human dignity is alleged to be derived from man's creation in the image of God." [14]

The inevitable question as to what science might have to say is illustrated by startling diversity as we consider what certain representatives report:

Why believe in democracy if its distinctive quality, the worth of the individual, and the moral responsibility of each person for his decisions and his acts, cannot qualify as true in the crucible of science? [15]

The religion of science leaves to us faith in the worth and dignity and almost boundless possibilities of man.[16]

Western Thought has emphasized the importance and dignity of the individual. . . . When we turn to what science has to offer, however, we do not find very comforting support for the traditional Western point of view. The hypothesis that man is not free is essential to the application of scientific method to the study of human behavior.[17]

Affirmations are not entirely from Western authors. As we turn to some writings from the Eastern hemisphere, we may expect to en-

[11] *Ibid.*, p. 238.

[12] Ferré, *op. cit.*, p. 147.

[13] J. K. Folsom, et al., *Youth, Family, and Education* (American Council on Education, 1941), p. 236.

[14] From a review of *These Young Lives: A Review of Catholic Education in the U.S.*, by Don Sharkey, published by W. H. Sadlier, 1950. The review appeared in Information Service, Department of Research and Education, Federal Council of Churches, XXIX, No. 41 (Dec. 16, 1950), 1, col. 2.

[15] Helen Howell Neal, *The Universe and You* (Laguna Beach, Calif.: Carlborg-Blades, Inc., 1954), p. 270. Based on the manuscript of Herbert Vincent Neal.

[16] Edwin G. Conklin, *Man, Real and Ideal* (New York: Charles Scribner's Sons, 1943), p. 205.

[17] B. F. Skinner: *Science and Human Behavior* (New York: The Macmillan Company, 1953), pp. 446-47.

counter the term "spirit" or some of its derivatives, especially from India. If we do not always find the precise phrase "dignity and worth of persons," we will find indications of why many Indian writers have been particularly responsive to the idealist tradition in the West. We find also some affirmations similar in at least one respect to the divine spark notion of Stoics: "Finite minds necessarily seek to be the infinite that they potentially are. The Infinite immanent in them goads them on and does not allow them to rest." [18] "The spiritual status is the essential dignity of man and the origin of his freedom. . . . The values of the human soul are not earth-bound but belong to the eternal world to which man can rise through discipline and disinterestedness." [19] "The individual soul, through a mode of the supreme, is real, unique, eternal, endowed with intelligence and self-consciousness, without parts, unchanging, imperceptible and atomic." [20]

This same author appeared on the international symposium honoring the two hundredth anniversary of Columbia University. His address, printed in *Man's Right to Knowledge,* contains the following:

> The one doctrine by which Indian culture is best known to the outside world is that of *tattvamasi.* The eternal is in one's self. The Real which is the inmost of all things is the essence of one's own soul. . . . Because there is the reflection of the divine in man, the individual becomes sacred.[21]

A visitor who spoke locally (October 22, 1956) said of his own people, the Lebanese, "The yearning of our people [is] for dignity. There is another yearning, at the same time, for technical competence —but this is a secondary objective." A *Journal of Opinion* carried the following news item: "The Prime Minister of Ceylon, Sir John Kotelawala, stated the peoples of Asia and Africa, for the first time in history, have the power to apply the spiritual values of life and the dignity of human personality to world problems." [22]

It cannot be claimed that all the quotations belong precisely in the same family, but there are family resemblances, in spite of wide differences of opinion of certain aspects, such as spiritualistic vs. natural-

[18] *Contemporary Indian Philosophy,* ed. S. Rādhākrishnan and J. H. Muirhead (New York: The Macmillan Company, 1936), p. 232.

[19] *Ibid.* pp. 266-67.

[20] Rādhākrishnan, *Indian Philosophy* (New York: The Macmillan Company, 1927), II, p. 690.

[21] "Tradition and Change" (First Series; New York: Herbert-Muschel).

[22] *Christianity and Crisis,* XV, No. 10 (June 13, 1955), p. 78.

istic interpretations. Also, one should ask whether there had been any mutual influences across cultural and geographical boundaries. Denis Saurat of the University of London, in a public lecture at Oxford in 1947, said that a characteristic of the "European Mind" was a sense of the high value of the individual, a sense of the sacredness of the individual soul. He further said this was properly realized from the thirteenth century on. This appears to be questioned by the following: "Today for the first time we are realizing what we mean, or can mean, by the belief in the value and worth of the human personality, what are the full implications of the dignity of man as seen in the light of our present day conception of man in nature and nature in man." [23]

There is a special series of works, the individual volumes of which have appeared annually since 1940. The general title of the series suggests that some attention might be given our theme under auspices of varied sorts. The Conference on Science, Philosophy and Religion, meeting annually, has been the occasion for the publication of what is now becoming a formidable library. We can give only a very brief sampling of the ways our theme is introduced in some of the volumes: "Human dignity is based upon man as a 'supranatural' being, in the sense of being essentially a spiritual being." [24] "Personality is the seat of value. . . . Value, as T. H. Green has so well said, is always 'for, of, or in person.'" [25] *"In the type of democratic religion, which is emerging, the concept of personality, or soul, carries with it the principle of intrinsic worth or dignity that is inviolable."* [26]

We should take note of dissenting voices. Because of their sources and the parts they play currently on the world scene, we cannot afford to close our eyes to them. The first appears in *Darkness at Noon,* a widely acclaimed novel by Arthur Koestler:

"I don't approve of mixing ideologies," Ivanov continued. "There are only two conceptions of human ethics, and they are at opposite poles. One of them is Christian and humane, declares the individual to be sacrosanct, and asserts that the rules of arithmetic are not to be applied to human units. The other starts from the basic principle that a collective aim justifies all means, and not only allows, but demands, that the individual should in every way be subordinated and sacrificed to the community—which may dispose of it

[23] Lawrence K. Frank, *Nature and Human Nature* (New Brunswick, N.J.: Rutgers University Press, 1951), p. 12.

[24] Maximilian Beck, Third Symposium, 1942, p. 254.

[25] Edgar S. Brightman, Fourth Symposium, 1943, p. 544.

[26] Mordecai M. Kaplan, Ninth Symposium, 1948, p. 318. Italics in the text.

as an experimental rabbit or a sacrificial lamb. . . . Humbugs and dilettantes have always tried to mix the two conceptions.[27]

The second is a complex of quotations from an author interested in interpretations of history and in certain historical developments. The common denominator is a negative response to the theme of the dignity and worth of the individual.

Plato was in line with Fascism in rejecting the principle of liberty and equality, tacitly denying the dignity and worth of the individual, even anticipating the technique of deliberately lying to the common people.[28]

Even the Webbs, in their sympathetic study of Soviet Communism, admit that hundreds of thousands were destroyed or deported to prison camps. They add, however, that while factions within the party disagreed over matters of practical policy, none argued for mercy for the kulaks. Certainly Lenin was never the type to plead the sanctity of the individual.[29]

Marx nurtured a cult of force that betrayed both his rationalism and his Romantic idealism. In effect he repudiated the faith in reason and reasonableness, denied the dignity and worth of the individual.[30]

Why the extensive and repeated references to this principle today? The presence of so much verbal "smoke" calls for the identification and location of the "fire." In the absence of ready references and explanations, the best we can do under present circumstances is to make a few suggestions.

To begin with, we may say that human relationships depend upon some basic postulates or principles. If there were none, then some natural principles would obtain, for example survival of the fittest, the claw and fang, to the victor belongs the spoils, the race to the swift, the devil take the hindmost. For constructive human relationships, however, there should be some principles which are recognized, generally accepted, and at least moderately abided by.

Perhaps our various quotations indicate a genuine search for a fundamental norm. Or they may indicate a recognition and reassertion of one already accepted at least nominally, except for dissenters. It has not been possible to conduct an inquiry into whether any other

[27] Tr. Daphne Hardy, pp. 156 ff. Copyright 1941 by The Macmillan Company and used by their permission.

[28] Herbert J. Muller, *The Uses of the Past* (New York: Oxford University Press, 1952), p. 127. Used by permission.

[29] *Ibid.*, p. 309.

[30] *Ibid.*, p. 318.

century gives evidence of such an outpouring of affirmation of our principle as this century.

We may suggest that the frequency of the reference to the principle, in the light of widespread action to the contrary in our violent century, is a reaffirmation of a principle threatened with atrophy and now recognized, however dimly, to be of priceless significance. In other words, it is entirely conceivable that the very violations of the principle have evoked the polar opposite of these violations in the twentieth-century mind.

Since the various statements included some quotations from areas outside the Western world, we may wonder if this idea has extended its influence beyond the Western world, or whether it had its origins in both hemispheres. We still cannot expect unanimity on the precise origins of the affirmation. Is it a prescientific or nonscientific idea? Must it now secure its credentials at the bar of science? Is it something apart from science? Is it a complex of things, partly wish, partly vague learning from experience, partly supposed fulfillment of need, partly a development? The prevailing categories in which it is considered are political and religious. This suggests that the principle is needed as basis and inspiration for protest and revolt against political oppression, and in the name of political justice; and that it is needed, too, as religious affirmation and aspiration to resolve tensions within the depths of man himself, wherein emotion wars against emotion, and hostilities turn inner life into a battleground, but also provoke internecine strife in the wider contexts of interpersonal relationships.

Very few books are devoted entirely or primarily to our principle, but we should mention three that are: *The Person or The Significance of Man,*[31] *The Dignity of the Human Person,*[32] and *The Phenomenon of Man.*[33] The first is written within the context of the philosophy of personalism; the second, the context of Thomistic rationalism and theism; and the third grows out of the lifelong concern of the author with evolutionary theory, that is, it claims to be scientifically grounded.

A Valid Principle?

Asking if the principle of the worth of persons is valid is not the same as asking if it can be proved true, by science or logic, for example.

[31] Ralph Tyler Flewelling (Los Angeles: The Ward Ritchie Press, 1952).

[32] Edward P. Cronan (New York: Philosophical Library, 1955).

[33] Pierre Teilhard de Chardin (New York: Harper & Brothers, 1959). English translation by Bernard Wall from the French *Le Phénomène Humain* (Paris: Editions du Seuil).

In the first place, worth is not a quality of objects or force in objects or events which can be detected by some objective measuring device. Attributes, qualities, and forces that can be detected by these devices constitute a limited area of knowledge and activity—one in which, to be sure, there has been a spectacular story of discovery and invention. The terminology of such discovery and invention includes a battery of technical words or phrases, from litmus paper to thermodynamics and cosmic radiation. There has been an understandable influence for the widely popular notions about quantification and how far such a process may be extended, to include the area of ethics, for example.

Worth is at once a simpler and more complex notion. It is simpler because the acceptance and practice of it does not require the type of analytical understanding required of, for example, a chemist who is to work with substances in terms of their chemical properties, or an engineer who builds bridges, or the physician who is trained in materia medica. Sheer technical knowledge is an indispensable requirement for these concerns.

It is a more complex notion, however, in that it relates to and involves both object and subject, both the locus of worth and its appreciation and acceptance by others. For adequate and proper functioning a "closed circuit" is required. It is more of a problem to answer the question, How may I develop interest in and appreciation of crude and alien people?—even though some people seem to do this with ease—than the question, How may I become an expert in the chemistry of soils? The existence of worth in an object can indeed be a vague notion even while recognition, appreciation, and action in behalf of worth are reaching a high stage of development. Frances of Assisi is not noted for his analytical definitions of "brother man," but the operating presence of the theme of worth was spectacular in his ministrations.

Another complicating factor, especially today, is to be seen in reductive explanations of St. Francis's behavior which endeavor to explain his behavior as perhaps compensatory measures or power devices operating as results of subconscious motivations. If these are pushed and accepted sufficiently, they could guarantee there would be no recurrences of any "St. Francis complex"—to coin a phrase. They tend to deny or ignore the concept of worth while at the same time devaluating the Franciscan exemplification of worth.

A further complexity is that, as of the present age, it seems that increase of knowledge is taking us farther away from questions regarding the worth and ultimate vocation of persons and away from the more expanded to the more reduced interpretations of life—and for that matter, away from the divine-personal to the natural-impersonal, from notions of purpose to those of accident, from notions of the coming of the Kingdom to the building of a kingdom, from the loving heart to the planning head, from theories of quality to those of quantity, from tenderness to toughness, from the fear of the Lord to the fear of fear, from supposed unrealistic otherworldly concerns to "thisworldly" realism, from the improvement of persons to the establishment of systems, from the wisdom of the ages to technological advancement, from justification and reconciliation to reconciliation through adjustment. The point is not whether all this indicates progress, as some would affirm, or retrogression, as others avow. It is not even whether it is accurate in all instances. Rather, the question is, What does it all signify? Adequate answers cannot be made and generally understood until some time in the future—at present, it is a case of *responsus absconditus*. This is not as deplorable as it might sound, unless we assume that adequate answers should be forthcoming now.

The affirmation of the worth of persons flies in the face of what seems to be evidence to the contrary. If we open the door to what has seemed to many people to be contrary evidence, a veritable scratch pack of candidates will come trooping through. A spectacular example has been preserved to the world by Origen of Alexandria. His extended refutation of the criticisms and arguments of Celsus includes many quotations from Celsus. The latter had argued that Origen's religion (Christianity) had put too high a value on man, that animals were superior to humanity in many ways. Origen said:

> How impious, indeed, is the assertion of this man, who charges us with impiety, that "not only are the irrational animals wiser than the human race, but that they are more beloved by God (than they)!" And who would not be repelled. . . from paying any attention to a man who declared that a serpent, and a fox, and a wolf, and an eagle, and a hawk, were more beloved by God than the human race? [34]

We need not recite the details of evidence of superiority as presented by Celsus, especially since many of these have long since been abandoned—such as predictive abilities of birds.

[34] *Origen Against Celsus,* bk. IV., ch. xcvii.

Famous satirists of history, from Lucian [35] to Lewis [36] have supplied readers with manifold examples, real and hypothetical, of stupidities and irrationalities of the supposed fair flower of creation, *homo sapiens,* which Henry L. Mencken, a master satirist of the twentieth century, changed to *homo boobiens.* These satirists may have thought they were doing nothing more than clothing the naked facts of human propensity and action in literary habiliments.

The actual records themselves have stimulated repeated recurrences of the thought and theme put into words by Robert Burns in "Man Was Made to Mourn":

Man's inhumanity to man
Makes countless thousands mourn.

If to many there has seemed to be evidence to the contrary, to many others there was a lack of evidence to support the thesis of the worth of persons. This point is more than ordinarily tied up with the problem of defining evidence, as well as with methods for securing evidence. The precise relationship of evidence and worth is a thorny problem from the beginning. If we say that there are varieties of evidence as well as of capacities for the recognition and acceptance of evidence, we will more than likely be accused of retreating. This is largely due to the fact that laboratory methods for the interpretation of evidence tend to dominate the current understanding of the term, even while it is supposedly understood that many aspects of life and experience are not amenable to this type of inquiry.

The ordinary and characteristic usages of the word are clear enough: in law, in crime detection, in ascertaining the presence and cause of illness, and many others. There is, however, a great difference between trying to adduce evidence for a fact and adducing it for a value or norm. The former would normally include data accessible primarily to the senses. The latter would raise questions that make the employment of sense experience difficult or perhaps irrelevant.

For sharp contrast in meaning and use of the term "evidence," let us recall the famous sentence, "Now faith is the substance of things hoped for, the evidence of things not seen." (Heb. 11:1, K.J.V.) The word "evidence" in this sentence is a far cry from the usage which speaks of scientific evidence. In the quoted verses there is a usage

[35] Lucian of Samosata, Syria, Greek satirical author, second century A.D.

[36] Sinclair Lewis (1885-1951), author of the novels *Mainstreet, Babbitt,* and numerous other satirizing works.

which reverses the usual and supposed order of events, wherein evidence leads to belief. In this sentence it is the faith or conviction which itself is the evidence. In other words, it is the faith which makes it possible to see the heretofore unseen things, whereas a modern notion would more likely be, "Let me see the unseen things first, then perhaps I can believe them."

As far as persons and their worth are concerned, there is a distinction deserving of far more than superficial attention between respecting persons who have proved or given evidence they are entitled to respect and recognizing the worth of persons who are not worthy, or whose records are yet unknown. Ordinarily it is considered entirely appropriate to expect, or even request, that people prove themselves. Such insistence on pragmatic validation even seems to have the support of a biblical injunction—"Ye shall know them by their fruits." (Matt. 7:16 K.J.V.). In fact to use such terminology as "respecting the worth of the unworthy" is to court trouble. Yet, it is approaching one of the profoundest of all religious ideas, and perhaps one of the most difficult to understand and accept fully. There is probably no one "best way" to state it, but it is related to and interwoven with such concepts as mercy, grace, love, forgiveness, and salvation. Even with as short a list as this, it is quite possible for people to have conflicting emotional attitudes toward individual terms in this list, or toward different instances calling for the application of one and the same term. For example, how many people have heaped praise on the "quality of mercy" speech of Portia in Shakespeare's *Merchant of Venice* without realizing that the person being asked to exhibit mercy is a striking symbol of a group to whom even the rudiments of mercy had so often been denied. The very implications constrain us to add the hypothetical remark, "Shylock, though we have been remarkably remiss in showing you and your group mercy, yet we certainly expect you to manifest it."

Today it is almost a mental fixation to assume that, What is the proof? is an entirely appropriate question to put to any claim. It is all too often assumed, also, that the processes of answering are all of the same type. This takes for granted that the proof precedes the belief, or should do so. But we never hear the quoted question put into such ultimate form as, What is the proof that it is always appropriate to ask for proof? It is quite likely that such a question would be called quibbling. But in so far as there is any presumed ultimacy for the first question, this second one is a logical implication. If it has any function, aside from quibbling, it would be to induce critical reappraisal.

Little attention is paid to the fact that much proof never proves. The canons of proof are strict and limited. Acceptance depends upon objective appraisal and rational agreement. But objective proof is often futile against the vitalities of entrenched interest, demanding desires, and the numerous irrationalities that have their place in the characterization of man. This in no sense takes away the importance of the problem of evidence, where relevant, but it is a reminder that something more is involved.

The affirmation of the worth of persons is not a factual proposition. It is an imperative. It does not so much affirm what is, in the ordinary sense, as what ought to obtain. It is not a simple affirmation of an attribute or quality, but a declaration of a principle that should prevail in the attitudes, appreciations, and conduct of persons toward persons. It is not a proposition about which we can afford to be purely objective and unconcerned as we might be regarding the weight of Jupiter's satellites. The ability to apprehend it is as important as the cogency of any rational and objective demonstration. The force and validity of this idea have been appreciated and articulated in distant times and widely separated places: "Thou shall not avenge, nor bear any grudge against the children of thy people, but thou shalt love thy neighbor as thyself." (Lev. 19:18, K.J.V.) "To feed men and not to love them is to treat them as if they were barnyard cattle. To love them and not to respect them is to treat them as if they were household pets." [37] These are not, or at least not said to be, the result of experimental verification—a famous and widely used phrase today.

The mode of justification for something like that indicated in the two quotations above is not primarily, if ever, an objective demonstration during which observant reason calmly waits, ready to yield full assent as soon as the cogency of the evidence becomes obvious. This is a charming thought, but a decidedly partial picture.

The validity of numerous value affirmations is often best proved or justified in the practice, and the constraint to try the practice may often be nothing more than unsupported trust, faith. The participant's faith serves him in the capacity of evidence and justification comes through involvement and performance. In something like swimming, an objective demonstration that organisms can swim is no necessarily

[37] Mencius, *Discourses.*

convincing proof to me that I can swim, or even learn. I will prove this to myself only by participation in the enterprise.

For the time being, then, we summarize some of the encouragements and supports that contribute to validation and justification of our declaration: worth of persons.

There are the testimonies of experience, notably and fundamentally in the love of the mother for her newborn. To label this a subjective argument is not *ipso facto* to deny it any and all validity. If it be said that in her concern for her young the human mother shares a propensity with the whole of animal species, we ask if this is intended to be a form of reductionism that takes significance away from human mother love. There is much of this kind of devaluing in recent generations—as though it argued some obvious form of depreciation. There is much less tendency to point out the achievements of human mother love wherein, for example, human mothers are able to generalize their concern into a concern for children everywhere, and not just their own. Though human motherhood shares in some of the features of reproductivity and behavior with animal creation, this is certainly no obvious argument for renunciation of special value claims.

Conversely, drastic experiences wherein children in their beginning years are denied affection and recognition, due to ignorance, hostility, or selfishness, tend to prove by contrast that affirmation of worth is essential in the nature of things. Spiritual wounds and scars come from the denial of this principle, not from its affirmation and practice. The patterns of violence that have been inflicted, in many cases even deliberately, against children in our century have given ample reason for saying that it is high time that agenda of international deliberations include serious and positive attention to the question of what sorts of psychological and spiritual climate we should establish for the growth and development of the children of the world. If this is ever taken seriously, then we will begin to wonder why we were so long getting at it.

Evidence can come from communal experience—if there is adequate capacity for interpretation and appreciation. By now there should be sufficient data for the articulation of sound arguments in behalf of the value of acceptance and practice of the principle of the worth of persons. Whether through sluggishness of capacity to learn, or through resistance provided by powerful contrary forces, we are caught in a tragic dilemma of affirmation on the one hand and violation on the other.

Again, supporting arguments are to be found in the insights and inspirations from the most varied sources in time and place. These tend to come to focus in the affirmation of worth, not the denial of it. That there have been denials we well know, but their sources and motivations make it quite clear that they are predominately if not entirely cases of malfunctioning of the human spirit. The most perceptive and appreciative of the sons and daughters of mankind see their fellow creatures as "children of God," or whatever the naturalistic correlate would be.

Moreover, will and faith risk all manner of opposition in the effort to proclaim and practice our fundamental principle, and not with the previously expressed intention of adducing proof. In the process, however, validation is provided by the end results, without necessarily appealing to some supposed antecedent guarantee. Spectators oftentimes, in their casualness and sideline observations, may think they see failure in prophet's martyrdoms, in rejections of saints, in Franciscan "impracticalities," in the slaughter of tenderness, and in all other occasions which seems to them to prove the rightness or power of alternative goals and methods—victories of flesh over spirit, quantity over quality, fist over friendship, score cards over rules of the game, death over growth, muscle over meditation, immediate decision over eventual judgment, haste over care. Yet, short-range decisions and victories must yield eventually to long-range judgment and temporary blindness to eventual sight. It may take time to understand this. We *do* live in a world in which the worst can happen, and where security is not naïvely promised in advance.

Does modern science provide any help? If we are to suppose that it is never science's function to concern itself with attempts to justify claims of worth and value this question is inappropriate and irrelevant. It is of course possible to define science with a certain kind of strictness, to limit its work to circumscribed areas and tasks wherein worth and value are merely insubstantial relativities. It is quite possible to define it as concerned only with the provable, the existent, the measurable, the objective, and not with the approvable, the not separably existent, the imponderable, the subjective, and to devalue the latter to an inferior status. In so doing we imply a drastic devaluation of the scientist. As suggested in Chapter VII, the enterprise of science can never get rid of the scientist, and the latter can never separate himself from concerns of purpose, worth, value, goals—except for those restricted tasks which require emotional neutrality and objectivity. The task of providing validation for claims of worth has not been considered to be science's prime task. The resultant assumption has been that worth and value claims are not of the "stuff of reality." Thus God and ghosts are placed in the same category—unrealities—as are the ghoulish and the good—relativities definable in the same general manner. Declarations of the valuable and the worthy are simply sentimental preferences. Thus, the faith that sees is, without exception, fooling itself. This is sometimes thought to be devastating even by those who accept it, and they doggedly cling to some kind of generalized preference for what are supposed to be particular sentimental choices. This amazing dilemma has not been put more graphically than in the following quotation:

> After all the present writer has no compelling argument to convince the reader that he should not be cruel or mean or cowardly. Such things are also in his own make-up in a large measure, but none the less he hates and fights against them with all his strength. He would rather our species ended its story in dignity, kindliness and generosity, and not like drunken cowards in a daze or poisoned rats in a sack. But this is a matter of individual predilection for everyone to decide for himself.[38]

This is not science speaking. These are the words of a well-known writer and a great popularizer of science. They are the words of one who sees no objective (scientific?) verification for the values his words extol. If he had hopes for his predilection, it was because there was some human propensity which he celebrated in a novel years earlier: "The passions and conflicts and discomforts of A.D. 1921 were the discomforts of the fever of an uninoculated world. The Age of Confusion on the Earth also would, in its own time, work itself out, thanks to a certain and indomitable righteousness in the blood of the human type." [39]

In other words, the slender support for a proper predilection is that in the "blood of the human type" is an "indomitable righteousness," but this cannot be supported by the kind of objective argument which is a specialty of science.

Yet, science itself can scarcely avoid some kind of concern with and affirmation of value and of particular values. They may not be held or argued in the name science. If not, and if strict science cannot, as science, justify value claims, either there are no ways to justify value claims, or there are other ways, including even the faith that sees.

[38] H. G. Wells, *Mind at the End of Its Tether* (New York: Didier, Publishers, 1946), p. 18.

[39] *Men Like Gods* (New York: The Macmillan Company, 1923) p. 229.

The simplest and commonest values associated with science have been (1) that knowledge and its systematic accumulation are good, and (2) that science has provided innumerable benefits which would not have been provided otherwise. These do not make much sense, however, apart from a principle of the worth of persons. Thus, if this latter is a valid principle, has science demonstrated its validity in some scientific manner? Has science accepted it on faith as a fundamental presupposition? Or has science taken it over from some other enterprise, such as religion? If some such pattern obtains it is not only possible, but it is essential to consider that these other enterprises have their own avenues to reality and their own modes of validation for the truth about worth.

Epilogue

BEFORE LIFE EXISTED ON THIS PLANET, OR IN THE COSMOS ANYWHERE, was there a great and subtle potential for life, for the mystery of organic functioning? There must have been, unless life was a creation out of nothing, or an accident that was "miraculous."

Before human life came to be on this planet or in the cosmos was there a great and subtle potential for the saintliness and sinfulness of human existence? Was there any apprehension of or plan for the coming drama of human experience in all its tragedy, comedy, pathos, and spiritual achievement? Any affirmative answer is neither objectively demonstrable nor logically necessary. It is rather an article of faith, if not a revelatory deliverance.

It seems easier to suppose that the human species began as a fortuitous occurrence—easier than to complicate the issue with personalized, teleological, anthropomorphic interpretations of man's appearance on the scene. On the basis of this mode of thought, articles of faith seem to be frail lances for engaging the "moderns" secure in their empirical chains of reasoning.

Concepts of worth develop in either case, though connotations may in part be mutually exclusive. Yet, if the sense of vocation, purpose, and worth develop within a context of unconscious purposelessness—this would challenge credulity beyond that essential for a more purposeful and theistic interpretation.

In any event, challenges to the understanding are overwhelming. While we may seem to have learned much in the past concerning the abilities of man to know and to understand, we are now in the process of learning from psychological sciences the significance of being understood. On the purely human level, to be understood and accepted, in some sense and to some degree, is a psychological essential—a form of spiritual food.

Speaking of the wider context, it is not possible to be completely understood in a world without God—the only name that allows a connotation of understanding on such a cosmic scale.[1] This of course is

[1] Pss. 8 and 139 are relevant to this.

not proof of the reality of God, but to relate the themes of understanding and being understood to the Idea of God is a supreme challenge to the human spirit. Not to do so could jettison man's rich cargo of spiritual treasure. To decide between such alternatives is not so much a matter of weighing evidence as of being responsive to conviction.

If the perfected [2] human person be thought of as a "living soul standing before God," this would be a religious concept of the most advanced sort. "Living soul" reflects the NEPHESH CHAYYAH of Gen. 2:7, rather than the "pigeon in a cage" dualism of Platonic usage, from which it should be sharply differentiated.[3]

There are strains of thought today which probably would favor a modernized translation of the foregoing, religiously oriented phraseology. That is, "living souls before God" might be rendered, reductively, into "tiny enclaves of negative entropy in the midst of a universal Second Law of Thermodynamics." [4] It would still be possible to introduce the themes of human potential and worth, but they would then seem greatly attenuated.

The human person, in the most comprehensive religious terms, is something like the sanctum sanctorum (the "holy of holies" of the historic Jewish Temple). This was (is) a holy place, or preferably, a place of holiness. Yet it has never been thought of as simply a place. Surrounding it with walls could never capture and confine the "holiness." Walls can be erected anywhere or not at all. Still the sacred "place" is where man at his best meets God whom he cannot see. When a muscular world, with signal lack of reverence and comprehension, attempts an invasion [5] it does not find anything, at least it does not

[2] In the sense of completion or fulfillment of potential rather than in the sense of without blemish. The former corresponds to the usage of Matt. 5:48.

[3] The soul-body dualism in Platonic thought was an even sharper dualism than the "pigeon-cage" figure suggests. The soul was not only immortal, it was preexistent, whereas the body (cage) was temporary and mortal. The Hebrew view, on the other hand, affirms or suggests God's endowing earthly being with vitality, so that diverse elements are brought into creative unity: dust-body-life-spirit. The resultant unity reflects the impress of the divine initiative. "Soul" is neither a necessary nor precise translation of any feature or result of this creative process.

[4] This formulation is inspired by Norbert Wiener's writings, though it is not a direct quotation, nor does it claim to represent Wiener's point of view. Special note has been taken of his *The Human Use of Human Beings* (Boston: Houghton Mifflin Company, 1950; reprinted as a Doubleday Anchor Book, 1954).

[5] Cf.: "Pompey . . . forced his way into the inmost shrine . . . amazed to find that there was nothing whatever—*vacua omnia!* The mass of native rock on which the Ark had once stood . . . alone was visible. The absence of everything else perhaps originated the notion that the Jews worshipped 'nothing except clouds and the Deity of Sky.'" F. W. Farrar, *The Early Days of Christianity* (Two volumes; London: Cassell, Petter, Galpin & Co., 1882), I, p. 417.

find what it may have thought it would—some esoteric, sensational object.

How can the spirit of the sanctum be captured within the materiality of surrounding walls? The question is relevant only because man has so persistently tried to do this. In Old Testament language, how can the *ruach* (spirit) be contained within the limits of *nephesh* (flesh)? Or, how can the invisibility of worth commend itself to organisms with eyes? How can it be objectively presented to passive observation? The answer is perennially available but also perennially elusive. In human and linguistic terms, it is best found with those in whom understanding and appreciation are transmuted into conviction, and who can express their meanings only in "similitudes." [6]

[6] Cf. the reference in *Hosea* 12:10 (K.J.V.): "I have also spoken by the prophets, and I have multiplied visions, and used similitudes, by the ministry of the prophets."

Bibliography

(Suggested titles for further reading—titles not heretofore listed.)

Allport, Gordon W. *Becoming*. New Haven, Conn.: Yale University Press, 1955.

———. *The Individual and His Religion*. New York: The Macmillan Company, 1950.

Baillie, John. *Natural Science and the Spiritual Life*. New York: Charles Scribner's Sons, 1952.

Boisen, Anton T. *The Exploration of the Inner World*. Chicago: Willett, Clark and Company, 1936.

Bosanquet, Bernard. *The Value and Destiny of the Individual*. Gifford Lectures. London: Macmillan and Company, 1913.

Brammer, L. M., and Shostrom, E. L. *Therapeutic Psychology*. Englewood Cliffs, N. J.: Prentice-Hall, Inc., 1960.

Breasted, James H. *The Dawn of Conscience*. New York: Charles Scribner's Sons, 1934.

Bridges, Robert. *The Spirit of Man: An Anthology*. London: Longmans, Green and Company, 1929.

Bury, J. B. *The Idea of Progress*. New York: The Macmillan Company, 1932.

Cadoux, Cecil J. *The Early Church and the World*. Edinburgh: T. & T. Clark, 1925.

Coffin, Henry Sloane. *God Confronts Man in History*. New York: Charles Scribner's Sons, 1947.

College Reading and Religion. Symposium. New Haven, Conn.: Yale University Press, 1948.

Dewey, John. *The Quest for Certainty*. Gifford Lectures. New York: Minton, Balch and Company, 1929.

Eiseley, Loren. *The Firmament of Time*. New York: Atheneum Publishers, 1960.

Hiltner, Seward. *Preface to Pastoral Theology*. Nashville: Abingdon Press, 1958.

Hocking, William Ernest. *The Coming World Civilization*. New York: Harper & Brothers, 1956.

———. *Human Nature and Its Remaking*. New Haven, Conn.: Yale University Press, 1918.

Hoijer, Harry. (ed.). *Language in Culture.* Chicago: University of Chicago Press, 1954.

Hügel, Friedrich von. *The Mystical Element of Religion.* 2 vols. London: J. M. Dent. New York: E. P. Dutton and Company, 1908.

James, William. *Varieties of Religious Experience.* Gifford Lectures. New York: Longmans, Green and Company, 1902.

Kunkel, Fritz, *In Search of Maturity.* New York: Charles Scribner's Sons, 1943.

McNeill, John T. *A History of the Cure of Souls.* New York: Harper & Brothers, 1951.

Mandler, George, and Kessen, William. *The Language of Psychology.* New York: John Wiley & Sons, Inc., 1959.

May, Rollo. *Man's Search for Himself.* New York: W. W. Norton & Company, 1953.

Murphy, Gardner. *Human Potentialities.* New York: Basic Books, Inc., 1958.

Ostow, O., and Scharfstein, B.: *The Need to Believe.* New York: International Universities Press, 1954.

Pasternak, Boris. *Doctor Zhivago.* Trans. Max Hayward and Manya Harari. New York: Pantheon Book, 1958. Especially pp. 43, 122, 296 ff., 404, 411.

Radin, Paul. *Primitive Man as Philosopher.* New York: Appleton & Co., 1927. New York: Dover Publications, 1957.

Rall, Harris F. *Religion as Salvation.* Nashville: Abingdon Press, 1953.

Randall, John Herman, Jr. *The Making of the Modern Mind.* Rev. ed. Boston: Houghton Mifflin Company, 1940.

Remmers, H. H., and Radler, D. H. *The American Teenager.* Indianapolis, Ind.: The Bobbs-Merrill Company, 1957.

Routh, H. V. *Towards the Twentieth Century.* New York: The Macmillan Company, 1937.

Royce, Josiah. *The World and the Individual.* 2 vols. Gifford Lectures. New York: The Macmillan Company, 1904.

Ruesch, J., and Kees, W. *Nonverbal Communication.* Berkeley, Calif.: University of California Press, 1956.

Shotwell, James T. *The Long Way to Freedom.* Indianapolis, Ind.: The Bobbs-Merrill Company, 1960.

Stace, W. T. *Religion and the Modern Mind.* Philadelphia: J. B. Lippincott, 1952.

Tournier, Paul. *The Meaning of Persons.* New York: Harper & Bros., 1957.

Turner, J. E. *Essentials in the Development of Religion.* New York: The Macmillan Company, 1934.

Weatherhead, Leslie D. *Psychology, Religion and Healing.* Nashville: Abingdon Press, 1951.

What, Then, Is Man? Symposium. St. Louis: Concordia Publishing House, 1958.

Whitehead, Alfred N. *Adventures of Ideas.* New York: The Macmillan Company, 1933.

Widgery, Alban G. *What is Religion?* New York: Harper & Brothers, 1953.

Woodbridge, F. J. E. *Nature and Mind.* New York: Columbia University Press, 1937.

Yeaxlee, B. A. *Religion and the Growing Mind.* Greenwich, Conn.: The Seabury Press, 1952.

Yinger, J. M. *Religion, Society and the Individual.* New York: The Macmillan Company, 1957.

Index of Subjects

Index of Scripture Passages